# BRANDS AND BRANDING

# OTHER ECONOMIST BOOKS

Guide to Analysing Companies
Guide to Business Modelling
Guide to Economic Indicators
Guide to the European Union
Guide to Financial Markets
Guide to Management Ideas
Numbers Guide
Style Guide

Dictionary of Business
Dictionary of Economics
International Dictionary of Finance

Business Ethics
Business Strategy
China's Stockmarket
E-Commerce
E-trends
Globalisation
Successful Innovation
Successful Mergers
Wall Street

Essential Director
Essential Finance
Essential Internet
Essential Investment

Pocket Asia
Pocket Europe in Figures
Pocket World in Figures

The
Economist

# BRANDS AND BRANDING

**Rita Clifton** and **John Simmons**

with

Sameena Ahmad

Tony Allen

Simon Anholt

Anne Bahr Thompson

Patrick Barwise

Tom Blackett

Deborah Bowker

Chuck Brymer

Deborah Doane

Kim Faulkner

Paul Feldwick

Steve Hilton

Jan Lindemann

Allan Poulter

Shaun Smith

THE ECONOMIST IN ASSOCIATION WITH
PROFILE BOOKS LTD

Published by Profile Books Ltd
3A Exmouth House, Pine Street, London EC1R 0JH
*www.profilebooks.com*

Typeset in EcoType by MacGuru Ltd
*info@macguru.org.uk*

Printed in Great Britain by
Clays, Bungay, Suffolk

A CIP catalogue record for this book is available
from the British Library

ISBN-10 1 86197 664 X
ISBN-13 978 186197 664 2

The paper this book is printed on is certified by the © 1996 Forest Stewardship
Council A.C. (FSC). It is ancient-forest friendly. The printer holds FSC chain of custody
SGS-COC-2061

FSC
Mixed Sources
Product group from well-managed
forests and other controlled sources

Cert no. SGS-COC-2061
www.fsc.org
© 1996 Forest Stewardship Council

# Contents

# The authors

**Rita Clifton** is a leading practitioner, author and commentator on brands and branding, and has worked with many of the world's most successful companies. After graduating from Cambridge, she spent her early career in advertising, becoming vice-chairman and strategic director at Saatchi & Saatchi. A frequent speaker at conferences around the world, she is also a regular contributor on CNN and the BBC and to all the major broadsheets and business magazines. Since 1997 she has been CEO and then chairman at Interbrand, a global brand consultancy, and she was the editor of its recent book *The Future of Brands*.

**John Simmons** pioneered the discipline of verbal identity and has consulted for brands around the world such as Guinness, Lever Fabergé and Air Products. He is a consultant and author, and his two books *We, Me, Them & It* and *The Invisible Grail* have become widely valued as authoritative and engaging texts on the role of language in branding. Previously he was a director of Newell and Sorrell and then of Interbrand, where he was verbal identity director and led major brand programmes for companies such as Royal Mail and Waterstone's.

**Sameena Ahmad** is a business correspondent with *The Economist*, who has written about marketing and brands. Formerly based in New York and London, she now covers Asian business from Hong Kong.

**Tony Allen** graduated from Cambridge University with a degree in Physical Anthropology. He then joined McCann-Erickson where he worked on some of the agency's biggest accounts, and was involved in launching Diet Coke into the UK. In 1985 he joined corporate identity company Newell and Sorrell, known for its work with such clients as British Airways and Waterstone's the book sellers. He set up the firm's office in Amsterdam in 1995 where he worked on a number of cross-border merger projects including those for PriceWaterhouse and Coopers & Lybrand and Pharmacia and Upjohn. Following the purchase of Newell and Sorrell by Interbrand in 1997, he returned to London to become the joint managing director of the new company in 1999 and then its CEO in 2002.

**Simon Anholt** is one of the UK's best-known international marketing thinkers. After graduating in modern languages at Oxford University, he worked as international creative co-ordinator at McCann-Erickson before founding World Writers, a culture consultancy, in 1989, which he ran until 2001. He has specialised in the branding of places for over a decade, and advises many cities, regions and countries on public diplomacy and brand strategy, including the governments of the UK (and separately Scotland), Slovenia, Croatia, the Czech Republic, Germany and New Zealand. He also advises the World Bank, the UN, the World Travel and Tourism Council, the World Technology Network and several other organisations. He is the author of the best-selling *AdWeek* book, *Another One Bites the Grass*, and *Brand New Justice: The Upside of Global Branding*, which was published in 2003. He is a founding director of Placebrands, an international consulting firm.

**Anne Bahr Thompson** has worked as a consultant and strategist in marketing, planning and research, and with brands including Chase, Citibank, Fidelity, Kraft Foods, Quaker Oats, Random House and UBS Switzerland. She was formerly vice-president of market research and planning at Bankers Trust and held product management and strategic planning posts at Chemical Bank. She has an MBA (International Business and Finance) from Darden Graduate School of Business at the University of Virginia and a BA in Communications and English from Rutgers University. She is currently head of consulting at Interbrand.

**Patrick Barwise** is professor of management and marketing and chairman of the Future Media Research Programme at London Business School. He joined LBS in 1976 having spent his early career with IBM. He is the author of *Television and its Audience, Accounting for Brands, Strategic Decisions, Predictions: Media* and *Advertising in a Recession*, as well as numerous articles and academic papers, mostly on brands, consumer/audience behaviour and new media. His current projects include a major study of global *Marketing Expenditure Trends* and *Simply Better*, a book on customer-driven strategy, to be published by Harvard Business School Press.

**Tom Blackett** has been a leading expert on brands and branding for over 20 years. He is the author of *Trademarks* and the co-editor of *Co-branding: the science of alliance* and *Brand Medicine* and a contributor to many other key texts about brands. During his career the international brand owners he has worked with include Heineken, Unilever, GlaxoWell-come, BP Amoco and Volvo. Now group deputy chairman of Interbrand, he is a regular conference speaker, media commentator and writer.

**Deborah Bowker** has experience in strategic planning, change communication, media and government relations. Before joining Burson-Marsteller she was director of PricewaterhouseCooper's Centre of Excellence for Strategic Communications and a technical adviser in communications and marketing planning to numerous PWC clients. She has also served as an assistant postmaster general and vice-president at the US Postal Service, and has directed major projects for USPS, a worldwide Olympic sponsorship and a national literacy programme. Her promotion of the Elvis postage stamp earned her a place in the Ad Age 100. She is a Sloan Fellow of the Massachusetts Institute of Technology, where she earned a Master of Science in Management.

**Charles (Chuck) Brymer** began his career at BBDO, opening its Houston office in 1982 before moving to the head office in New York. Since moving into branding, he has led branding programmes for MCI, Compaq, Samsung, Discover, Procter & Gamble, Gillette and AT&T. As group chief executive of the Interbrand Group based in New York, he is responsible for managing the company's global interests as well as remaining involved in client projects. He has written and lectured extensively on brands, corporate identity, naming and brand valuation.

**Deborah Doane** is programme director, Transforming Markets, at the New Economics Foundation, a leading think-tank aiming to build a just and sustainable economy. She is an active campaigner and researcher in the area of corporate social responsibility and chair of the CORE (Corporate Responsibility) Coalition, campaigning for stronger corporate accountability of business. She is a frequent speaker at international conferences, to both business and government audiences and contributes to broadcast and broadsheet media, including the BBC, the *Guardian* and the *Independent*. Previously, she was head of the International Humanitarian Ombudsman Project, and she started her career as a senior policy analyst with the Canadian government. She earned a Masters in Development Studies from the London School of Economics.

**Kim Faulkner** has 20 years of experience in branding, marketing communications and design management, working with a diverse range of international and local client organisations in Asia. She was a founding partner of Interbrand's office in Singapore and is now chairman of the office, as well as sitting on the board of directors of International Enterprise Singapore. She is also a council member of the DesignSingapore Council and of the Action Community for Entrepreneurship, Singapore.

**Paul Feldwick** joined BMP (then known as Boase Massimi Pollitt), an advertising agency, in 1974. Today he is executive planning director for the same company (BMP DDB) and worldwide brand planning director for DDB. He has been chairman of the Association for Qualitative Research and of the Account Planning Group, and is a Fellow of the IPA and the Market Research Society. He has spoken at the US Account Planning Group Conference and twice won "best" paper at the Market Research Society Conference (UK). He is the author of *What is Brand Equity, Anyway?*.

**Steve Hilton** is the founding partner of Good Business, a leading corporate responsibility consultancy. He is a prominent commentator on the social role of business, and the author *Good Business – Your World Needs You*, a constructive riposte to the anti-globalisation movement. Previously, he was campaign co-ordinator for the Conservative Party's successful 1992 general election campaign and then worked at Saatchi & Saatchi, where he combined commercial and social marketing disciplines with clients ranging from British Airways to Boris Yeltsin.

**Jan Lindemann** is global managing director, brand valuation, at Interbrand Group, responsible for the company's brand valuation practice worldwide. He has extensive experience in advising on brands, marketing and financial issues in all major industries and countries, with clients who include American Express, AT&T, AXA, Bank of America, BBC, BP, BT, Gucci, Fujitsu, GE, Heineken, IBM, Japan Tobacco, L'Oreal, MasterCard, Nestlé, NYCE, Olivetti, Orange, Pilsner Urquell, Prada, Powergen, Prudential, RHM, Samsung Electronics, Texas Instruments, TNT, Vodafone and Wells Fargo. His work has been widely published on these subjects and he is a frequent lecturer, commentator and broadcaster on brand related issues, including the creation of the league table on the leading global brands. Previously he worked as mergers & acquisitions adviser for Chase Manhattan Bank.

**Allan Poulter** is a partner at Field Fisher Waterhouse, a London-based law firm, practising within its Trade Marks and Brand Protection Group. He is qualified as a solicitor and as a registered trade mark attorney, and was previously managing director of Markforce Associates. He has managed the international trade mark portfolios of several household-name clients and has particular expertise in Community Trade Mark proceedings. He is a member of International Trade Mark Association's publications board and is editor of the INTA publication on the Community Trade Mark. Conferences he has spoken at around the world include Eurolegal's Annual Trade Mark Conference and INTA's Madrid Protocol Forum in Washington, Chicago and San Francisco.

**Shaun Smith** is a leading expert in helping organisations create and deliver customer experiences that differentiate their brands. A consultant to a wide range of organisations covering many different industry sectors, he is also author of *Managing the Customer Experience* and *Uncommon Practice*. He started his career at British Airways, becoming head of Customer Service, Sales and Marketing Training worldwide before moving to Asia for 11 years as managing director of Cathay-Performa consulting. He later joined the Forum Corporation as senior vice-president of The Customer Experience Business with responsibility for their customer experience consulting practice in Europe. He now runs his own businesss focussing on speaking internationally and advising companies in the area of brand experience.

# Preface

This collection of essays comes at an interesting time for brands. The past few years have seen the apparent triumph of the brand concept: everyone from countries to political parties to individuals in organisations is now encouraged to think of themselves as a brand. At its best this means caring about, measuring and understanding how others see you, and adapting what you do to take account of it, without abandoning what you stand for. At its worst it means putting a cynical gloss or spin on your product or your actions to mislead or manipulate those you seek to exploit. These are hardly new ideas. What is new is the ubiquitous and often confused use of branding terminology to describe them.

This timely book aims to bring greater understanding into this complex and, to some, emotive area. Written by leading practitioners and analysts, it puts brands and branding into their historical context, describes current thinking and best practice, and ventures some thoughts about the future.

Part of the confusion about brands is that the word is used in at least three separate but interrelated senses:

- In most everyday use (for example, "which brand did you buy?") a brand is a named product or service.
- In some contexts (for example, "which brand shall we use for this new product?") brands are trade marks.
- In other contexts (for example, "how will this strengthen or weaken our brand?"), brand refers to customers' and others' beliefs and expectations about products and services sold under a specific trade mark or about the company which provides them; the best term for this is "brand equity".

The use of the same word to mean three categorically different things does not aid clear thinking; and the thinking gets muddier when the anti-globalisation movement refers to "brands as bullies", when really they are attacking the mostly American multinationals that own global brands.

Again, brand valuation is an attempt to attribute part of the total value of a firm to brand equity. But brand equity – especially for a corporation, such as Microsoft, IBM or GE, as opposed to a product, such as Windows or Persil – is like reputation: it cannot be bought or sold. In contrast, a trade mark can be sold but has little inherent value apart from the associated brand equity.

This is not to deny that brands – that is, brand equity – can be an extremely important component of a firm's value. Most successful businesses today are valued by the market at far more than the value of their tangible assets. Brand equity, whether it is or is not a separable asset to which we can assign a single valid financial value, is often the most important intangible factor accounting for this difference. The financial markets now understand this and are starting to require top management to act as good stewards of this crucial aspect of business performance.

If top managers are becoming brand stewards, what issues should they think about?

**Brand measurement, accountability and understanding.** To manage brand equity (or anything) requires current, valid data. This includes diagnostic data about why the brand is where it is. Few brand owners do this well. Part of the failure of American "public diplomacy" (government PR aimed at foreigners) stems from not having bothered to understand systematically how "Brand America" is perceived. This failure poses a potential threat to American lifestyle brands such as Coca-Cola, Marlboro and McDonald's, although it is too soon to tell how real the threat is. Another accountability issue relates to marketing metrics such as market share, customer loyalty, relative price and relative perceived quality. Managers should see these metrics regularly and report the main ones to shareholders.

**Brand support.** Including a range of marketing metrics in performance measurement systems such as the balanced scorecard (to complement short-term financial measures) should make it easier to maintain investment in activities that will build and develop brand equity. The main trends are a gradual shift of resources away from traditional media advertising towards direct and interactive marketing, and a gradual concentration of resources on fewer, bigger brands, each capable of supporting more products. Relating back to measurement and accountability, managers should insist on quantitative evaluations (post-audits) of all brand investments even though these are unlikely to pin down the full long-term effects. The three criteria for a post-audit should be effectiveness (did the campaign reach its objectives?), efficiency (was it good value for money?) and learning (what have we learned which will help us do better in future?).

**The brand owner's social and ethical stance.** There is no consensus about the net social impact of businesses, brands or branding, either in general or in particular cases. Nor is there consensus about the implications for public policy (for example, regulation, investment incentives) or for businesses themselves; but because of attacks from diverse groups (both consumerist and anti-consumerist) brand owners must address these issues. Brand owners rightly argue that many of the criticisms of them are confused and ill-informed; that, for instance, the labour and environmental standards of multinationals in developing countries are usually higher than those of local competitors; and that those who criticise their involvement in these countries rarely spell out the likely consequences if that involvement were to cease. These arguments, however, are insufficient either to address the substantive issues or to win the battle for hearts and minds. Brand owners today need to take account of the fact that these issues are starting to affect not only the brand choices of some consumers but also areas such as graduate recruitment and government relations, and that in a digitally connected world anti-brand websites and e-mail campaigns can have a dramatic impact within a few days.

**Making the experience of buying and using the brand reliably live up to the promise.** A recurrent theme in this book is that successful brand management goes well beyond the cosmetics of branding (brand name, packaging, advertising, and so on). All great brands are built on a bedrock of trust derived from customers' experience of buying and using products and services sold under the brand name. The resulting brand equity is then reinforced by excellent branding, usually playing a supporting role. Of those brands ranked the top ten in 2002 by Interbrand, a brand consultancy firm, in association with JP Morgan (see page 29) only Coca-Cola and Marlboro have been created primarily by branding, supported by a good product and great distribution. Intel owes some of its strength to its Intel Inside "ingredient branding" campaign, but more to its products' price-performance, its strategic alliance with Microsoft and its dominance of standards. The rest of this top ten – Microsoft, IBM, GE, Nokia, Disney, McDonald's and Mercedes-Benz – are primarily customer experience brands.

This represents the biggest opportunity for top management as brand stewards. After 25 years of total quality management (TQM), customer relationship management (CRM) and other such management prescriptions, there is still a huge gap between promise and delivery for most brands, especially service brands.

I recently read a review of a book on "building great customer experiences". The reviewer tells how he settled down to read the book coming back from Brussels to London by Eurostar, having had his original train cancelled and … don't ask. (This was a few weeks after Eurostar left several hundred passengers stranded for five hours.) Imagine his reactions on finding the managing director of Eurostar quoted three times in the book on his company's wonderful customer-led culture. Did this MD have any idea of customers' actual experience with the brand?

My hope and expectation is that the next big brand thing will be top managers, as brand stewards, working to close the gap between the promised and the delivered brand experience.

Brands create customer value because they reduce both the effort and the risk of buying things, and therefore give suppliers an incentive to invest in quality and innovation. Branding can also enhance the customer's experience aesthetically and psychologically. Today, there is far more interest in brands and recognition of their importance than there was 10 or 20 years ago, but there is still great ignorance and misunderstanding of many of the issues. This book is aimed at any open-minded person who seeks a better understanding of the social and financial value of brands, current best practice in branding, and some of the emerging issues around this important, complex and ever fascinating topic.

PATRICK BARWISE
*September 2003*

# Introduction

*Rita Clifton*

In great part, this book, and its treatment of the subject of brands and branding, was inspired by the leader article "Pro Logo" which appeared in *The Economist* on 8th September 2001. The date of publication may give some clue as to why the subject did not generate as much follow-up debate as it might have done.

But there were, and are, other factors which have subdued the kind of support that the article advocated for brands. The title "Pro Logo" was a witty response to the title and arguments in Naomi Klein's 1999 book *No Logo*. The book had become an unofficial "bible" for the anti-capitalist and anti-globalisation movement, arguing that global brands essentially had too much power and were the cause of a variety of evils and injustices in world society. *The Economist* article essentially advised Naomi Klein and her followers to grow up, and to recognise the importance of globalisation and brands to the economic and social development of all nations. Brands have been successful because people want them; and every organisation's need to protect its reputation (and so its corporate value) is a rather efficient impetus for them to behave well.

The fact that *The Economist* article was a rare example of a sophisticated publication clearly highlighting the nonsense that lay behind so many of the anti-capitalist arguments was also thought-provoking in its own right. Why is it that there seems to be less high-level advocacy for the collective importance of brands than seems justified by the facts?

Is it a lack of understanding of their nature and role? Is it a form of personal denial about how much we are influenced by brands, a kind of developed-world guilt? Certainly, there is little evidence of this kind of soul-searching in a country like China, where the government has explicitly stated that it sees "branded commodities" as China's way forward in world success.

Contrast this with the sentiment of a letter from a FTSE company CEO in response to an approach from a brand consultancy. No one could blame the CEO for rebuffing such an approach from a supplier, but it was the reason given that was illuminating: "Branding is not our main preoccupation at the moment." The letter was polite, but the implication was clear. Basically, in the face of difficult market conditions, the CEO was preoccupied with "more important" things such as, presumably, cutting costs and restructuring. In contrast, branding was, to him, a discretionary cost and most probably to do with expensive logo-twiddling. To equate "brand" with such superficial cosmetics is the equivalent of saying that people are really only the sum of their name, face and clothes.

Thinking about all of these differently expressed (and indeed unexpressed) views, it seemed important for this book to air and explore the many different angles on brands and branding, both positive and negative, for a range of different audiences. This is indeed what the book has set out to do, as is reflected in the chapter subjects and contributors.

However, we should be clear that there is a central tenet for this book, whether it is reflected in the individual contributions or not. The brand is the most important and sustainable asset of any organisation – whether a product- or service-based corporation or a not-for-profit concern – and it should be the central organising principle behind every decision and every action. Any organisation wanting to add value to day-to-day process and cost needs to think of itself as a brand.

## The economic importance of brands

Certainly, all the hard economic evidence is there for the central importance of the brand. While the brand clearly belongs in the "intangible" assets of an organisation, this hardly makes its economic contribution and importance any less real. For example, the intangible element of the combined market capitalisation of the FTSE 100 companies has increased to around 70%, compared with some 40% 20 years ago, and it is likely to grow even further as tangible distinctions between businesses become less sustainable. The brand element of that combined market value amounts to around one-third of the total, which confirms the brand as the most important single corporate asset. Globally, brands are estimated to account for approximately one-third of all wealth; and that is just looking at their commercial definition. Some of the world's most recognised and influential brands are, of course, those of not-for-profit organisations, such as Oxfam and the Red Cross. This is an aspect of "global brands" all too rarely considered in the public debate about brands and branding.

The economic importance of brands on a national and international stage is undeniable. As an example, when the GDP of Thailand was around $115 billion in 2001, the combined value of the world's two most valuable brands (Coca-Cola and Microsoft) was $134 billion. If the financial clout wielded by these companies makes some commentators nervous, it should not. The owners of brands are also highly accountable institutions. If a brand delivers what it promises, behaves in a responsible fashion, and continues to innovate and add value, people will continue to vote for it with their wallets, their respect and even their affection. If, however, a brand begins to take its position for granted and becomes complacent, greedy or less scrupulous in its corporate practices, people will stop voting for it, with potentially disastrous effects for the brand and its owner.

In a word-processed, all-seeing digital world, where the ghosts of corporate malpractice are never laid to rest, there is every incentive for companies to behave well. One of the ironies of the recent anti-globalisation movement, in its original targeting of global brands, is the failure to acknowledge that the importance of brand reputation provides the strongest incentive for a company to do everything to protect the reputation of its brand, its most valuable corporate asset. If the ability to increase the value of that asset is the "carrot" for companies, then the "stick" is the knowledge of how worthless the once-proud names of Andersen and Enron have now become.

From an investment perspective, the brand provides a more reliable and stable indicator of the future health of a business. Inspection of brand value, equity measures and audience relationships will give a more complete and realistic basis for underlying value than short-term financial results, which often reflect short-term priorities. A recent study by Harvard and South Carolina Universities compared the financial performance of the world's most valuable 100 brands with the average of the Morgan Stanley Capital Index and the Standard & Poor's 500. The dramatic difference in performance gives further quantified substance to what is qualitatively obvious. Strong brands mean more return, for less risk.

## The social and political aspects of brands

Brands, however, are not simply economic entities.

Apart from the obvious social benefits of wealth creation on improvements in standards of living both nationally and internationally, there are less recognised social effects and benefits. Most of the world's most valuable brands have been around for more than 50 years. Brands are the most stable and sustainable assets in business, living on long after the passing of most management teams, offices, technological breakthroughs and short-term economic troughs. Clearly, to deliver this sustainable wealth, they need to be managed properly. But achieving sustainable wealth means more reliable income for companies, which means more reliable earnings. All this in turn leads to more security and stability of employment, which in itself is an important social benefit.

Related to the social perspective, there is also strong political significance in brands. Quite apart from the fact that political parties all over the world now employ professional branding practices, there have been many articles and studies on issues such as "Brand America". These have looked at the role and global dominance of American brands, and at how these are being used as political symbols, for good or ill. Although initially the presence of McDonald's was greeted enthusiastically in the former Soviet Union as symbolic of Russia's new found "liberation", more recently McDonald's has been targeted for anti-American demonstrations, despite its best efforts at emphasising local management structures and locally sensitive approaches to tailoring product offers and practices.

An interesting development that goes beyond the idea of boycotting has been the launch of competitive initiatives such as Mecca-Cola, introduced in 2002 by Tawfik Mathlouthi, a French entrepreneur; this is another demonstration of the highest level of symbolic and economic importance of brands. The strongest brands have always worked at the level of personal identity. So even if Mecca-Cola is not an immediate financial challenge to the $70 billion brand value of Coca-Cola, it has highlighted new possibilities for actively expressing fundamental differences of view, with the nicely ironic touch that the "alternative statement" brand has almost exactly the same physical characteristics as the mainstream one. However, before commentators get too carried away in this area, the nature of competition in brands has always meant competition between product characteristics and broader brand values, image and associations. Whatever the motivation for launching a competitive brand, its long-term success will depend on its ability to satisfy a critical mass of customers on product, service and image grounds.

But a powerful political point about brands is their ability to cross borders, and potentially to bind people and cultures together more quickly and effectively than national governments, or the bureaucratic wheels of international law, ever could.

Increasingly, TV has acted as the second superpower. Whereas it used to take decades and centuries for one culture to seep into another, now lasting and transforming images of different cultures can be transferred in seconds. America's dominance of the TV and media markets has ensured that American brands (and, indeed, Brand America) have dominated global markets in their turn; and although the production and servicing facilities for brands benefit from regional flexibility, those that own the brands own the greatest wealth. However, any successful brand, of any provenance, must continue to understand and anticipate changes in its audiences in order to remain successful. It is beyond irony that the internet – essentially an American invention and "supplied" by America – has become such an instrument of challenge to its brands and its institutions. It will be interesting indeed to see how the world's most valuable brands continue to adapt to the complex and unsettling changes in the new world order.

This book will explore these and other issues, such as how Asian brands could emerge as serious global players. What is certain, however, is that the strongest brands have, in their lifetime, already seen off seismic changes in political, social and economic circumstances, and continue to thrive through deserving trust and long-term relationships. Brands of all kinds do have extraordinary power: economic power, political power and social power. It is no exaggeration to say that brands have the power to change people's lives, and indeed the world. For this claim, think not just about the "one free world" images introduced by Coca-Cola advertising over the years, and the universality of the Red Cross, but also consider the more recent emergence of Microsoft and Nokia as inspirers and enablers of social change.

## Understanding the role of brands

If brands are so demonstrably powerful, and since the definition and benefit of brands embrace every type of business and organisation, the question to ask is why every business and organisation would not want to concentrate their resources, structure and financial accountability around this most important asset. Indeed, there is a clear need for organisations to be consistently preoccupied with maintaining the sustainable competitive advantage offered by the brand. The clarity of focus that a strong brand positioning gives organisations will always create more effectiveness, efficiency and competitive advantage across all operations; and from a pragmatic financial perspective, research among investment communities confirms that clarity of strategy is one of the first criteria for judging companies.

So why are brands sometimes not taken as seriously as the data show us they should be? There seem to be several potential explanations.

### Lack of understanding

Perhaps the first and most obvious is a lack of full understanding among some senior managers about what successful branding really is. If branding is treated as a cosmetic exercise only, and regarded merely as a new name/logo, stationery and possibly a new advertising campaign, then it will have only a superficial effect at best. Indeed, if this "cosmetic" approach is applied in an effort to make a bad or confused business look more attractive, it is easy to see why these so-called "rebranding" exercises encourage such cynicism. Reputation is, after all, reality with a lag effect. Branding needs to start with a clear point of view on what an organisation should be about and how it will deliver sustainable competitive advantage; then it is about organising all product, service and corporate operations to deliver that. The visual (and verbal) elements of branding should, of course, then symbolise that difference, lodge it memorably in people's minds and protect it in law through the trade mark.

### Terminology

The second explanation for why branding is sometimes not central in the corporate agenda seems to be to do with terminology. The term "brand" has now permeated just about every aspect of society, and can be as easily applied to utilities, charities, football teams and even government initiatives as it has been in the past to packaged goods. Yet there still seems to be a residual and stubborn belief that brands are relevant only to consumer goods and commerce. Clearly, this is nonsense when every organisation has "consumers" of some kind; furthermore, some of the world's most valuable brands are business to business, but that does not make them any less "consumers". However, rather than get deeply embroiled in the broader meanings of consumption, it is probably more helpful to talk about audiences for brands today. These can be consuming audiences, influencing audiences or internal audiences. All of these audiences need to be engaged by the brand – whether it is a product, service, corporate or not-for-profit brand – for it to fulfil its potential.

If there are still those who would say "yes, but why does it have to be called brand?", it is worth remembering that every successful business and organisation needs to be set up and organised around a distinctive idea of some kind. To distinguish itself effectively and efficiently from other organisations, it is helpful to have some kind of shorthand: visual or verbal symbols, perhaps an icon that can be registered and protected. To make up another term for all this would seem perverse, as branding is already in existence. Rather, it is worth exploring why some people and organisations might have this aversion or misunderstanding and tackle the root cause. In the case of some arts and charitable organisations, there can be a problem with commercial overtones; for commercial organisations working in the business-to-business arena, or in heavy or technical services, there may be concerns that branding feels too soft and intangible to be relevant. With the former, it is a harsh truth of the new arts and not-for-profit worlds that they are competing for talent, funding, supporters and audiences, and need to focus their efforts and investment with the effectiveness and efficiency that brand discipline brings. With the latter, there is nothing "soft" about the financial value that strong branding brings, in all and any sector; nor is it "soft" to use all possible competitive levers to gain every customer in a hypercompetitive international market. Price will always be a factor in choice. But acting like a commodity, rather than a trusted and differentiated brand, will eventually lead only to the lower-price road to perdition.

### Ownership

The third area to examine is that of ownership within organisations. Whereas the more established consumer goods companies grew up around their individual brands, more complex and technical organisations may often be run by people who have little experience in marketing or selling. As a result, the brand may simply be regarded as the specialist province of the marketing team, or, since the visual aspects of brands are the most obvious manifestation, brand management may be delegated to the design manager. This is not to cast aspersions on the specialist marketing and design functions, since their skills are vital in maintaining the currency and aesthetics of the brand; however, unless the chief executive of the organisation is perceived to be the brand champion, the brand will remain a departmental province rather than the driving purpose of everyone in an organisation. Although marketing is critical in shaping and presenting a brand to its audiences in the most powerful way, brands and marketing are not the same thing. And as far as the need for CEO attention is concerned, if the brand is the most important organisational asset, it makes rational sense for it to be the central management preoccupation. Business strategy is, or should be, brand strategy, and vice versa. Effective and efficient corporate governance is brand-driven governance.

## Tangible and intangible elements

The last area to cover in explaining any remaining ambivalence about brands relates to their particular combination of tangible and intangible elements. The tangible area is always easier, since today's senior business culture is still often happier concentrating on the tangible, rational and quantifiable aspects of business. As far as quantification is concerned, brands can certainly now be measured, and it is critically important that they are. If their financial contribution is not already self-evident, there are many formally recognised ways to put a hard and quantifiable value on them.

It is the intangible, more creative, visual and verbal elements of brands that can sometimes be taken less seriously by senior management than they deserve. Yet it is these elements that will engage and inspire people, externally and internally, to the advantage of the organisation. When John McGrath, former CEO of Diageo, describes the creation of the Diageo corporate brand, and the vision and values to support it, he speaks warmly of the vision that clarified and inspired the company for a new future. He adds wryly that the £1m that was paid to brand consultants for helping the company create this was a high-profile topic of media discussion at the time. This was in contrast to the many more millions of pounds in fees and commissions that were reportedly paid to lawyers and financiers, and which passed with barely a murmur. Creativity and imagination are crucial to the success of a brand. It is the easiest thing in the world for people to approach new naming, product development, design and advertising ideas with an open mouth and a closed mind. In turn, brand practitioners need to have the courage of their convictions in publicly presenting new ideas, and to recognise that the most effective creative solution may even challenge their own professional conventions.

## About this book

The following chapters in this book are divided into three parts.

Part 1 looks at the history and definition of brands, and their financial and social importance. Also examined are the world's most valuable brands and the lessons that can be learned from their experiences and the challenges they face.

Part 2 examines a number of crucial practical areas of brand management such as the disciplines of brand positioning and brand value management. This includes the need for brand alignment through all aspects of an organisation's operations, stretching across products and services, human resources practices and corporate behaviour, environments and communications. Also covered is the role of visual and verbal brand identity in engaging audiences and the ever more complex area of brand communications in the round. A chapter on public relations highlights the increasing need to ensure that internal and external messages are consistent in their representation of the brand. Another chapter looks at the importance of taking the necessary steps to ensure that a brand is legally protected.

Part 3 considers the future for brands of all kinds. It analyses the effects and opportunities of globalisation and examines the potential for Asian brands. One chapter considers the area of corporate social responsibility and the effect of the anti-capitalism and anti-globalisation movements; another puts the case for nations to take advantage of brand disciplines. The last chapter pulls together the trends that will shape the future of brands, business and society, and highlights what organisations need to focus on if they are to make the most of their most valuable asset: their brand.

# 1
# THE CASE FOR BRANDS

# 1 What is a brand?

*Tom Blackett*

## Ancient and modern

The *Oxford American Dictionary* (1980) contains the following definition:

> **Brand** *(noun): a trade mark, goods of a particular make: a mark of identification made with a hot iron, the iron used for this: a piece of burning or charred wood, (verb): to mark with a hot iron, or to label with a trade mark.*

Similarly, *The Pocket Oxford Dictionary of Current English* (1934) says:

> **Brand.** *1. n. Piece of burning or smouldering wood, torch, (literary); sword (poet.); iron stamp used red-hot to leave an indelible mark, mark left by it, stigma, trade-mark, particular kind of goods (all of the best bb.). 2. v.t. Stamp (mark, object, skin), with b., impress indelibly (is branded on my memory)*

These two entries, in the order in which they list the definitions and in the definitions themselves, illustrate how, over 50 years, the primary use of the word "brand" now has a commercial application. However, the definitions also underline a common origin. Almost irrespective of how the word is used today, it has always meant, in its passive form, the object by which an impression is formed, and in its active form the process of forming this impression.

The following pages develop the use of the word brand, both passive and active (albeit in human consciousness rather than on the flank of an animal), and explain how "branding" has become so important to business strategy. But first, there is a short history of brands.

## A short history of brands

The word brand comes from the Old Norse *brandr*, meaning to burn, and from these origins made its way into Anglo-Saxon. It was of course by burning that early man stamped ownership on his livestock, and with the development of trade buyers would use brands as a means of distinguishing between the cattle of one farmer and another. A farmer with a particularly good reputation for the quality of his animals would find his brand much sought after, while the brands of farmers with a lesser reputation were to be avoided or treated with caution. Thus the utility of brands as a guide to choice was established, a role that has remained unchanged to the present day.

Some of the earliest manufactured goods in "mass" production were clay pots, the remains of which can be found in great abundance around the Mediterranean region, particularly in the ancient civilisations of Etruria, Greece and Rome. There is considerable evidence among these remains of the use of brands, which in their earliest form were the potter's mark. A potter would identify his pots by putting his thumbprint into the wet clay on the bottom of the pot or by making his mark: a fish, a star or cross, for example. From this we can safely say that symbols (rather than initials or names) were the earliest visual form of brands.

In Ancient Rome, principles of commercial law developed that acknowledged the origin and title of potters' marks, but this did not deter makers of inferior pots from imitating the marks of well-known makers in order to dupe the public. In the British Museum there are even examples of imitation Roman pottery bearing imitation Roman marks, which were made in Belgium and exported to Britain in the first century AD. Thus as trade followed the flag – or Roman Eagle – so the practice of unlawful imitation lurked close behind, a practice that remains commonplace despite the strictures of our modern, highly developed legal systems.

With the fall of the Roman Empire, the elaborate and highly sophisticated system of trade that had bound together in mutual interdependence the Mediterranean and west European peoples gradually crumbled. Brands continued to be used but mainly on a local scale. The exceptions were the distinguishing marks used by kings, emperors and governments. The fleur-de-lis in France, the Hapsburg eagle in Austria-Hungary and the Imperial chrysanthemum in Japan indicated ownership or control. (Interestingly, the chrysanthemum signifies death in Korea, intermittently over the centuries a Japanese colony.) In a similar fashion the cockleshell, derived from the legend attached to the shrine of St James at Santiago de Compostella in north-west Spain, a favourite medieval centre of pilgrimage when the holy places of Palestine were closed to pilgrims by the Muslims, was widely used in pre-Renaissance Europe as a symbol of piety and faith.

In the 17th and 18th centuries, when the volume manufacture of fine porcelain, furniture and tapestries began in France and Belgium, largely because of royal patronage, factories increasingly used brands to indicate quality and origin. At the same time, laws relating to the hallmarking of gold and silver objects were enforced more rigidly to give the purchaser confidence in the product.

However, the widescale use of brands is essentially a phenomenon of the late 19th and early 20th centuries. The industrial revolution, with its improvements in manufacturing and communications, opened up the western world and allowed the mass-marketing of consumer products. Many of today's best-known consumer brands date from this period: Singer sewing-machines, Coca-Cola soft drinks, Bass beer, Quaker oats, Cook's tours, Sunlight soap, Shredded Wheat breakfast cereal, Kodak film, American Express travellers' cheques, Heinz baked beans and Prudential Insurance are just a few examples.

Hand in hand with the introduction of these brands came early trade mark legislation. This allowed the owners of these brands to protect them in law (indeed, the Bass "Red Triangle" trade mark was the very first registered in the UK in 1876, and the beaming Quaker, who adorns the pack of the eponymous oats, is now well into his second century). The birth of advertising agencies such as J Walter Thompson and NW Ayer in the late 19th century gave further impetus to the development of brands.

But it is the period since the end of the second world war that has seen the real explosion in the use of brands. Propelled by the collapse of communism, the arrival of the internet and mass broadcasting systems, and greatly improved transportation and communications, brands have come to symbolise the convergence of the world's economies on the demand-led rather than the command-led model. But brands have not escaped criticism. Recent anti-globalisation protests have been significant events. They have provided a timely reminder to the big brand owners that in the conduct of their affairs they have a duty to society, as well as customers and shareholders.

## Elements of the brand

The dictionary definitions quoted above suggest that brands are intrinsically striking and that their role is to create an indelible impression.

### Intrinsically striking

The visual distinctiveness of a brand may be a combination of any of the following: name, letters, numbers, a symbol, a signature, a shape, a

slogan, a colour, a particular typeface. But the name is the most important element of the brand as its use in language provides a universal reference point. The name is also the one element of the brand that should
never change. All other elements can change over time (Shell's famous
logo has evolved significantly from the early line drawing and Pepsi-
Cola switched to all-blue livery a few years ago), but the brand name
should be like Caesar: "as constant as the northern star".

This is not to say that brands achieve true visual distinctiveness
through their names alone. Nike without its tick-like swoosh, Camel
cigarettes without "Old Joe", the supercilious dromedary, Michelin without exuberant Monsieur Bibendum, McDonald's without its Golden
Arches would be paler properties indeed. Brands like these – and many
thousands of others – rely for their visual distinctiveness on the harmonious combination of these elements and the consistency with which
this is maintained.

This said, in certain markets where the use of branding is highly
developed and consumers are particularly sophisticated, these rules are
sometimes tested. In the fashion-clothing market, for example, brands
like Mambo and Diesel have experimented with the use of completely
different logos; Diesel even changed the name for a season (although all
other visual aspects of the brand remained the same). The success of
such tactics depends upon the awareness of the consumer. These two
brands enjoy almost "cult" status, and the loyalty with which they are
followed by their devotees has assured success.

Name changes of products and services are rare; they are uncommon
too among companies, but perhaps a little more frequent. With products
and services, the main reasons for change are either to extend the
appeal of a brand to new markets where the original name may not be
optimal, or to standardise the company's international trade mark portfolio. The Lucky Dog Phone Company, an AT&T subsidiary, changed its
name to Lucky Guy in the United States because no counterpart to the
lucky dog exists in the American Chinese, Japanese and Korean markets,
all important targets. Mars changed the Marathon name to Snickers in
the UK to bring the product's name into line with the rest of the world.

Companies generally change their names either because their function or their ownership has changed, or because their name is in some
way misleading. Sometimes they revert to initials: Minnesota Mining
and Manufacturing became 3M, a name that is both handier and more
flexible strategically. Sometimes they combine the names of the merging
companies: GlaxoSmithKline. Sometimes they opt for an entirely new

name: Altria is now the name of the tobacco, beer and foods group once known as Philip Morris. There is no right or wrong way of renaming businesses; it is as much a matter of what the company feels comfortable with and what it feels it can make work. The key is commitment and good communications.

Sometimes these rules are not observed as faithfully as they should be. When Guinness merged with Grand Metropolitan the holding company adopted the name Diageo. Shareholders were not impressed, thinking that the decision to adopt a meaningless, foreign-sounding name, when perfectly good names like Grand Met or Guinness were available, amounted to corporate treachery. At the extraordinary general meeting held to approve the new name outbursts of booing enlivened the proceedings at each mention of "Diageo".

Name changes following mergers can be highly charged events, and closer communication with all stakeholder groups – particularly private shareholders, who may also be pensioners of the firms involved – may help ease the transition. In the case of Diageo, a name that has now "bedded down", the company should have explained why it had decided to adopt a neutral name for the new holding company and issued firm reassurances regarding the famous trading names – particularly Guinness – that it would continue to use.

Diageo, like Aviva, an insurance business, and Altria, mentioned above, is strictly a holding company name (as was the unfortunate Consignia, a name briefly adopted by the Post Office and now consigned to history). These names are not intended for "public consumption" – although a mischievous press made great play of post offices becoming "consignias" – so clarity is paramount; the rationale for change must be communicated to – and understood by – all stakeholder groups.

### Creating an indelible impression

In developed economies consumers have an astonishing – often bewildering – array of choice. There are, for example, dozens of car manufacturers, hundreds of car models and thousands of different vehicle specifications to choose from; the days when Henry Ford offered "any colour you want as long as it's black" are now long gone. This diversity of choice puts pressure on those making or selling products or services to offer high quality, excellent value and wide availability. It also puts pressure on them to find more potent ways of differentiating themselves and securing competitive advantage. According to *Fortune* magazine (in 1997):

*In the twenty-first century, branding ultimately will be the only unique differentiator between companies. Brand equity is now a key asset.*

Much of the skill of marketing and branding nowadays is concerned with building "equity" for products whose characteristics, pricing, distribution and availability are really quite close to each other. Take cola drinks, for example. Coca-Cola and Pepsi-Cola are able to dominate the worldwide cola market. The power of their bottling and distribution systems no doubt plays a part in this, but the main factor is the strength and appeal of the two brands to consumers. The strong, instantly recognisable names, logos and colours of these two brands symbolise their makers' promise that consumers' expectations will be fulfilled, whatever the subtleties of these might be.

Brands allow the consumer to shop with confidence, and they provide a route map through a bewildering variety of choices. The customer does not have to be an expert on the complexities of mobile telecommunications to choose between one service supplier and another. The brand name, the tariff and the method of payment are all that is required to make an informed choice. And as tariffs and methods of payment are largely the same among competing companies, it is the brand – and consumers' appreciation of its underlying appeals – that will ultimately drive the purchase decision. It is the inculcation of these "underlying appeals" – the bedrock of brand equity – that concerns brand owners and has become the subject of unceasing attention and investment. Brands with strong equity embed themselves deeply in the hearts and minds of consumers.

The real power of successful brands is that they meet the expectations of those that buy them or, to put it another way, they represent a promise kept. As such they are a contract between a seller and a buyer: if the seller keeps to its side of the bargain, the buyer will be satisfied; if not, the buyer will in future look elsewhere.

## Brands as business assets

The value to businesses of owning strong brands is incontestable. Brands that keep their promise attract loyal buyers who will return to them at regular intervals. The benefit to the brand owner is that forecasting cash flows becomes easier, and it becomes possible to plan and manage the development of the business with greater confidence. Thus brands, with their ability to secure income, can be classed as productive assets in exactly the same way as any other, more traditional assets of a business (plant, equipment, cash, investments and so on). The asset value of brands is now widely recognised, not just by brand owners but by investors. Brands can generate high-quality earnings that can directly affect the overall performance of the business and thus influence the share price.

The stockmarket value of The Coca-Cola Company, for example, was around $136 billion in mid-2002, yet the book value (the net asset value) of the business was only $10.5 billion. A vast proportion of the value of the business (around $125 billion) is therefore dependent upon shareholders' confidence in the intangible assets of the business, and the ability of the company to manage these profitably. Coca-Cola owns few intangibles other than its "secret recipe", its contracts with its global network of bottlers and its brand names. An independent analysis estimated that the value of the Coca-Cola brand name in mid-2002 was almost $70 billion, well over half of its intangible value. Similarly, high-profile consumer brands like McDonald's can attribute a huge proportion (around 70%) of their market value to their brands. At the other end of the scale, for two of the world's largest companies, General Electric and Intel, the ratio of brand values to intangible value is much lower. Both GE and Intel are rich in intangibles, but as these are linked to the technology in which these companies excel, they probably take the form of patents and know-how agreements.

It is not surprising that much of the merger and acquisition activity of the past 20 years or so has involved brand-owning businesses. The durability of brands, the quality of their earning power (unlike short-lived technology assets such as patents) and their widespread appeal make them highly desirable properties. The globalisation of trade is driving consolidation in many industries; a recent example is the purchase, for $21 billion, of Bestfoods by Unilever. Bestfoods owns many famous food brands, notably Knorr stock cubes and Hellmann's mayonnaise. These brands have truly global potential, which is more likely to be tapped by a company of the size and scale of Unilever than by Bestfoods, which is large but lacks Unilever's global resources.

Equally, in 1998 Volkswagen concluded a deal to acquire Rolls-Royce Motor Cars from Vickers, a UK engineering group, for around £400m. VW's interest was not in acquiring a pile of fully depreciated manufacturing assets in Derby, the home of Rolls-Royce, but in the famous Rolls-Royce and Bentley brands, crown jewels of the global automotive industry. However, although Vickers owned the Bentley name, it only had a licence for Rolls-Royce. In an interesting twist to this tale, Rolls-Royce Aero Engines, the owner of the Rolls-Royce brand name, refused to grant a licence in perpetuity to VW, handing this instead to BMW, VW's old German rival. There can be little doubt that these brands will thrive under new ownership, as both BMW and VW have state-of-the-art manufacturing and truly global resources far exceeding those of the former maker.

## The explosion of branding

The scale of adoption of branding has been breathtaking. An activity that for three-quarters of the 20th century was mainly confined to consumer goods and services now features in industrial and business-to-business sectors, the public and voluntary sectors, utilities and non-governmental organisations. Within the consumer sector, the development of technology has added thousands of new products and services: computer games, laptops, mobile telephones, the internet and the myriad services it distributes. Football teams, political parties and pop stars all now consider themselves brands; and the Church of England was recently urged in the media to adopt a more "branded" approach to the recruitment of clergy.

In parallel, we have seen the emergence of two new practices in branding: the application of branding techniques to corporations, and the "internalisation" of brands and their management, particularly within services businesses where the employee is pivotal in delivering customer satisfaction.

### Corporate branding

Corporations have learned how important it is to be understood and appreciated, not just by investors, customers, suppliers and employees but also by opinion formers, activist groups and the general public. In shareholding societies there is intense interest in both the behaviour and the performance of quoted companies; and with the advent of the internet such companies find themselves increasingly in the "global fishbowl", where damaging news or opinions travel fast and wide. Reputation is paramount, and companies that are known for the quality of their products and services, their integrity and the transparency of their actions are the ones best placed to sustain a competitive advantage.

In the pharmaceuticals industry, for example, large corporations such as GlaxoSmithKline, Merck, Pfizer, Roche and Novartis all depend upon the development of successful new drugs for future profitability. With the declining productivity of in-house R&D, they compete fiercely for promising new products being developed by smaller, research-based organisations, such as those specialising in biotechnology. Here the reputation of the bidder is as critical as the price and the royalty terms being offered. The bidder must have a spotless record for the quality and effectiveness of its products, and for the way it conducts itself in the public arena. The reputations of several of the leading pharmaceuticals companies were damaged recently through their involvement in the supply of HIV and AIDS drugs to southern Africa. The South African government threatened to overrule their patents and allow local manufacturers to produce the drugs, unless these companies reduced their prices, which – after negotiations that involved Oxfam, itself a conspicuous brand – they eventually did.

Even the mighty Coca-Cola has been brought up short by inattention to the particular needs and sensitivities of its stakeholders. In 1999 it was forced to withdraw Coke from the Belgian market following a contamination scare. The scare was dealt with quickly and efficiently, but it succeeded in attracting a great deal of attention. Around the same time the company had been involved variously in a discriminatory employment suit, an antitrust investigation in France and a failed attempt to buy the soft drink brand Orangina. The Belgian affair, exacerbated by some clumsy remarks by the then CEO, led analysts and investors to question the grip the Coca-Cola board had on its business. The share price fell and a planned acquisition – of Quaker – was abandoned. As a result the board was shaken up and the management of the company's global businesses devolved to a more local level to get closer to the consumer.

The companies referred to above have largely recovered the reputational ground they lost. The same cannot be said of such notorious casualties as Enron and WorldCom. Both these corporations were relative newcomers, but cheating your shareholders (your owners) so spectacularly represents a betrayal of trust that not even long-established brands can survive.

### Services branding

The developed world has seen a huge shift in output from industry and manufacturing to services, and as demand for financial and leisure services increases, brands will play an increasing role in a "brand savvy" world in which people have become more and more discriminating and difficult to please. Brand owners therefore need to ensure that they deliver high-quality services that are aligned with a compelling vision and delivered with a genuine commitment to customer satisfaction. Thus the next journey for the brand is inside. Some of the most successful branded companies use the brand as their central organising principle. Richard Branson's determination to give the man in the street a better deal – whether it is in financial services, train services or air travel – animates the organisation and acts as a filter for corporate development. Not all of Branson's enterprises have been successful, notably Virgin Rail, but he is widely admired for his commitment and enthusiasm, even if these qualities are not always matched by service delivery. Fliers with Virgin Atlantic can readily sense the difference; not only is the flight cheaper, but the whole experience is different. It may not be to everyone's taste, but the friendliness and informality of the staff reflect the personality of Branson himself. The result is a well-managed customer experience, distinctive and memorable.

Contrast this with the financial services sector. Banks, in particular, have struggled to create and deliver a well-differentiated customer experience. Years of overclaiming in advertising – "the bank that likes to say 'yes'", "Come and talk to the listening bank" – have led to customer cynicism. Unlike the Virgin Atlantic experience, which is almost palpable, banks seem to lack a really big idea. (Perhaps this is the result of over a century of trying not to be different.) Some have experimented with telephone and internet banking, and it is notable that the most successful have been those that have adopted new names, such as First Direct and Egg, and have distanced themselves from their owners (Midland Bank and Prudential Assurance respectively). But in truth it is exceptionally difficult for banks to differentiate; all have broadly the same products, premises and services, and all seek to recruit the same type of employee. Employees can make a difference, however, as anyone who has had a memorable experience when dealing with their bank branch will know. Employees can make or mar a long-standing relationship, and as banking has traditionally been the business of "relationships", investment in staff training is clearly one of the most important commitments to brand management that a bank can make.

Other than our health, our wealth (or lack of it) is an aspect of life that is closest to most people's hearts. It is also an aspect of life where we frequently need advice and where "trust" carries a high premium. Brands have always been about trust, and it is instructive to reflect on how the level of trust we may have in our medical adviser contrasts with the level of trust we may have in our bank and other financial advisers. The financial institutions were once greatly esteemed by their customers – "safe as the Bank of England" – but with the general drive towards greater operational efficiencies (downsizing) the personal contact with customers on which relationship building depends is now greatly reduced. Automatic teller machines and remote banking (via the internet) may be a boon to banks' balance sheets, but they remove the opportunity to help customers with the more complicated decisions they need to make in their lives, particularly those concerning investments and pensions. Increasing familiarity, and comfort, with the internet may eventually enable banks and other financial services providers to engage with customers at a more intimate level. But in the meantime, a return to good old-fashioned relationship building, based on staff training that embraces business and social skills, will help restore some of the credibility these brands once had.

Overall, the best services brands are built around a unique business idea or a compelling vision. When employees are excited by the proposition they will help to sustain it and communicate it to customers, suppliers and others through their enthusiasm and commitment.

## Guidelines for good brand management

Some of the guidelines given below are eternal truths that apply equally to product, services and corporate brands, and some apply particularly to one category of brand or another.

- **Protect your brand.** Trade mark law offers provision for the protection of your brand and corporate names, your logo and colours, the shape of your packaging, smells, and the advertising jingle you use. This protection can last indefinitely, subject to payment of a fee and the observation of some none too onerous rules of use. Patent law allows you to protect your product for periods of up to 20 years, provided the product is your invention and is a novel or non-obvious idea. Copyrights allow you to protect artistic, literary, dramatic and musical works for up to 50 years after the death of the author or originator. Protect these elements of your brand on a wide geographical scale: you may not yet be an international player, but the real opportunities are for brands whose appeals are potentially universal.
- **Honour your stakeholders.** Your customers expect attractive, well-differentiated products and services that will live up to their expectations and are well priced. Your employees want to work

for a company with a compelling business idea, where they feel engaged and where they can make a difference. Your shareholders expect sound corporate governance and a well-managed company with a commitment to growing shareholder value. Your trade partners want fairness and respect in their dealings with you, and they want your reputation to enhance their own. Opinion leaders and industry commentators expect performance, innovation, transparency and a sense of social responsibility. Interest groups want you to listen and to act.

◪ **Treat your brand as an investment, not a cost.** Brands are among the most important assets that a business can own, and strong brands can ensure business continuity in times of difficulty. Brands must remain relevant to their customers, contemporary and appealing. This means that sufficient investment must be made in advertising and marketing as well as in new product development. For many businesses active in mature markets, brand support and development is often the single biggest item of overhead cost. Investors and analysts will, quite rightly, expect the management of the business to account for the effectiveness of this expenditure; but they will look in vain at the balance sheet for evidence of this. Periodic valuations of the brands in the business will help explain how successfully management is steering the brands for the benefit of shareholders.

◪ **Exploit the financial potential of your brand.** As well as seeking ways to extend the brand through new product development, companies should look at opportunities to exploit the equity in their brands through co-branding, licensing and franchising. Co-branding can be a highly cost-effective way of entering new markets and geographical areas; the art is in finding a suitably compatible partner. Licensing is the granting of a right to use a brand in relation to similar goods or services. However, the licensor must retain control over the quality of the goods and services produced by the licensee and marketed under the brand (the practice is common in the brewing industry). Franchising is the granting of a right to a number of licensees in different geographical areas to use the brand together with a business system developed by the licensor (this practice is common in fast foods, print shops, florists and so on). Co-branding, licensing and franchising can be highly lucrative ways of exploiting a brand, broadening its exposure and enhancing its message.

◪ **Understand that successful brand management nowadays is a complex task.** It requires skills not normally associated with the traditional marketing function. The ability to brief market-research companies, advertising agencies and designers, to liaise with the sales and distribution people and to survive the odd skirmish with the "bean counters" is no longer enough. Brand managers certainly need to be adept in all these areas, but they also need to understand how a brand can be managed for the benefit of shareholders. This requires an understanding of how, in financial terms, a brand contributes to the success of a business and the creation of shareholder value. Managers of services brands need to become adept at internal communication and training, to ensure that customer satisfaction is delivered consistently in support of their brand's promise. And if the brand is the corporation, the brand manager needs to understand not just the subtle art of corporate communications but the infinitely more demanding role of stakeholder accountability.

# 2 Brand valuation

*Jan Lindemann*

If this business were split up, I would give you the land and bricks and mortar, and I would take the brands and trade marks, and I would fare better than you.

John Stuart, chairman of Quaker (ca. 1900)

In the last quarter of the 20th century there was a dramatic shift in the understanding of the creation of shareholder value. For most of the century, tangible assets were regarded as the main source of business value. These included manufacturing assets, land and buildings or financial assets such as receivables and investments. They would be valued at cost or outstanding value as shown in the balance sheet. The market was aware of intangibles, but their specific value remained unclear and was not specifically quantified. Even today, the evaluation of profitability and performance of businesses focuses on indicators such as return on investment, assets or equity that exclude intangibles from the denominator. Measures of price relatives (for example, price-to-book ratio) also exclude the value of intangible assets as these are absent from accounting book values.

This does not mean that management failed to recognise the importance of intangibles. Brands, technology, patents and employees were always at the heart of corporate success, but rarely explicitly valued. Their value was subsumed in the overall asset value. Major brand owners like The Coca Cola Company, Procter & Gamble, Unilever and Nestlé were aware of the importance of their brands, as indicated by their creation of brand managers, but on the stockmarket investors focused their value assessment on the exploitation of tangible assets.

## Evidence of brand value

The increasing recognition of the value of intangibles came with the continuous increase in the gap between companies' book values and their stockmarket valuations, as well as sharp increases in premiums above the stockmarket value that were paid in mergers and acquisitions in the late 1980s. A study by the US Federal Reserve Board (see Figure 2.1) shows the dramatic increase in the importance of intangibles to overall corporate value in the second half of the 20th century.

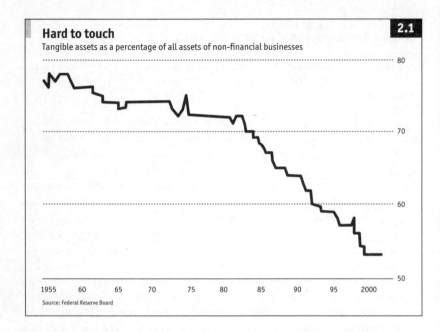

**Hard to touch**

2.1

Tangible assets as a percentage of all assets of non-financial businesses

Source: Federal Reserve Board

Today it is possible to argue that in general the majority of business value is derived from intangibles. Management attention to these assets has certainly increased substantially.

The brand is a special intangible that in many businesses is the most important asset. This is because of the economic impact that brands have. They influence the choices of customers, employees, investors and government authorities. In a world of abundant choices, such influence is crucial for commercial success and creation of shareholder value. Even non-profit organisations have started embracing the brand as a key asset for obtaining donations, sponsorships and volunteers.

Some brands have also demonstrated an astonishing durability. The world's most valuable brand,[1] Coca-Cola, is more than 118 years old; and the majority of the world's most valuable brands have been around for more than 60 years. This compares with an estimated average life span for a corporation of 25 years or so.[2] Many brands have survived a string of different corporate owners.

Several studies have tried to estimate the contribution that brands make to shareholder value. A study by Interbrand in association with JP Morgan (see Table 2.1) concluded that on average brands account for more than one-third of shareholder value. The study reveals that brands

Table 2.1 **The contribution of brands to shareholder value**

| Company | 2002 brand value ($bn) | Brand contribution to market capitalisation of parent company (%) | 2001 brand value ($bn) |
|---|---|---|---|
| Coca-Cola | 69.6 | 51 | 69.0 |
| Microsoft | 64.1 | 21 | 65.1 |
| IBM | 51.2 | 39 | 52.8 |
| GE | 41.3 | 14 | 42.4 |
| Intel | 30.9 | 22 | 34.7 |
| Nokia | 30.0 | 51 | 35.0 |
| Disney | 29.3 | 68 | 32.6 |
| McDonald's | 26.4 | 71 | 25.3 |
| Marlboro | 24.2 | 20 | 22.1 |
| Mercedes-Benz | 21.0 | 47 | 21.7 |

Source: *Business Week*, Interbrand/JP Morgan league table, 2002

create significant value either as consumer or corporate brands or as a combination of both.

Table 2.1 shows how big the economic contribution made by brands to companies can be. The McDonald's brand accounts for more than 70% of shareholder value. The Coca-Cola brand alone accounts for 51% of the stockmarket value of the Coca-Cola Company. This is despite the fact that the company owns a large portfolio of other drinks brands such as Sprite and Fanta.

Studies by academics from Harvard and the University of South Carolina[3] and by Interbrand[4] of the companies featured in the "Best Global Brands" league table indicate that companies with strong brands outperform the market in respect of several indices. It has also been shown that a portfolio weighted by the brand values of the Best Global Brands performs significantly better than Morgan Stanley's global MSCI index and the American-focused S&P 500 index.

Today leading companies focus their management efforts on intangible assets. For example, the Ford Motor Company has reduced its physical asset base in favour of investing in intangible assets. In the past few years, it has spent well over $12 billion to acquire prestigious brand names such as Jaguar, Aston Martin, Volvo and Land Rover. Samsung, a leading electronics group, invests heavily in its intangibles, spending about 7.5% of annual revenues on R&D and another 5% on communications.[5] In packaged consumer goods, companies spend up to 10% of annual revenues on marketing support. As John Akasie wrote in an article in *Forbes* magazine:[6]

> *It's about brands and brand building and consumer relationships ... Decapitalised, brand owning companies can earn huge returns on their capital and grow faster, unencumbered by factories and masses of manual workers. Those are the things that the stockmarket rewards with high price/earnings ratios.*

## Brands on the balance sheet

The wave of brand acquisitions in the late 1980s resulted in large amounts of goodwill that most accounting standards could not deal with in an economically sensible way. Transactions that sparked the debate about accounting for goodwill on the balance sheet included Nestlé's purchase of Rowntree, United Biscuits' acquisition and later divestiture of Keebler, Grand Metropolitan acquiring Pillsbury and Danone buying Nabisco's European businesses.

Accounting practice for so-called goodwill did not deal with the increasing importance of intangible assets, with the result that companies were penalised for making what they believed to be value-enhancing acquisitions. They either had to suffer massive amortisation charges on their profit and loss accounts (income statements), or they had to write off the amount to reserves and in many cases ended up with a lower asset base than before the acquisition.

In countries such as the UK, France, Australia and New Zealand it was, and still is, possible to recognise the value of acquired brands as "identifiable intangible assets" and to put these on the balance sheet of the acquiring company. This helped to resolve the problem of goodwill. Then the recognition of brands as intangible assets made use of a grey area of accounting, at least in the UK and France, whereby companies were not encouraged to include brands on the balance sheet but nor were they prevented from doing so. In the mid-1980s, Reckitt & Colman, a UK-based company, put a value on its balance sheet for the Airwick brand that it had recently bought; Grand Metropolitan did the same with the Smirnoff brand, which it had acquired as part of Heublein. At the same time, some newspaper groups put the value of their acquired mastheads on their balance sheets.

By the late 1980s, the recognition of the value of acquired brands on

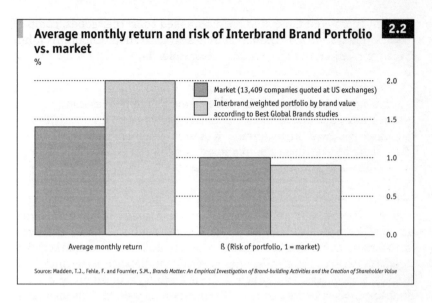

Average monthly return and risk of Interbrand Brand Portfolio **2.2** vs. market
%

Market (13,409 companies quoted at US exchanges)
Interbrand weighted portfolio by brand value according to Best Global Brands studies

2.0
1.5
1.0
0.5
0.0

Average monthly return       ß (Risk of portfolio, 1 = market)

Source: Madden, T.J., Fehle, F. and Fournier, S.M., *Brands Matter: An Empirical Investigation of Brand-building Activities and the Creation of Shareholder Value*

the balance sheet prompted a similar recognition of internally generated brands as valuable financial assets within a company. In 1988, Rank Hovis McDougall (RHM), a leading UK food conglomerate, played heavily on the power of its brands to successfully defend a hostile takeover bid by Goodman Fielder Wattie (GFW). RHM's defence strategy involved carrying out an exercise that demonstrated the value of RHM's brand portfolio. This was the first independent brand valuation establishing that it was possible to value brands not only when they had been acquired, but also when they had been created by the company itself. After successfully fending off the GFW bid, RHM included in its 1988 financial accounts the value of both the internally generated and acquired brands under "intangible assets" on the balance sheet.

In 1989, the London Stock Exchange endorsed the concept of brand valuation as used by RHM by allowing the inclusion of intangible assets in the class tests for shareholder approvals during takeovers. This proved to be the impetus for a wave of major branded-goods companies to recognise the value of brands as intangible assets on their balance sheets. In the UK, these included Cadbury Schweppes, Grand Metropolitan (when it acquired Pillsbury for $5 billion), Guinness, Ladbrokes (when it acquired Hilton) and United Biscuits (including the Smith's brand).

Today, many companies including LVMH, L'Oréal, Gucci, Prada and

PPR have recognised acquired brands on their balance sheet. Some companies have used the balance-sheet recognition of their brands as an investor-relations tool by providing historic brand values and using brand value as a financial performance indicator.

In terms of accounting standards, the UK, Australia and New Zealand have been leading the way by allowing acquired brands to appear on the balance sheet and providing detailed guidelines on how to deal with acquired goodwill. In 1999, the UK Accounting Standards Board introduced FRS 10 and 11 on the treatment of acquired goodwill on the balance sheet. The International Accounting Standards Board followed suit with IAS 38. And in spring 2002, the US Accounting Standards Board introduced FASB 141 and 142, abandoning pooling accounting and laying out detailed rules about recognising acquired goodwill on the balance sheet. There are indications that most accounting standards, including international and UK standards, will eventually convert to the US model. This is because most international companies that wish to raise funds in the US capital markets or have operations in the United States will be required to adhere to US Generally Accepted Accounting Principles (GAAP).

The principal stipulations of all these accounting standards are that acquired goodwill needs to be capitalised on the balance sheet and amortised according to its useful life. However, intangible assets such as brands that can claim infinite life do not have to be subjected to amortisation. Instead, companies need to perform annual impairment tests. If the value is the same or higher than the initial valuation, the asset value on the balance sheet remains the same. If the impairment value is lower, the asset needs to be written down to the lower value. Recommended valuation methods are discounted cash flow (DCF) and market value approaches. The valuations need to be performed on the business unit (or subsidiary) that generates the revenues and profit.

The accounting treatment of goodwill upon acquisition is an important step in improving the financial reporting of intangibles such as brands. It is still insufficient, as only acquired goodwill is recognised and the detail of the reporting is reduced to a minor footnote in the accounts. This leads to the distortion that the McDonald's brand does not appear on the company's balance sheet, even though it is estimated to account for about 70% of the firm's stockmarket value (see Table 2.1), yet the Burger King brand is recognised on the balance sheet. There is also still a problem with the quality of brand valuations for balance-sheet recognition. Although some companies use a brand-specific valuation approach, others use less sophisticated valuation techniques that often produce questionable values. The debate about bringing financial reporting more in line with the reality of long-term corporate value is likely to continue, but if there is greater consistency in brand-valuation approaches and greater reporting of brand values, corporate asset values will become much more transparent.

## The social value of brands

The economic value of brands to their owners is now widely accepted, but their social value is less clear. Do brands create value for anyone other than their owners, and is the value they create at the expense of society at large?[7] The ubiquity of global mega-brands has made branding the focus of discontent for many people around the world. They see a direct link between brands and such issues as the exploitation of workers in developing countries and the homogenisation of cultures. Furthermore, brands are accused of stifling competition and tarnishing the virtues of the capitalist system by encouraging monopoly and limiting consumer choice. The opposing argument is that brands create substantial social as well as economic value as a result of increased competition, improved product performance and the pressure on brand owners to behave in socially responsible ways.

Competition on the basis of performance as well as price, which is the nature of brand competition, fosters product development and improvement. And there is evidence that companies that promote their brands more heavily than others in their categories do also tend to be the more innovative in their categories. A study by PIMS Europe for the European Brands Association[8] revealed that less-branded businesses launch fewer products, invest significantly less in development and have fewer product advantages than their branded counterparts. Almost half of the "non-branded" sample spent nothing on product R&D compared with less than a quarter of the "branded" sample. And while 26% of non-branded producers never introduced significant new products, this figure was far lower at 7% for the branded set.

The need to keep brands relevant promotes increased investments in R&D, which in turn leads to a continuous process of product improvement and development. Brand owners are accountable for both the quality and the performance of their branded products and services and for their ethical practices. Given the direct link between brand value and both sales and share price, the potential costs of behaving unethically far outweigh any benefits, and outweigh the monitoring costs associated with an ethical business.

A number of high-profile brands have been accused of unethical practices. Interestingly, among these are some of the brands that have been pioneering the use of voluntary codes of conduct and internal monitoring systems. This is not to say that these brands have successfully eradicated unethical business practices, but at least they are demonstrating the will to deal with the problem.

The more honest companies are in admitting the gap they have to bridge in terms of ethical behaviour, the more credible they will seem. Nike, a company once criticised for the employment practices of some of its suppliers in developing countries, now posts results of external audits and interviews with factory workers at www.nikebiz.com. The concern of multinational companies is understandable, considering that a 5% drop in sales could result in a loss of brand value exceeding $1 billion. It is clearly in their economic interests to behave ethically.

## Approaches to brand valuation

Financial values have to some extent always been attached to brands and to other intangible assets, but it was only in the late 1980s that valuation approaches were established that could fairly claim to understand and assess the specific value of brands. The idea of putting a separate value on brands is now widely accepted. For those concerned with accounting, transfer pricing and licensing agreements, mergers and acquisitions and value-based management, brand valuation plays a key role in business today.

Unlike other assets such as stocks, bonds, commodities and real estate, there is no active market in brands that would provide "comparable" values. So to arrive at an authoritative and valid approach, a number of brand evaluation models have been developed. Most have fallen into two categories:

◪ research-based brand equity evaluations;
◪ purely financially driven approaches.

## Research-based approaches

There are numerous brand equity models that use consumer research to assess the relative performance of brands. These do not put a financial value on brands; instead, they measure consumer behaviour and attitudes that have an impact on the economic performance of brands.

Although the sophistication and complexity of such models vary, they all try to explain, interpret and measure consumers' perceptions that influence purchase behaviour. They include a wide range of perceptive measures such as different levels of awareness (unaided, aided, top of mind), knowledge, familiarity, relevance, specific image attributes, purchase consideration, preference, satisfaction and recommendation. Some models add behavioural measures such as market share and relative price.

Through different stages and depths of statistical modelling, these measures are arranged either in hierarchic order, to provide hurdles that lead from awareness to preference and purchase, or relative to their impact on overall consumer perception, to provide an overall brand equity score or measure. A change in one or a combination of indicators is expected to influence consumers' purchasing behaviour, which in turn will affect the financial value of the brand in question. However, these approaches do not differentiate between the effects of other influential factors such as R&D and design and the brand. They therefore do not provide a clear link between the specific marketing indicators and the financial performance of the brand. A brand can perform strongly according to these indicators but still fail to create financial and shareholder value.

The understanding, interpretation and measurement of brand equity indicators are crucial for assessing the financial value of brands. After all, they are key measures of consumers' purchasing behaviour upon which the success of the brand depends. However, unless they are integrated into an economic model, they are insufficient for assessing the economic value of brands.

### Financially driven approaches

**Cost-based approaches** define the value of a brand as the aggregation of all historic costs incurred or replacement costs required in bringing the brand to its current state: that is, the sum of the development costs, marketing costs, advertising and other communication costs, and so on. These approaches fail because there is no direct correlation between the financial investment made and the value added by a brand. Financial investment is an important component in building brand value, provided it is effectively targeted. If it isn't, it may not make a bean of difference. The investment needs to go beyond the obvious advertising and promotion and include R&D, employee training, packaging and product design, retail design, and so on.

**Comparables.** Another approach is to arrive at a value for a brand on the basis of something comparable. But comparability is difficult in the case of brands as by definition they should be differentiated and thus not comparable. Furthermore, the value creation of brands in the same category can be very different, even if most other aspects of the underlying business such as target groups, advertising spend, price promotions and distribution channel are similar or identical. Comparables can provide an interesting cross-check, however, even though they should never be relied on solely for valuing brands.

**Premium price.** In the premium price method, the value is calculated as the net present value of future price premiums that a branded product would command over an unbranded or generic equivalent. However, the primary purpose of many brands is not necessarily to obtain a price premium but rather to secure the highest level of future demand. The value generation of these brands lies in securing future volumes rather than securing a premium price. This is true for many durable and non-durable consumer goods categories.

This method is flawed because there are rarely generic equivalents to which the premium price of a branded product can be compared. Today, almost everything is branded, and in some cases store brands can be as strong as producer brands charging the same or similar prices. The price difference between a brand and competing products can be an indicator of its strength, but it does not represent the only and most important value contribution a brand makes to the underlying business.

**Economic use.** Approaches that are driven exclusively by brand equity measures or financial measures lack either the financial or the marketing component to provide a complete and robust assessment of the economic value of brands. The economic use approach, which was developed in 1988, combines brand equity and financial measures, and has become the most widely recognised and accepted methodology for brand valuation. It has been used in more than 3,500 brand valuations worldwide. The economic use approach is based on fundamental marketing and financial principles:

- ◿ The marketing principle relates to the commercial function that brands perform within businesses. First, brands help to generate customer demand; customers can be individual consumers as well as corporate consumers depending on the nature of the

## Brand valuation process

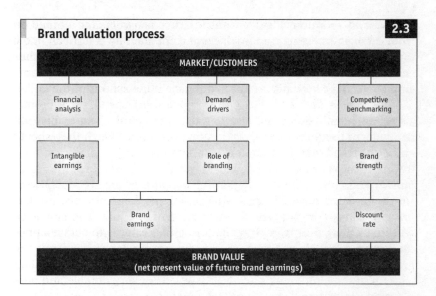

business and the purchase situation. Customer demand translates into revenues through purchase volume, price and frequency. Second, brands secure customer demand for the long term through repurchase and loyalty.

◪ The financial principle relates to the net present value of future expected earnings, a concept widely used in business. The brand's future earnings are identified and then discounted to a net present value using a discount rate that reflects the risk of those earnings being realised.

To capture the complex value creation of a brand, take the following five steps:

**1 Market segmentation.** Brands influence customer choice, but the influence varies depending on the market in which the brand operates. Split the brand's markets into non-overlapping and homogeneous groups of consumers according to applicable criteria such as product or service, distribution channels, consumption patterns, purchase sophistication, geography, existing and new customers, and so on. The brand is valued in each segment and the sum of the segment valuations constitutes the total value of the brand.

**2 Financial analysis.** Identify and forecast revenues and "earnings from intangibles" generated by the brand for each of the distinct segments determined in step 1. Intangible earnings are defined as brand revenue less operating costs, applicable taxes and a charge for the capital employed. The concept is similar to the notion of economic profit.

**3 Demand analysis.** Assess the role that the brand plays in driving demand for products and services in the markets in which it operates, and determine what proportion of intangible earnings is attributable to the brand measured by an indicator referred to as the "role of branding index". This is done by first identifying the various drivers of demand for the branded business, then determining the degree to which each driver is directly influenced by the brand. The role of branding index represents the percentage of intangible earnings that are generated by the brand. Brand earnings are calculated by multiplying the role of branding index by intangible earnings.

**4 Competitive benchmarking.** Determine the competitive strengths and weaknesses of the brand to derive the specific brand discount rate that reflects the risk profile of its expected future earnings (this is measured by an indicator referred to as the "brand strength score"). This comprises extensive competitive benchmarking and a structured evaluation of the brand's market, stability, leadership position, growth trend, support, geographic footprint and legal protectability.

**5 Brand value calculation.** Brand value is the net present value (NPV) of the forecast brand earnings, discounted by the brand discount rate. The NPV calculation comprises both the forecast period and the period beyond, reflecting the ability of brands to continue generating future earnings.

An example of a hypothetical valuation of a brand in one market segment is shown in Table 2.2.

This calculation is useful for brand value modelling in a wide range of situations, such as:

- ◼ predicting the effect of marketing and investment strategies;
- ◼ determining and assessing communication budgets;
- ◼ calculating the return on brand investment;
- ◼ assessing opportunities in new or underexploited markets;
- ◼ tracking brand value management.

## Applications

The range of applications for brand valuation has widened considerably since its creation in 1988, and it is now used in most strategic marketing and financial decisions. There are two main categories of applications:

◪ Strategic brand management, where brand valuation focuses mainly on internal audiences by providing tools and processes to manage and increase the economic value of brands.

◪ Financial transactions, where brand valuation helps in a variety of brand-related transactions with external parties.

### Strategic brand management

Recognition of the economic value of brands has increased the demand for effective management of the brand asset. In the pursuit of increasing shareholder value, companies are keen to establish procedures for the management of brands that are aligned with those for other business assets, as well as for the company as a whole. As traditional purely research-based measurements proved insufficient for understanding and managing the economic value of brands, companies have adopted brand valuation as a brand management tool. Brand valuation helps them establish value-based systems for brand management. Economic value creation becomes the focus of brand management and all brand-related investment decisions. Companies as diverse as American Express, IBM, Samsung Electronics, Accenture, United Way of America, BP, Fujitsu and Duke Energy have used brand valuation to help them refocus their businesses on their brands and to create an economic rationale for branding decisions and investments. Many companies have made brand value creation part of the remuneration criteria for senior marketing executives. These companies find brand valuation helpful for the following:

◪ Making decisions on business investments. By making the brand asset comparable to other intangible and tangible company assets, resource allocation between the different asset types can follow the same economic criteria and rationale, for example, capital allocation and return requirements.

◪ Measuring the return on brand investments based on brand value to arrive at an ROI that can be directly compared with other investments. Brand management and marketing service providers

Table 2.2 **Sample brand value calculation**

| | Year 1 | Year 2 | Year 3 | Year 4 | Year 5 |
|---|---|---|---|---|---|
| Market (Units) | 250,000,000 | 258,750,000 | 267,806,250 | 277,179,469 | 286,880,750 |
| Market growth rate | | 4% | 4% | 4% | 4% |
| Market share (Volume) | 15% | 17% | 19% | 21% | 20% |
| Volume | 37,500,000 | 43,987,500 | 50,883,188 | 58,207,688 | 57,376,150 |
| Price ($) | 10 | 10 | 10 | 11 | 11 |
| Price change | | 3% | 2% | 2% | 2% |
| **Branded Revenues** | **375,000,000** | **450,871,875** | **531,983,725** | **621,341,172** | **625,326,631** |
| Cost of sales | 150,000,000 | 180,348,750 | 212,793,490 | 248,536,469 | 250,130,653 |
| Gross margin | 225,000,000 | 270,523,125 | 319,190,235 | 372,804,703 | 375,195,979 |
| Marketing costs | 67,500,000 | 81,156,938 | 95,757,071 | 111,841,411 | 112,558,794 |
| Depreciation | 2,812,500 | 3,381,539 | 3,989,878 | 4,660,059 | 4,689,950 |
| Other overheads | 18,750,000 | 22,543,594 | 26,599,186 | 31,067,059 | 31,266,332 |
| Central cost allocation | 3,750,000 | 4,508,719 | 5,319,837 | 6,213,412 | 6,253,266 |
| **EBITA (Earnings Before Interest, Tax and Amortisation)** | **132,187,500** | **158,932,336** | **187,524,263** | **219,022,763** | **220,427,638** |
| Applicable taxes    35% | 46,265,625 | 55,626,318 | 65,633,492 | 76,657,967 | 77,149,673 |
| **NOPAT (Net Operating Profit After Tax)** | **85,921,875** | **103,306,018** | **121,890,771** | **142,364,796** | **143,277,964** |

| | Year 1 | Year 2 | Year 3 | Year 4 | Year 5 |
|---|---|---|---|---|---|
| **Capital Employed** | **131,250,000** | **157,805,156** | **186,194,304** | **217,469,410** | **218,864,321** |
| Working capital | 112,500,000 | 135,261,563 | 159,595,118 | 186,402,351 | 187,597,989 |
| Net PPE | 18,750,000 | 22,543,594 | 26,599,186 | 31,067,059 | 31,266,332 |
| **Capital Charge** 8% | **10,500,000** | **12,624,413** | **14,895,544** | **17,397,553** | **17,509,146** |
| **Intangible Earnings** | **75,421,875** | **90,681,606** | **106,995,227** | **124,967,243** | **125,768,819** |
| **Role of Branding Index** 79% | | | | | |
| **Brand Earnings** | **59,583,281** | **71,638,469** | **84,526,229** | **98,724,122** | **99,357,367** |
| **Brand Strength Score** 66 | | | | | |
| **Brand Discount Rate** 7.4% | | | | | |
| **Discounted Brand Earnings** | **55,477,916** | **62,106,597** | **68,230,515** | **74,200,384** | **69,531,031** |
| NPV of Discounted Brand Earnings (Years 1–5) | 329,546,442 | | | | |
| Long term growth rate 2.5% | | | | | |
| NPV of Terminal Brand Value (beyond Year 5) | 1,454,475,639 | | | | |
| **Brand Value** | **1,784,022,082** | | | | |

can be measured against clearly identified performance targets related to the value of the brand asset.

- Making decisions on brand investments. By prioritising them by brand, customer segment, geographic market, product or service, distribution channel, and so on, brand investments can be assessed for cost and impact and judged on which will produce the highest returns.
- Making decisions on licensing the brand to subsidiary companies. Under a licence the subsidiaries will be accountable for the brand's management and use, and an asset that has to be paid for will be managed more rigorously than one that is free.
- Turning the marketing department from a cost into a profit centre by connecting brand investments and brand returns (royalties from the use of the brand by subsidiaries). The relationship between investments in and returns from the brand becomes transparent and manageable. Remuneration and career development of marketing staff can be linked to and measured by brand value development.
- Allocating marketing expenditures according to the benefit each business unit derives from the brand asset.
- Organising and optimising the use of different brands in the business (for example, corporate, product and subsidiary brands) according to their respective economic value contribution.
- Assessing co-branding initiatives according to their economic benefits and risks to the value of the company's brand.
- Deciding the appropriate branding after a merger according to a clear economic rationale.
- Managing brand migration more successfully as a result of a better understanding of the value of different brands, and therefore of what can be lost or gained if brand migration occurs.
- Establishing brand value scorecards based on the understanding of the drivers of brand value that provide focused and actionable measures for optimal brand performance.
- Managing a portfolio of brands across a variety of markets. Brand performance and brand investments can be assessed on an equally comparable basis to enhance the overall return from the brand portfolio.
- Communicating where appropriate the economic value creation of the brand to the capital markets in order to support share prices and obtain funding.

## Financial transactions

The financial uses of brand valuation include the following:

- Assessing fair transfer prices for the use of brands in subsidiary companies. Brand royalties can be repatriated as income to corporate headquarters in a tax-effective way. Brands can be licensed to international subsidiaries and, in the United States, to subsidiaries in different states.
- Determining brand royalty rates for optimal exploitation of the brand asset through licensing the brand to third parties.
- Capitalising brand assets on the balance sheet according to US GAAP, IAS and many country-specific accounting standards. Brand valuation is used for both the initial valuation and the periodical impairment tests for the derived values.
- Determining a price for brand assets in mergers and acquisitions as well as clearly identifying the value that brands add to a transaction.
- Determining the contribution of brands to joint ventures to establish profit share, investment requirements and shareholding in the venture.
- Using brands for securitisation of debt facilities in which the rights for the economic exploitations of brands are used as collateral.

## Conclusion

As global competition becomes tougher and many competitive advantages, such as technology, become more short-lived, the brand's contribution to shareholder value will increase. The brand is one of the few assets that can provide long-term competitive advantage.

Despite the commercial importance of brands, the management of them still lags behind that of their tangible counterparts. Even though measurement has become the mantra of modern management, it is astonishing how few agreed systems and processes exist to manage the brand asset. When it comes to managing and measuring factory output the choice of measures is staggering, as are the investments in sophisticated computer systems that measure and analyse every detail of the manufacturing process. The same is true for financial controlling. But, strangely, this cannot be said for the management of the brand asset. Although many brand measures are available, few can link the brand to long-term financial value creation. Nor has investment in brand management reached a level or sophistication comparable with other controlling measures. As the importance of intangibles to companies increases, managers will want to install more value-based brand management systems that can align the management of the brand asset with that of other corporate assets.

There is a similar lack of detail about the contribution of brands in the financial reporting of company results. Investments in and returns from tangible assets are reported at sophisticated and detailed levels, but this is not true for intangible assets. For example, Coca-Cola's balance sheet, income statement and cash flow calculation tell us about working capital, net fixed assets and financial investments, but little about the performance of the most important company asset, the Coca-Cola brand. The same is true for most other brand-owning companies. Current accounting regulations are deficient in their treatment of intangible assets. The increasing value placed on intangibles through mergers and acquisitions over the past two decades has forced accounting standards to acknowledge and deal with intangible assets on the balance sheet. However, the standards deal only with the bare minimum accounting for acquired intangibles, formerly known as goodwill. As a bizarre consequence, the value of acquired brands is included in companies' balance sheets but the value of internally generated brands remains unaccounted for.

Overall, there is an increasing need for brand valuation from both a management and transactional point of view. With the development of the economic use approach, there is at last a standard that can be used for brand valuation. This may well become the most important brand management tool in the future.

## Notes and references

1 "The Best Global brands", *BusinessWeek*, August 6th 2002.
2 Foster, R. and Kaplan, S., *Creative Destruction: Why Companies That Are Built to Last Underperform the Market – And How to Successfully Transform Them*, Doubleday, 2001.
3 Madden, T.J. (University of South Carolina), Fehle, F. (University of South Carolina) and Fournier, S.M. (Harvard University), *Brands Matter: An Empirical Investigation of Brand-Building Activities and the Creation of Shareholder Value*, unpublished paper, May 2nd 2002.
4 Interbrand, *Brand Valuation*, March 2003, p. 3.
5 K.W. Suh, manager, global marketing, Samsung Electronics, interview, August 6th 2003.

6  Akasia, J.F., "Ford's Model E", *Forbes*, July 17th 2000, pp. 30-34.
7  Examples are Klein, N., *No Logo*, Picador, 1999; Philip Kotler, interview in the *Financial Times*, May 31st 2003.
8  PIMS (Profit Impact of Marketing Strategy), "Evidence on the contribution of branded consumer business to economic growth", PIMS Europe, London, September 1998.

# 3 The social value of brands

*Steve Hilton*

Few propositions are more likely to unleash a barrage of anti-globalisation chuntering than the suggestion that brands have a social value. Ask consumers to explain their brand preferences in the limited context of their own personal experience, and they will happily extol the virtues of McDonald's, Coca-Cola, Nike, and so on: "great value", "a refreshing treat", "cool shoes" are typical responses. But tip the conversation into the more abstract arena of the role that these brands play in society, and you may well get the response "the Americans are taking over the world", "junk food is making our kids fat" and "third-world workers are being exploited". Open any newspaper and you may find praise in the business pages for a leading brand's financial performance, tempered elsewhere in the same publication by agonised hand-wringing over the impact of this or that brand on our communities, our values and our way of life. Brands, it seems, are great for "us" but disastrous for "them" – good for business, bad for society.

When so much of the wealth that underpins personal and family well-being derives from the commercial success of brands, it is curious that brands' overall social impact is generally regarded in a negative light. When so many of the innovations that improve the quality of life for individuals and communities around the world are generated by brands, it seems extreme to label them all as members of a sinister and destructive McAxis of Evil. Given the energy, brainpower and creativity that are devoted to creating and building brands, there must be a more constructive analysis available than an angry assumption that big business is basically bad. Could it not be argued that the very things that are easiest to dislike about brands – their cultural power, their economic clout, their global reach – might actually serve as positive forces for good in society?

These are the questions that this chapter tackles. The aim is to offer a positive re-evaluation of the role of brands in society, a counterpoint to the criticism of brands that has aroused such attention in recent years. Of course, it would be fatuous to suggest that brands' social role is consistently and universally positive. But any balanced assessment of their true social value has to start by acknowledging that brands are not, a priori, the enemies of social progress. It is possible to go further than this and argue that brands are in fact a great ally of social progress:

- Brands foster customer loyalty, leading to more reliable company earnings and therefore higher and more sustainable levels of employment and wealth creation.
- Brands are a spur to innovation, ensuring that companies can capture appropriate returns from investments they make in improved products and services.
- Brands provide a reliable mechanism for consumer protection.
- Brands create pressure for corporate social responsibility.
- Brands provide a platform for corporate social leadership.
- Brands play a progressive social role through the opportunities they create for the not-for-profit sector.
- Lastly, there is a sense in which brands promote social cohesion, both nationally and globally, by enabling shared participation in aspirational and democratic narratives.

These are the "seven social wins" of brands, and it is no exaggeration to argue that branding, in these seven crucial ways, represents one of the most powerful and wide-ranging forces at our disposal for positive social change.

## Brands and wealth creation

The rise of the consumer society in the developed world is frequently blamed for many ills but rarely praised for its principal social contribution: generating the wealth that pays for and sustains social progress. Long-term improvements in health, education, living standards and opportunities depend on the process of wealth creation, and although wealth creation is a process normally associated with "capitalism" alone, the connection between capitalism, consumers and brands is rarely made explicit. But capitalism cannot work without a consumer society, and a consumer society is impossible without brands.

Brands arose in the 19th century as a form of consumer protection in the industrial age. Mass migration to cities meant that people no longer knew the precise provenance of the various products they bought, and branding provided a useful substitute for personal knowledge of producers. But branding also provided the crucial component for economic growth and development: the possibility of scale. Without brands, producers of consumer goods would have been limited to selling their products to a small pool of local customers. Through their newly created brands, pioneers like Cadbury's and Kellogg's were able to expand their operations from the local to the national and then the global. More customers led to increased sales and to more need for the industrial infrastructure to meet growing consumer demand. Workers became more productive, and because there were more than enough customers who wanted to buy the goods they made, the workers became more valuable, and were therefore paid more. This in turn made more money available to pay for the increased supply of goods produced, and so on. At the same time, global trade meant that goods could be bought from and sold to people in other countries, and raw materials could be imported in order to turn them into higher-priced goods that other people wanted to buy. This upward spiral – actually nothing more complicated than people making, buying and selling more of the things they wanted – made possible a huge growth in tax revenues that could be spent on social goods such as sanitation, health care and education.

This first great leap forward in global prosperity and living standards was of course limited to North America and Europe, and it is no coincidence that the world's biggest and most successful brands today are based in the world's richest countries. But these brands aren't there because the countries are rich: the countries are rich because they have the brands. Without brands, modern capitalism falls apart. No brand: no way to create mass customer loyalty; no customer loyalty: no guarantee of reliable earnings; no reliable earnings: less investment and employment; less investment and employment: less wealth created; less wealth: lower government receipts to spend on social goods.

## Brands and socially beneficial innovation

The social value of brands in the process of wealth creation is important, but indirect. It lies principally in brands' contribution to the public purse. When it comes to innovation, however, the social value of brands can be seen more directly. Here, it lies in brands' contribution to personal and community well-being through the development of socially beneficial new products and services.

This contribution is by no means universally understood or accepted. Indeed, it is easy to criticise the seemingly unstoppable brand marketing juggernaut that forces new and increasingly decadent branded fripperies into the shopping baskets of gullible consumers. Detractors might ponder whether a world in which billions of people still do not have a reliable source of clean water really needs toilet paper infused with aloe vera; or whether the invention of mobile phones that alert their owners to an incoming call with demotic approximations of much-loved tunes is a sensible priority when developing countries cannot offer basic education to most of their children.

But it is more constructive to examine how brands affect the process of innovation, which can lead directly to better social outcomes. In doing so, it is important to remember that the brand, not the company or its inventors, is the essential component. Without a brand, companies would not risk innovating, since they would not be able to associate new products and services with their own efforts and investments, and would therefore not be able to capture the benefits of innovation.

In Brazil, Unilever's Ala brand detergent was created specifically to meet the needs of low-income consumers who wanted an affordable but effective product for laundry that is often washed by hand in river water. In India, Unilever's sales in rural areas represent as much as 55% of turnover. The company has therefore developed specifically affordable products, such as low-cost tooth powder and fortified staple foods, including flour enriched with extra iron and vitamins (six in every ten women and children in India are iron-deficient). It has also created a range of pack sizes for products such as salt enriched with iodine that can be bought in small, affordable units. In Tanzania, where half the population earns less than $1 a day, Unilever's new company has set up a bicycle brigade of salespeople drawn from local unemployed youngsters to supply small shops with products such as Key soap, sold in small units for a few cents. A year after its launch, the soap's affordability and availability earned it a market share of around 10%. All these branded innovations deliver direct business benefits to Unilever through increased sales. And yet they deliver powerful social benefits too, contributing to improved hygiene and nutrition and thereby helping to tackle disease and infant mortality.

In the UK, mobile phone brand $O_2$ is pioneering ways to harness its technology for social applications. One example is an innovation that benefits asthma sufferers. Using an electronic peak-flow meter connected to $O_2$'s xda product (a colour personal digital assistant or PDA with integrated PC capability and mobile handset), patients can gather, record and submit accurate asthma data in real time, allowing their doctor to monitor their health and manage their treatment in a more proactive and responsive way than has previously been possible.

Patients benefit through greater reassurance and improved quality of life, and the health-care system benefits through fewer avoidable emergency hospitalisations and call-outs, resulting in time and cost efficiencies. Mobile phone picture messaging, on the surface a candidate for the useless fripperies pile, is demonstrating its social value in an increasingly broad range of contexts. For example, it enables local-authority tree surgeons to take pictures of fallen trees and send them immediately to colleagues to help assess the type of response needed, saving time and taxpayers' money, and improving local environments.

Behind every great brand lies a valuable social benefit delivered through innovation. Procter & Gamble's Pampers brand of nappies bases all its innovation and marketing on a simple proposition: a dry baby is a happy baby. As a result, millions of mothers all over the world have happier babies thanks to Pampers products. Take away the Pampers brand, and you take away any incentive for Procter & Gamble to develop new products that make babies (and mothers) happy. Even the most trenchant critics of Bill Gates and Microsoft would acknowledge the social value unleashed by enabling individuals, businesses and social organisations to transform their effectiveness through personal computing and accessible software. But would any of it have happened if consumers had not been able to associate the new computing products with the Microsoft name? For those on the Apple side of the global software divide, the point remains the same: it's the Apple brand that enables people to "Think Different". Wal-Mart, the world's biggest company, is as successful as it is because it continues to find new ways to deliver what is an indisputably social brand mission: to lower the cost of living for everyone.

Value, choice, effectiveness, taste, functionality, convenience: in order to prosper, businesses have to offer consumers these benefits, and when they do, people's lives are improved. Without brands, there would simply be no point in businesses competing, investing and innovating in order to offer ever-greater numbers of people around the world more and more of these valuable social benefits.

## Brands and consumer protection

As well as any specific social benefits that brands may create, they can also act as a powerful mechanism for consumer protection. It is often assumed that regulation is the consumer's best protection against poor-quality goods and services. Of course it is true that regulation plays a vital role in enforcing and raising standards in this field as in many others. But how could regulation work without brands? What would the regulators regulate? What could the inspectors inspect?

Even without a regulatory constraint, brands provide an in-built market mechanism for consumer protection. The need of brands to create and maintain customer loyalty is a powerful incentive for them to guarantee quality and reliability. Sony endeavours to ensure that its televisions do not malfunction so that those who buy them might subsequently return to the Sony brand for a video-games console that they know will work. The management of Electrolux does not need a regulator to force it to make domestic appliances that do not electrocute their users. When something does go wrong, as in well-known instances such as Johnson & Johnson discovering that bottles of its Tylenol painkiller capsules had been laced with cyanide, or Perrier water and benzene contamination, consumers are best protected when a brand is involved, as the company that owns the brand will urgently want to put things right.

In this sense, famous and striking brands perform a far more positive social role than, as their detractors often claim, simply polluting public space with garish logos and images. Brands are a mark of standards of quality and reliability as powerful as any regulator's kitemark or stamp of approval. Certain types of western tourists, keen to visit parts of the world that afford them a different cultural and aesthetic experience from the one back home, may throw their hands up in horror when they see the famous and ubiquitous Coca-Cola logo dogging their every footstep as they press on optimistically in search of an unspoiled ancient civilisation, desert, temple, jungle or beach. But with the promise of elephants bathing in the local river the following day, there is a surprising lack of revulsion at the ubiquitous yellow of the Kodak film boxes that fill the local shops. Kodak yellow means the film will work; Coca-Cola red means the drink will quench your thirst and not poison you; Nivea blue means the cream will not give you a rash. These are not trivial advantages, and they are guaranteed by brands.

Anti-corporate campaigners regularly advise consumers to boycott big brands and to support small, local businesses. There may be a number of good reasons to do this, but consumer protection is not one of them. In May 2003, the UK's Food Standards Agency published a report warning of the severe dangers to public health associated with fast-food outlets in the UK. Guess what? The agency was not talking about McDonald's with its valuable brand to protect: it was warning consumers about the small, local fast-food outlets that have a barely nodding acquaintance with health and safety regulations. If we are concerned about consumer protection, it is not well-known brand-name companies we should be worried about, but the little-known or unbranded ones.

## Brand pressure for corporate social responsibility

Product health and safety is one dimension of a tide that is lapping ever more insistently at the feet of policymakers in the private, public and not-for-profit sectors alike: corporate social responsibility (CSR). To observers of a sceptical disposition, CSR represents either the apogee of cynical spin, or just the latest gimcrack management fad. It highlights the alleged social costs of brands, rather than their social value, since CSR is chiefly concerned with identifying and making good these social costs.

Frankly, the costs are often real ones. There is no need to don a balaclava and participate in a May Day protest in order to be troubled by many aspects of contemporary business behaviour. Companies both large and small behave in ways that fully deserve the strongest condemnation. Too many think nothing of despoiling the environment, damaging local communities, covering up health risks associated with their products, exploiting their workers, misleading their customers and generally trying to make a quick buck whatever the social or environmental consequences. The purpose of CSR is to reduce such negative impacts of business activity by making the case, and providing the management tools, for companies to minimise risks arising from their social and environmental performance.

But the pressure for CSR is felt most by companies that have brand reputations to build and protect, because they have the greatest incentive to ensure that their social and environmental impact is as positive as possible. This works in two ways.

First, there is a straightforward, and positive, commercial process at work. Building and protecting a brand reputation, as described elsewhere in this book, is not just a question of maintaining a consistent visual identity and commissioning memorable advertising campaigns. It means being seen as a decent place to work, a trustworthy business partner and a good neighbour, welcome in any community. These values (along with useful and reliable products and services) are the building blocks of CSR, and are instinctively the practice of most successful brands. For decades, and certainly long before the current prominence in business discourse of the language of CSR, brands like Shell, McDonald's and Nike have been carrying out what would today be

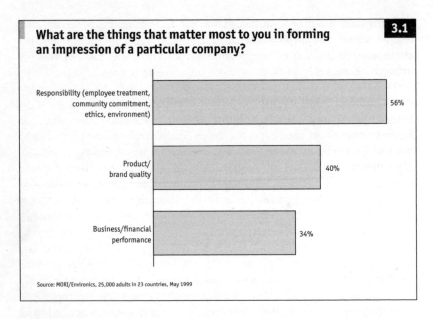

**3.1**

**What are the things that matter most to you in forming an impression of a particular company?**

Responsibility (employee treatment, community commitment, ethics, environment) — 56%

Product/ brand quality — 40%

Business/financial performance — 34%

Source: MORI/Environics, 25,000 adults in 23 countries, May 1999

described as CSR activities, simply because they are part and parcel of building a successful brand. Shell's commitment to its employees, McDonald's support for the local communities near its restaurants and Nike's emphasis on environmental stewardship are good examples.

The selection of these three brands is deliberately provocative, since they illustrate the second way in which brands create pressure for CSR: by ensuring that companies react to criticism and adapt to society's changing expectations (Figure 3.1). Although this second process is more defensive than the one outlined above, it too highlights an important aspect of the social value of brands.

Shell, shocked by activists' campaigning against both its planned disposal of the Brent Spar oil platform in the North Sea and its human rights record in Nigeria, has in recent years transformed itself from corporate pariah to corporate paragon, inspiring and teaching a wide range of global companies to follow suit. But without the Shell brand to try to tarnish, the activists would have struggled to make an impact, and the now considerable body of progressive work on CSR that Shell has pioneered would never have been undertaken.

McDonald's, stung by criticism of its supply chain policies, has pioneered new standards of animal welfare that have won the praise of former critics such as Compassion in World Farming. Its commitment to

CSR, combined with its marketplace clout as a global brand leader, has led to significant improvements throughout the agricultural supply chain around the world, the benefits of which extend far beyond the immediate requirements of McDonald's itself. Indeed, the fact that McDonald's is a successful global brand means that it exports higher CSR standards when it enters new, less-developed markets. Critics in the United States may not think that a "McJob" adds up to much, but in former communist countries, the training and superior working conditions at McDonald's make employment there one of the most sought-after options available. Similarly, the need to achieve cost efficiencies through global standardisation means that environmental or health and safety standards will usually be set in line with the most stringent global requirements, meaning that in many countries the local McDonald's restaurant is a beacon of best practice.

Nike, reeling from the "sweatshops" scandals of the 1990s, has become a leading player in tackling the complex causes of poor working conditions and human rights abuse in the developing world. This is not to condone practices like child labour and forced overtime, merely to note that these were not created by Nike (or any other western brand that sources its products in East Asia) and that without brands, there would be precious little awareness of the problems today. The brutal truth is a simple one: no logo, no knowledge of what is going on in the developing world. Global brands make the connection on a mass scale between consumer choices "here" and economic and social realities "there". Brands are the transmission mechanism through which we can most clearly understand the consequences – good and bad – of business behaviour, and work to eliminate the bad in favour of the good.

In other words, the argument is the opposite of the one that anti-globalisation and anti-capitalist activists would have us believe. Far from causing bad outcomes for society, brands are revealing them. Brands do not lead to social and environmental damage; they are helping to deal with it in their capacity as the public face of private-sector activity. Brands are a battering ram for positive social change. In part, positive social change is a process that goes hand in hand with economic development, in the same way that social conditions in the rich West have improved since the Victorian era. But in the developing world today, it is happening more quickly than it otherwise would specifically because of corporations' need to protect brand value by meeting consumers' expectations of how companies should behave.

Importantly, these positive CSR effects can be seen not simply in the direct activities of brands themselves, but in the activities of all the other companies that are involved in producing the products or services that a brand represents. Brands face risks both from their own behaviour in society, and from the behaviour of their multiplicity of suppliers. So brand owners are now working to help their business partners improve their own social and environmental performance, in the process spreading best practice around the world and down to the grass roots. No one doubts that there is an enormous distance to travel before we can confidently assure ourselves that the social and environmental impact of business is wholly positive; but equally, no one should doubt the vital role of brands in this optimistic journey.

However, there is more to the social value of brands than the pressure they create for companies to be more responsible. They offer the opportunity for companies to go further than simply complying with society's expectations. They offer companies a way to carry out, and benefit from, activities that make a direct and active business contribution to tackling social and environmental problems. Brands can be the platform for corporate social leadership.

## Brands and corporate social leadership

The difference between corporate social responsibility and corporate social leadership is the difference between defence and attack in football. One is mainly reactive: responding to attacks; the other is always proactive: actively scoring goals. Responsibility and leadership, defence and attack: every good business, like every good football team, needs both. But while the contours of the CSR landscape are becoming increasingly well defined, the exhilarating opportunities for corporate social leadership by brands are not yet well enough understood. The three most important ways in which brands create social leadership opportunities for corporations are:

- harnessing the cultural power of brands for positive social change;
- harnessing innovation for social gain;
- applying brand power to the urgent task of spreading the benefits of globalisation more widely.

Elsewhere in this book, readers will gain an understanding of the economic value of brands; how many calculate their worth with forensic actuarial rigour so they can be included on corporations' balance sheets;

how these valuations often place the brand way above tangible assets as a source of long-term value. Marketing professionals treat their brands' customer relationships with the greatest respect, often going to extraordinary lengths to understand consumer needs and desires. More often than not, they seek to imbue brands with a sense of meaning that conveys more than just the functional benefits of whatever is being promoted. Brands lay claim to a social role too. However, it is rare to see these claims backed up by concrete social action. More usually, they are artificial constructs designed solely to identify with consumers' social concerns, rather than to do anything about them. This does not make brands a bad thing, but it does help explain why some anti-corporate critics profess to hate them so much.

When communicating with consumer audiences, companies invest far more time, effort and money in building a positive image for their brands than they do in promoting their reputation as a corporation. Indeed, one of the primary aims of anti-globalisation campaigners is to expose what they see as the vast gulf between the wholesome, upbeat images that companies develop for their brands, and the allegedly destructive, irresponsible behaviour of the brands' corporate parents. They are starting to succeed, with opinion polls regularly recording low levels of trust in "large companies" (Figure 3.2). But when consumers are asked for their opinions of individual brands, their views are far more favourable – particularly in the United States (Figure 3.3); and this trust in brands, as opposed to business generally, gives corporations a ready-made tool for social leadership. Consumer trust in brands could become a valuable asset in campaigns for social change, and campaigning for social change could become an additional source of value for the corporations behind the brands.

Think about the range of social issues that governments and not-for-profit organisations wrestle with on a daily basis. Many of them are hard to deal with using conventional tools: passing laws and spending money. Issues such as literacy, where in rich societies the greatest need is not for more books, but for more parents to read with their children from an early age. Issues such as health, where more informed and positive lifestyle choices, rather than more effective (and expensive) treatments, are the real policy prize. Issues such as youth crime and anti-social behaviour, care for the environment, giving young people a sense of purpose, galvanising community spirit, mental health problems and drug abuse. For all these and more, the social policy requirement is for a change of attitude and a change of behaviour. It is the same in the

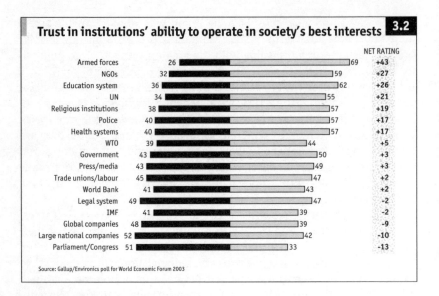

**Trust in institutions' ability to operate in society's best interests** `3.2`

|  | | NET RATING |
|---|---|---|
| Armed forces | 26 / 69 | +43 |
| NGOs | 32 / 59 | +27 |
| Education system | 36 / 62 | +26 |
| UN | 34 / 55 | +21 |
| Religious institutions | 38 / 57 | +19 |
| Police | 40 / 57 | +17 |
| Health systems | 40 / 57 | +17 |
| WTO | 39 / 44 | +5 |
| Government | 43 / 50 | +3 |
| Press/media | 43 / 49 | +3 |
| Trade unions/labour | 45 / 47 | +2 |
| World Bank | 41 / 43 | +2 |
| Legal system | 49 / 47 | -2 |
| IMF | 41 / 39 | -2 |
| Global companies | 48 / 39 | -9 |
| Large national companies | 52 / 42 | -10 |
| Parliament/Congress | 51 / 33 | -13 |

Source: Gallup/Environics poll for World Economic Forum 2003

developing world: governments and aid agencies can pump billions into disease-eradication programmes, but these will only work if attitudes and behaviours also change.

The institutions that are best placed to help change people's attitudes and behaviour are brands, and this is why brands' cultural power, as well as their economic power, is potentially such a huge component of their social value. Using their brands for social change is one of the most effective ways in which corporations can quickly move beyond CSR to demonstrate real leadership. This is emphatically not the same as brands linking up with charities or good causes for mutually beneficial promotional campaigns. This is about a corporation using its brand's ability to change consumer behaviour as a way of changing social behaviour at the same time, thereby strengthening that brand's reputation.

Still the best example of this approach in action is the "pro-social" (as it calls it) brand agenda of MTV. For two decades, MTV has placed social-issue campaigning at the heart of its brand, and has used this technique as a powerful and distinctive method of communicating and identifying with its target audience. In the process, it has done more than any other commercial organisation to tackle cultural taboos and change youth attitudes on issues such as HIV and AIDS, environmental protection and human rights – not to mention its pioneering role in pro-

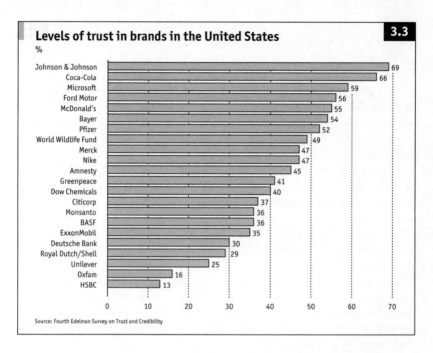

**Levels of trust in brands in the United States**  3.3

%

|  |  |
|-------|-------|
| Johnson & Johnson | 69 |
| Coca-Cola | 66 |
| Microsoft | 59 |
| Ford Motor | 56 |
| McDonald's | 55 |
| Bayer | 54 |
| Pfizer | 52 |
| World Wildlife Fund | 49 |
| Merck | 47 |
| Nike | 47 |
| Amnesty | 45 |
| Greenpeace | 41 |
| Dow Chemicals | 40 |
| Citicorp | 37 |
| Monsanto | 36 |
| BASF | 36 |
| ExxonMobil | 35 |
| Deutsche Bank | 30 |
| Royal Dutch/Shell | 29 |
| Unilever | 25 |
| Oxfam | 16 |
| HSBC | 13 |

Source: Fourth Edelman Survey on Trust and Credibility

moting youth participation in the electoral process through its high profile "Rock the Vote" campaign.

More recent examples demonstrate the range of potential applications:

- the UK's Sky satellite service harnessing the youth appeal of its
  brand to inspire teenagers about their future choices through its
  "Reach For The Sky" initiative;
- Kia cars encouraging its customers to use their vehicles
  responsibly through its "Think Before You Drive" campaigning,
  and its support for walking buses that enable children to walk to
  school safely, reducing traffic congestion from the school run;
- Coca-Cola using its marketing expertise to help create sexual
  health campaigns in Africa, the best long-term solution to the
  AIDS pandemic;
- Avon cosmetics raising awareness of breast cancer and offering
  its customers practical advice and support;
- Asda supermarkets in the UK using their trusted role in local
  communities to campaign on issues from crime prevention to
  domestic violence.

It is simply a question of finding creative connections between brand trust and those social issues where a change of attitude can make all the difference.

The second way in which brands can demonstrate social leadership is through making explicit one of the aspects of brands' social value reviewed earlier: their role in producing socially beneficial product and service innovation. By incorporating social needs in the innovation process, commercial brands can often make a more tangible and sustainable impact on social and environmental problems than governments can. On a grand scale, this can be seen in the development by the world's leading car manufacturers of vehicles that run on alternative fuels, or the investment by oil companies like BP and Shell in solar power and other renewable energy sources. On a more localised level, the creation by HSBC of financial services products, including mortgages, that are consistent with Sharia law, shows how it is possible for brands in any sector to turn social needs into market opportunities.

The third way in which brands can deliver corporate social leadership is the most ambitious, but it is also the most important. Just as brands have become the transmission mechanism for raising awareness of issues such as sweatshops and child labour, they could also be the transmission mechanism for raising awareness and spurring action on the principal cause of global poverty, the real reason why globalisation's benefits are not spread more widely. This is the stark division of the global economy between the formal and informal sectors. This division is rarely one between countries; rather it is one that is present within all countries, the proportions varying depending on whether you happen to be in the developed West or the developing rest of the world. In the formal economy, most things work: rights to physical and intellectual property can be enforced; assets can be used to borrow money and generate wealth; taxes are collected; and utility and other essential business services are provided. But in the informal economy (which represents most of the global economy), many or all of these preconditions for a successful and prosperous consumer society are absent. Eliminating this division will be the central global policy challenge of the 21st century.

Brands are well placed to help tackle this vast challenge, since they are often the only institutions present on both sides of the divide. Coca-Cola, for example, is as much a part of life in the slums as of life in the skyscrapers. Brands could use their grass-roots presence to foster local institutions that start to break down the barriers between these divided worlds. They could use their media and cultural power to argue more firmly and more publicly for good governance and commercial infra-structure. Through their trading relationships, they could forge closer links between the two divided sectors of the world economy, enabling more and more people to enjoy the benefits of globalisation. Most of all, brands could take on a campaigning role: raising awareness, mobilising opinion and forcing the pace of change.

These three dimensions of corporate social leadership – harnessing cultural power, harnessing innovation and campaigning for social change – are often best demonstrated by the brands that have used a social or environmental platform to define and differentiate themselves in the marketplace. For example, the Co-operative Bank raising aware-ness of ethical investment; the Body Shop creating cosmetics products not tested on animals; and Café Direct demonstrating through Fairtrade that an inclusive global business model is achievable. With the increas-ing interest of consumers in the social and environmental consequences of their purchasing decisions, the successful brands of the future are likely to be those that embrace corporate social leadership as a core component of their strategy, thereby adding a powerful additional dimension to the social value of brands.

## Social brands

So far, the discussion has focused on the social value created by brands in the commercial sector. But in the not-for-profit sector too, brands create value for society by enabling charities, non-governmental organ-isations (NGOs) and multilateral institutions to accomplish their goals more effectively. Indeed, some activists have remarked with chagrin that leading NGOs, with their professional logos and identities, sophisti-cated communications strategies and partnerships with commercial brands are themselves beginning to resemble the big corporations that they have traditionally seen as their enemies. That this should be a cause for regret probably says more about the prejudices of such activists than their commitment to social progress, since polling evi-dence shows that the public's trust in and respect for NGOs – crucial fac-tors in their ability to influence positive social change – have risen enormously in recent years as the NGOs have embraced the benefits of branding.

There are three important ways in which brands confer benefits to not-for-profit organisations, and thereby to society. They are all linked to trust, the essential component of brand strength in any sector.

### *Giving NGOs a role as social arbiters*

Trust in NGO brands gives them a powerful role as arbiters in complex social and environmental issues where competing claims are being made. Global brands such as the Red Cross, Médecins Sans Frontières and the UN are increasingly called upon to make sense of international events where trust is in short supply. This may be either because information is scarce and these organisations have first-hand, on-the-ground knowledge and expertise, or because other organisations (like governments or private-sector companies) have a vested interest in one particular outcome, whereas these social brands are assumed to be motivated by the best interests of society. This independent, arbiter role is essential in a world of instant information and opinion, and is only made possible by the brand. A report or comment by the Red Cross on a particular humanitarian situation is more likely to be believed, and acted upon, than that of, say, a famous academic. The credibility of the Red Cross derives not from the qualifications or expertise of individual Red Cross employees, but from global trust in the Red Cross brand. Of course, this high degree of trust comes with significant responsibilities, and this is an area, as we shall see, where social brands have some progress to make.

Another important manifestation of social brands' arbiter role is in their interactions with the private sector. Commercial brands seeking to thread their way through the minefields of corporate social responsibility are increasingly turning to trusted NGO brands to serve as their guide. Shell pioneered this approach, entering into constructive dialogue with formerly implacable NGO critics such as Greenpeace and Amnesty International in order to better understand the social and environmental issues connected with its business and to seek advice on how to deal with them. This trend towards constructive engagement and open dialogue rather than the traditional confrontation is now seen as best practice in the private sector. It extends to companies seeking the public endorsement of trusted NGO brands for their corporate responsibility activities. Many company social and environmental reports now feature commentary, some of it critical, from social brands. The proliferation of cause-related marketing schemes, whereby charities and NGOs establish fundraising or public education campaigns in partnership with leading commercial brands, is another example. These developments are an implicit recognition by large corporations of the higher levels of trust that reside in the not-for-profit sector when it comes to social and environmental matters.

Clearly, this changing relationship between companies and not-for-profit organisations needs to be nurtured carefully. NGOs need to ensure that their trust is not compromised by sacrificing their independence and credibility in exchange for a seat at the boardroom table or a sizeable corporate donation. Equally, businesses need to make sure that in an effort to accommodate their critics, they do not lurch into an unthinking acceptance of often highly partisan, unrepresentative and essentially political points of view. But overall, there can be no doubt that real social value is being created by the application of social brands' experience and expertise to the social and environmental challenges faced by business, and that in an increasingly complex and interconnected world, social brands often perform a vital arbiter role.

### Providing a campaigning platform

The second way in which social brands deliver social value is through their campaigning platform. By using their trust and credibility to raise awareness of important public issues, they make a vital contribution to tackling those issues. Sometimes this can be a direct appeal to citizens, as in the case of the US charity MADD (Mothers Against Drunk Driving) and its high-profile campaigning to seek an end (as the charity's brutally direct branding suggests) to the scourge of drink-driving. But it also encompasses less direct campaigning activity, where the objective is to change public policy (or the policy of corporations) in order to advance social or environmental objectives. Examples include the work of development NGOs such as Oxfam, Christian Aid or Jubilee 2000 on issues such as third-world debt, trade policy or corporate behaviour in developing countries. Again, it is the platform provided by the brands associated with these causes that ensures the effectiveness of the campaigns. A lone scientist, however well qualified, would struggle to make an impact on public consciousness, regardless of the merits of his or her case. Backed by the Greenpeace brand, however, the impact would be transformed.

### Enabling the provision of beneficial social services

The third way in which social value is created by brands in the not-for-profit sector is through their role in enabling beneficial social services (and sometimes products) to be provided directly. At a grass-roots level, charities around the world are working at the sharp end of the social problems that policymakers seek to tackle. To do this they need income, just as a business needs sales to deliver its products and services. And just as commercial organisations use branding to compete for consumer

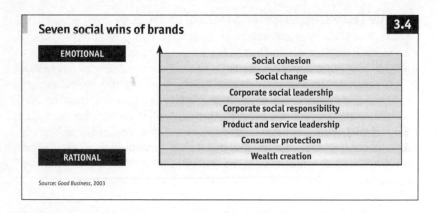

**Seven social wins of brands** — 3.4

| EMOTIONAL | |
|---|---|
| | Social cohesion |
| | Social change |
| | Corporate social leadership |
| | Corporate social responsibility |
| | Product and service leadership |
| | Consumer protection |
| RATIONAL | Wealth creation |

Source: *Good Business*, 2003

expenditure, so charities are increasingly using their brands to compete for philanthropic spending, either in the form of direct donations from citizens, or through partnerships and contractual arrangements with companies and government. The reasons brands are important to charities in this regard are exactly the same as in the private sector: they serve as signals of quality, effectiveness and trust.

## Brands and social cohesion

The last component of brands' social value is perhaps the least tangible, but it relates to a fundamental human desire: to come together with other people. This is the positive counterpoint to one of the most frequently cited criticisms of brands: that they impose homogeneity on a diverse world. The important point to remember is that if to some extent they do this, it is because individual people have chosen to do it. Brands promote social cohesion, both nationally and globally, by enabling shared participation in aspirational and democratic narratives.

The greatest brands in the world today seek to be social unifiers. Coca-Cola sought to teach the world to sing; Nike celebrates human endeavour; Nokia connects people; Lux soap gives Asian women self-confidence; Budweiser made heroes of the blue-collar workers who built the land of the free.

In the years ahead, the challenge for brands will be to champion new ideas, new stories, and new and more inclusive ways to achieve social solidarity. In so doing, they will continue to make an incalculable contribution to social progress.

# 4 What makes brands great

*Chuck Brymer*

In a global economy subject to changing market dynamics and heightened competition, the role of brands has never been greater. They serve as a route map for purchasing behaviour and, when managed properly, generally accrue significant value to their owners. But how do you evaluate a brand and evaluate what makes it special?

Chapter 2 dealt with brand valuation. This chapter examines what makes brands great, but first it is helpful to briefly review valuation and evaluation approaches. For years, most brand owners relied on marketing-oriented measures such as awareness and esteem. Today they use more innovative and financially driven techniques to better quantify the value that brands represent.

These new techniques draw from a mix of traditional business valuation models and economic tools that measure brand performance in terms of monetary quantification, historical benchmarking, competitive assessment and return-on-investment analyses. This has enabled companies to evaluate their brands more rigorously and to establish criteria with which to govern their development in the future.

But what is the right answer for evaluating brand performance? Some would argue that financial models in isolation are unreliable, given fluctuations in corporate profitability. Some would contend that marketing measures alone are unsuited to the realities of today's management needs. Others would argue that no single methodology is credible enough to encompass all the dimensions and complexities of a full evaluation of a brand. These different points of view mean that today there is a proliferation of measurement approaches that attempt to bridge the traditionally separate considerations of finance and marketing needed to provide a more holistic view of brand performance.

For the purposes of this chapter, 23 models that assessed the value and benefits of brands were examined (see list at end of this chapter). Some were more financially driven and others employed traditional marketing techniques. Many offered brand rankings based on their methodologies. From those rankings, the brands that repeatedly appear at the top of the different list of rankings (see Table 4.1) were identified

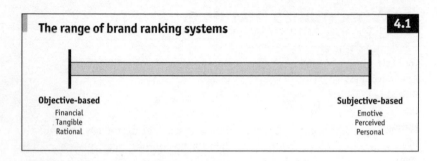

**The range of brand ranking systems**　　　4.1

**Objective-based**　　　　　　　　　　　　　　**Subjective-based**
Financial　　　　　　　　　　　　　　　　　　Emotive
Tangible　　　　　　　　　　　　　　　　　　Perceived
Rational　　　　　　　　　　　　　　　　　　Personal

in order to determine why they come out on top regardless of the criteria used to rank them.

That they do is perhaps no surprise, as they are widely recognised as being leaders in best practices in brand investment and management. These "usual suspects" among brand leaders appear to perform consistently well against a broad range of factors, including tangible equity, customer purchasing habits and market stature. The reason is that they share certain characteristics and approaches that contribute to their success as a brand and as a business.

**What great brands share**
There are five notable qualities that leading brands share.

*Three principal attributes ...*
**1 A compelling idea.** Behind every brand is a compelling idea, which captures customers' attention and loyalty by filling an unmet or unsatisfied need.

**2 A resolute core purpose and supporting values.** These remain in place even though the business strategy and tactics have to be regularly revised to address and take advantage of the circumstances of a changing, and in the detail often largely unanticipated, world and business environment.

From the 7 Series to the Mini, the BMW brand stands for "the ultimate driving machine". The target audience for each BMW model differs and the communications about them project different expectations, but the core purpose remains the same: to deliver an outstanding experience through superior car performance. The Mini represented an opportunity to sell to a new market segment and to introduce people to the BMW experience. The company set out to accomplish this by marrying the

Table 4.1 **Brands most often cited as leading or great**

| | |
|---|---|
| Coca-Cola | Disney |
| American Express | FedEx |
| BMW | Hewlett-Packard |
| IBM | Kellogg's |
| Microsoft | Sony |
| Nike | Starbucks |
| Pepsi | Intel |
| Toyota | Kodak |
| Colgate-Palmolive | Nokia |

values and aspirations of a younger, hipper demographic to the experience promised by owning a Mini. The imagery, typography and tone of the communications identify who is a "Mini" kind of person. This strategy illustrates an opportunity captured by connecting with a wider market without eroding the core purpose and positioning of the parent company.

**3 A central organisational principle.** The brand position, purpose and values are employed as management levers to guide decision-making. This becomes so ingrained in leading organisations that they consciously ask themselves, "How will this decision impact upon the brand?" or "Is this on-brand?" According to Shelly Lazarus, chairman of Ogilvy & Mather, "Once the enterprise understands what the brand is all about, it gives direction to the whole enterprise. You know what products you're supposed to make and not make. You know how you're supposed to answer your telephone. You know how you're going to package things. It gives a set of principles to an entire enterprise."

**... and two characteristics**
**1 Most leading brands are American.** Of the 20 leading brands, 15 are American. Does this mean that although a leading brand can originate from anywhere, the United States is better at the practice of branding than other countries? Its dominance of the list of leading brands may be attributed to the nature of American society. Its entrepreneurial culture recognises and rewards those successful in business, and encourages risk-taking and the kind of innovation that produces the big idea from which a leading brand may develop. In effect, the United States has an

established and natural incubator for business innovation rooted in the core purpose and values of the country.

There is also the fact that Americans are credited if not with inventing the practice of branding, certainly with embracing it as a management discipline. The rise of consumer-product brands in the United States after the second world war was simultaneously a response to prosperous times and a signal to consumers to spend because times were indeed better. Goods were plentiful, and choice, in the form of brands, was apparent on shelves across the country.

Brands and branding practices within the United States became more sophisticated through product and line extensions, corporate identity programmes and pitched advertising wars that were waged throughout the 50 states and the world. American companies recognised that to succeed in business they needed to differentiate themselves in ways that could not be copied by other companies. Management books of the last 30 years reflect this primary tenet. Whether it is a differentiated strategy, product, service, technology or process, it will have been based on "what we have" versus "what they don't have" or the fact that "we just do it better".

If differentiation is the goal, branding is the process. And if a brand is a major source of value, it requires investment and dedicated management. This is precisely what the mostly American firms that own the leading brands do: they nurture the brand, grow its value and evaluate its performance like any other holding.

2 **Most leading brands are commodities.** Coca-Cola, Pepsi and Starbucks products and services are easily substituted; BMW, Toyota and Harley-Davidson face plenty of competition; and there are many cellular phone alternatives to Nokia. Brands are about choice, and these brands have to compete in a crowded and noisy space. They have therefore had to continually search out what makes them special to so many people and how they can continue to innovate and meet these people's needs. They know that customers have a choice, and that if the benefits of their product or service are not readily apparent and consistently delivered, people will choose something else.

### What makes brands great

Leading brands have three attributes and two common characteristics as described above. They also reflect five distinctive traits.

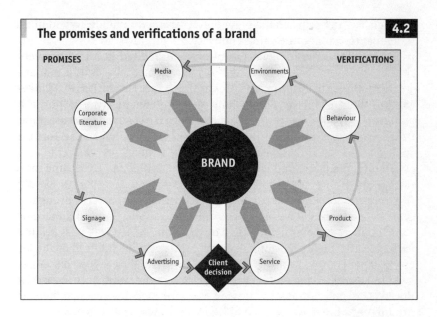

**4.2**

The promises and verifications of a brand

PROMISES

Media

Corporate literature

Signage

Advertising

BRAND

Client decision

VERIFICATIONS

Environments

Behaviour

Product

Service

**1 Consistency in delivering on their promise.** Leading brands communicate their promise to the market, encouraging customers to purchase the product or service. At the time of customer decision, they must do everything within their power to deliver on the promise. Everything the customer experiences in the process of evaluation, trial, purchase and adoption is a verification of the original promise (see Figure 4.2).

By observing the habits of the 20 leading brands listed earlier in Table 4.1, it is clear that to deliver on their individual promises requires taking a stand and not wavering for short-term benefit. It demands consistency and clarity within the organisation to succinctly articulate benefits. Nike has consistently delivered on its promise with healthy doses of innovation along the way. In the process it has achieved near legendary status as a company and a brand. Nike represents a destination never fully reached in the pursuit of individual fitness and wellness goals. The idea is inspirational and aspirational, appealing to a wide audience seeking personal betterment.

**2 Superior products and processes.** Brand leaders are well aware of the sources of brand value. To attract customers and maintain their loyalty, brand leaders must offer them products or services that are superior to others, thereby reducing the risk that the customer will not be satisfied. Nokia has taken the view that it cannot rely solely on suppliers to deliver the components that comprise the products, so it is buying up its suppliers in order to have control of the whole process.

3 **Distinctive positioning and customer experience.** Brand leaders capture what is special about their offering, convey it to the desired audience and allow customers to experience it. Ikea has opened up the furniture showroom to touch like no other retailer. Chairs are pounded with machinery to demonstrate durability, displays are elaborate and constantly changing, and customers are invited to stay by means of a restaurant, events and product-knowledge sessions.

Unlike many retailers, Ikea has developed an emotional connection with its customers. The offering is elevated above the mundane and functional while being competitive on price and selection. The shopping experience is highly customer-centric and personal. Most large retail environments are confusing, noisy and impersonal, yet Ikea has managed to customise the experience even though the product is mass-produced. The ability to deliver a wide range of well-designed, functional products at a low cost has paid off; Ikea's turnover tripled between 1994 and 2002, from €4 billion to €12 billion.

4 **Alignment of internal and external commitment to the brand.** Marketing and branding managers focus their strategies on the customer. In general, employees have been the last to know about the latest marketing campaign or have not been appropriately trained in the brand values. Leading brands understand that an internal culture supportive of the brand strategy has a far better chance of delivering a consistent yet differentiated experience. The internal values are aligned with brand values to shape the organisation's culture and embed the core purpose. The true test of a leading brand is whether employees' commitment to the brand is high, as that will help keep customer commitment high. If those who make and sell the brand are not committed to it, why should anyone else be? In other words, those who live the brand will deliver the brand.

Harley-Davidson has created a cult following because of the consistency between its internal beliefs and practices and what it communicates and delivers externally. Both Harley customers and Harley employees embody the basic attitudes of freedom, individualism, enjoyment, self-expression and self-confidence. This has resulted in an enviable loyalty rate where 45% of current owners have previously owned a Harley. The brand is also popular with non-bike owners as a significant component of revenue is derived from the licensing of merchandise and clothing.

If branding is about belonging to a club, then Harley-Davidson has established an active and loyal membership largely because of the connection that employees and customers make and maintain. John Russell, vice-president and managing director of Harley-Davidson Europe, says:

> We actively engage with our customers; we encourage our people to spend time with our customers, riding with our customers, being with our customers whenever the opportunity arises.

This marriage of the internal employee experience and the external customer experience strengthens brand loyalty, as Russell confirms:

> If you move from being a commodity product to an emotional product, through to the real attachment and engagement that comes from creating an experience, the degree of differences might appear to be quite small but the results are going to be much greater.

**5 An ability to stay relevant.** Leading brands constantly maintain their relevance to a targeted set of customers, ensuring ownership of clear points of difference compared with the competition. They sustain their credibility by increasing customers' trust of and loyalty to them.

However, for every great brand there are scores of failures. Even once-successful brands lose their way, and in most cases the causes are obvious but are recognised too late.

## What makes brands leaders lose their way

The most common cause of lost leadership is taking the brand for granted. This can happen when the brand owners treat the asset as a cash cow. This causes erosion of the original brand idea as it marginalises the customer experience. There is a popular story told in business schools around the world. For many years a man ran a successful roadside restaurant. Word-of-mouth recommendations from regular customers were so effective that the restaurant itself became the destination, rather than a passing stop, for its good value, high-quality home cooking and its smart, well-trained and well-paid staff. It was not a showy place but standards were high. It was a decently profitable business.

The owner was proud when his son got a place at a good business school and he gladly paid for the education he had never received. Following his studies, the son joined his father in the business, perhaps with the goal of franchising the concept. Following a detailed analysis of the restaurant, he recommended reducing the number of staff and bringing in more junior people who could be paid less, and buying lower-grade food which would be cheaper. The father was wary of the changes and concerned for his current staff, but he went along with them.

The result was that standards of food, service and cleanliness all went down and staff turnover became a big problem. Regulars deserted their once-favourite restaurant and word-of-mouth recommendations stopped. The son decided to advertise on billboards in the city and along the road to the restaurant, and to run special promotional offers. At first, there was a small lift to the business, but the new customers were quick to decide that their expectations were not met. The restaurant limped along until it was forced to close.

This story is used to encourage business students not to be rigid in their approach and to be sure to include employees and customers in any changes. But the tale also has brand lessons. The son saw a cash cow that could be manipulated for greater profit. He did not recognise that if he disturbed what made the "brand" great in the first place, he ran the risk of breaking its promise. It also shows that a good product is only as good as the accompanying service. This issue is being faced today by McDonald's. As *The Economist* wrote on April 10th 2003:

> McDonald's, once a byword for good service, has been ranked
> the worst company for customer satisfaction in America for
> nearly a decade – below even health insurers and banks.

The current management is endeavouring to return to the basics that once made the concept and the chain great.

There is no magic formula for creating a successful brand. However, brands that lose their shine should compare their past with their present and look to the future with regard to three things: relevance, differentiation and credibility. Once a brand loses touch with its customer or ignores a potential new audience, it has lost relevance. Successful brands understand the wants and needs of their stakeholders and tailor their offering to maintain its relevance. Differentiation is a critical component of the branding process. And, because brands are based on promises and trust, they must be credible. Customers grant companies the right to provide them with what they need. As Adam Smith wrote many, many years ago in *The Wealth of Nations*: "Money is merely a claim on goods and services." Today we know that customers who experience a breach in trust will take that claim elsewhere.

### Recovering lost ground

Jim Collins, a business author, says in his book *Good to be Great* that to build a great company you "have to have a strong set of core values" that you never compromise.

> *If you are not willing to sacrifice your profits, if you're not willing to endure the pain for those values, then you will not build a great company.*

Brands that lose direction often do so because they depart from their core values. Thus it follows that they can recover by returning to them and by asking and answering such questions as: what is our lasting influence? What void will exist if we were to disappear? A frank appraisal of what made the brand great in the first place, coupled with an innovative reinvention of it, can make it as relevant and great as it used to be.

IBM is an example of a great brand bouncing back. The company dominated the mainframe computer market but was outflanked in the personal computer age by companies such as Compaq and Dell. It has since reinvented itself as an IT services provider. It was a high-risk strategy and a challenging journey, during which IBM invented and pioneered large-scale brand management. It centralised brand strategy and focused the marketing spend for overall leverage. It used the brand as a central management tool to drive behaviour internally and communicate consistently. It provided enough flexibility to be nimble in the fast-moving technologies segments but maintained control and discipline to ensure integrity. Brand equity was measured to gauge performance and ensure a brand-driven culture, which would never again take the customer for granted.

As a result, IBM has become the largest IT service provider in the world, and the brand communicates both innovation and reliability.

Table 4.2 **Great brands: summary of attributes, observations and practices**

| The three attributes of the great brands | Three observations of the great brands | The five great practices of the great brands |
| --- | --- | --- |
| Built from a great idea | Largely American | Continually deliver on the brand promise |
| Holds true to core purpose and values | Predominantly commodity businesses and industries | Possess superior products, services and technologies |
| Employs brand as the central organising principle | Represent clear choices | Own a distinct position and deliver a unique customer experience |
| | | Focus on "internal" branding |
| | | Improve and innovate |

When it claims that it can provide "deeper" services to clients, IBM comes across as highly credible.

## Brand-building skills

Anyone with responsibility for building a brand needs to be creative, intelligent, innovative, venturesome, nurturing, disciplined and service-focused. They must also master three primary tasks:

- Embody the brand itself. This is the most important task. The communications and the actions of the individual must align with the core purpose and values reflecting the brand. The organisation looks to brand managers as role models who portray appropriate behaviour and act in the best interests of the brand and company. Conversely, they must also challenge convention to keep the brand fresh by questioning what has become the status quo.
- Understand the underlying sources of brand value and protect and build on them.
- Continually search out what makes the brand unique. Customer preferences, competitive frameworks and market conditions are incredibly dynamic. Renewing and refreshing the brand to ensure continuing relevance, differentiation and credibility are the most strategic tasks and perhaps the most consuming tactically. Brand

managers must determine what cannot change and what must change.

## References

### Specific rankings
Brandchannel.com, Brand of the Year
BrandEconomics, Valuation Model
Interbrand, World's Most Valuable Brands
Semion, Brand Evaluation
Young & Rubicam, Brand Asset Valuator
Wunderman, Brand Experience Scorecard

### Brand valuation models, rankings and surveys
The A.C. Nielson Brand Balance Sheet
The A.C. Nielson Brand Performance
Aker, Brand Equity Approach
BBDO, Brand Equitation Evaluation Systems (BEES) ranking
BBDO, Brand Equity Evaluator
BBDO, Five-level Model
Brandchannel.com, Brand of the Year Survey
Consor, Licence-based Brand Valuation
Emnin/Horiont, Brand Barometer
Emnin/Horiont, Brand Positioning Models
icon, Brand Trek Approach
Interbrand, Brand Valuation
Kapferer, Brand Equity Model
Keller, Brand Equity Approach
Kern, Brand valuation based on the concept of enterprise value
McKinsey Consulting, Brand Valuation System
Repenn, Brand valuation based on the concept of enterprise value
Sander, Crimmins and Herp, Price Premium-oriented Brand Valuation
The Sattler Brand Value Approach
The Semion Brand Value Approach
Simon and Sullivan, Capital Market-oriented Brand Valuation
Wunderman, Brand Experience Scorecard
Young & Rubicam, Brand Asset Valuator

### Bibliography
BBDO, *Brand Equity Evaluation*, November 2001.

BBDO, *Brand Equity Analysis*, September 2002.

Brandchannel.com, website

BrandEconomics, website

"Famous Brands – Half Off!", *Fortune Magazine*, August 13th 2002.

"The Brand Report Card", *Harvard Business Review*, January–February 2000.

Interbrand, *Brands – The New Wealth Creators*, 1998.

Interbrand, *Brand Valuation*, 1997.

Interbrand, *The Future of Brands*, 2000.

Interbrand, *The World's Greatest Brands*, 1997.

Interbrand, *Uncommon Practice*, 2002.

"AC Puts Number of Global Brands at 43", *Wall Street Journal*, November 1st 2001

Wunderman, website

# 2
# BEST PRACTICE IN BRANDING

# 5 Brand positioning and brand creation

*Anne Bahr Thompson*

If a brand is to be a source of value for an organisation, its positioning in the market and the minds of consumers will be critical to the actual value created.

There are many definitions of brand positioning, each a variation on the same basic themes. It is interesting, though, to pick out a couple of definitions from different decades and from different sides of the Atlantic.

> *Positioning starts with a product. A piece of merchandise, a service, an institution, or even a person. But positioning is not what you do to a product. Positioning is what you do to the mind of the prospect.*

This was the definition given by Al Ries and Jack Trout in their 1981 book *Positioning: The Battle for Your Mind*.[1] More than 15 years later, the following definition was given in *Understanding Brands*:[2]

> *Positioning means owning a credible and profitable "position" in the consumer's mind, either by getting there first, or by adopting a position relative to the competition, or by re-positioning the competition.*

Clearly, both definitions emphasise that, first and foremost, you must think about the minds and emotions of your audience. The former still feels contemporary in its broad definition of product (that it is as much to do with institutions and people as with things). The latter adds the dimension that sometimes you must try to define markets through your stance, rather than just mapping your brand in an existing market or category in relation to the current competition.

If there are elements that should be added or emphasised today, they would be broadening the definition of "consumer", and the importance of "taking up a position" for your brand – and that means a leadership position of some kind – over and above product categories.

In the constant search for competitive advantage, the importance of an organisation's employees with regard to brand positioning cannot be overstated, whether an organisation owns many brands or just one. "Taking up a position", in the sense of showing leadership and vision in how your brand will deliver its promise, meet people's needs and satisfy their expectations and desires, is increasingly important. This is not only because today people expect (or at least desire) higher standards, but also, crucially, because of blurring and fusing marketplaces. This means that a strong category positioning in relation to your competitors now may be inadequate if your market is attacked from outside by a brand with a strong position and customer relationship in a previously discrete category. The traditional financial services brands in the UK found this to their cost when "retail" brands such as Tesco and Marks & Spencer entered the market with a strong service proposition, and indeed when Virgin entered the market with its brand positioning of "consumer champion".

The Virgin example reinforces another crucial point about brand positioning in today's business environment. Although complex and multi-layered brand positioning models and frameworks can be useful, brand positioning must always be capable of being explained and expressed in a couple of words, a sharp sentence, or a clear image – not a slogan or an advertising end line or tag line, but the core idea of the brand. This might be called the "CEO test". What would the CEO say when asked: "So what is this brand/organisation really about?" Whether it is to shareholders, to investors, to the media, to employees or to consumers, the response must clearly and vividly set out how this brand is different and better.

Such focus has helped Richard Branson turn Virgin into the category-leaping brand it is today; "consumer champion" is a positioning that is simple to grasp, and it can work in just about every category. This is assuming, of course, that the product and service reality is delivered. Even allowing for the trials and errors of markets that the Virgin brand has entered, the clarity of its brand positioning has provided an effective and efficient platform for innovative product and service development. Indeed, such category-defying positioning acts as a spur to innovation and entrepreneurship, and it is interesting that classic consumer goods companies have started to embrace this broader philosophy. For instance, Procter & Gamble has adopted a "happy baby" brand positioning for its Pampers brand, thus allowing the brand to reach beyond the nappy category and stretch into all kinds of products and services that make babies happy.

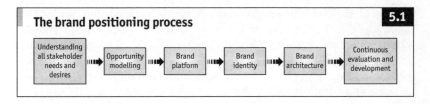

**The brand positioning process**

There are many methodologies for brand positioning, but the basic process involves:

- ◪ the need to understand your stakeholders in the broadest sense, both internally and externally;
- ◪ the generation of information, insights, ideas and possibilities;
- ◪ an active definition of your "position" or your brand platform, and the expression of that position through visual and verbal identity, products, services and behaviours;
- ◪ the disciplined application of a brand architecture system to optimise the value of the positioning;
- ◪ the continuous development, management and evaluation of the positioning over time.

Figure 5.1 illustrates the positioning process. The rest of the chapter is concerned with the "how".

**Stakeholders**

The brand positioning process begins with identifying an organisation's stakeholders, or audiences, assessing how important different stakeholders are, and defining the ideal relationship needed with each to enable business goals and objectives to be met. Different stakeholders will define the brand differently, according to their needs and their distinctive agendas. Deciding the priority each brand audience should be given is not as easy as it may seem, particularly when the brand is a corporation rather than a product.

So although the brand must address the varying needs of many stakeholders simultaneously, the roles it plays with each audience clearly need not be identical. For example, a corporate brand such as Procter & Gamble primarily has resonance with employees, investors, channel partners and suppliers, whereas the company's product brands such as Tide and Ariel speak to consumers. Although consumers may trust Procter & Gamble products, many continue to be unaware that the company now manufactures Oil of Olay. Would this knowledge change their purchase decision when choosing Oil of Olay over Nivea? Probably not, as Oil of Olay was an established brand before being purchased by Procter & Gamble. Investors, however, will always be keenly interested in understanding the breadth and depth of and the strategy behind Procter & Gamble's portfolio. Thus they would have wanted to know why Procter & Gamble purchased Richardson Vicks and how and where Oil of Olay fits in. Richardson Vicks employees, however, would have wanted to know how secure their jobs were and which company's performance evaluation criteria would form the basis for their next review. When it comes to sales and distribution, are channel partners more likely to offer Oil of Olay extra display space when approached by a Procter & Gamble salesman rather than a Richardson Vicks one?

Once the different key stakeholder audiences have been identified, however, positioning should not be based on the lowest common denominator that unites them but, rather, should aim to focus their differing points of view towards shared perceptions in the future.

## Modelling the opportunity for positioning

Almost every strong brand begins with a great idea, and for it to succeed it needs to have great positioning. To some extent inspired intuition can help identify the positioning opportunity, but in practice it requires the perspiration of systematic research and analysis that takes into account strategic options, core competencies, current and future market trends, and customers' wants, needs and perceptions.

Those involved in strategic planning or financial analysis generally use languages and terms that are well understood – by themselves, at least. For example, business strategists have the Boston Consulting Group model, McKinsey's 7S Strategy Framework, or Porter Analysis to work with. Brand planning has no such equivalents and this lack of commonly used frameworks often limits the ability of brand managers to identify, and indeed justify, a core idea that will effectively assist them in positioning their brand to achieve business goals and objectives.

To identify the core idea for positioning, there are four things to focus on.

- **Relevance.** Strong brands connect with customers. They meet functional needs and also tap into, and satisfy, emotional needs and desires. By understanding how existing and potential customers define ideal experiences and perceive the world with which they interact, you can determine what they are missing from existing products and services and thereby identify suitable opportunities to stake an unclaimed (or underclaimed) territory.

◪ **Differentiation.** Strong brands add value, which makes them stand out from their competitors. By evaluating the current and future competitive landscape and the strengths and weaknesses of product and service offerings – in view of customers' perceptions, customers' needs, and real organisational competencies – we can identify leadership opportunities to change the category debate, or, indeed, to supersede existing categories.

◪ **Credibility.** For customers to be loyal to a brand, the brand must be true to itself and keep the promises it makes. Analysing an organisation's aspirations in the context of its financial resources, core competencies, research and development, and values, then pairing these findings with customer insight to understand the gaps between real and perceived competencies, allows the development of a believable proposition. It also identifies areas where competencies must be improved or expanded.

◪ **Stretch.** A brand's continued success lies in its ability not only to remain relevant in a changing world but also to foster innovation and to bring new products and line extensions into its value proposition. To determine where and how the brand can be stretched requires a good understanding of current and potential customers, good judgment about future market trends, good information about all these things and, above all, inspiration.

Together these criteria form a framework, which can be called opportunity modelling (see Figure 5.2). It provides the lenses through which to review internal data, customer knowledge, marketplace intelligence and trend analysis in a structured way to identify a brand opportunity that lives in the future as well as the present. The core idea for brand positioning is often first recognised through relevance and differentiation, through developing a deep appreciation for customers' functional and emotional needs and a thorough grasp of the marketplace and competitive dynamics. It is then balanced with credibility and stretch; in other words, it is scrutinised on the basis of organisational priorities, resources and aspirations.

A ladder of customer needs is a useful way to identify relevance and

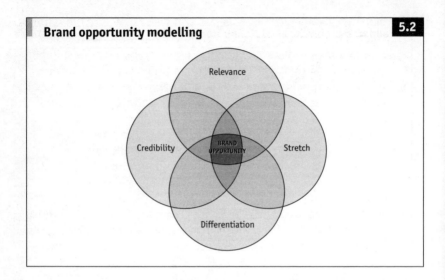

**Brand opportunity modelling**  5.2

connect divergent audience perspectives (see Figure 5.3). As you move up a hierarchy of needs, the emotional and aspirational benefits for different audience groups start to mingle. Furthermore, ideas for differentiation and stretch – added value services or new business models to explore – often emerge from an understanding of desired functional and emotional benefits.

Overall, the sources of information for opportunity modelling are broad. Management interviews, employee focus groups, business plans, syndicated and other industry studies, and desk research all contribute to forming a picture for each of the four lenses.

As far as customer research is concerned, attitudes and perceptions of brands are often based on experiences and prejudices, and will only take you so far. Hence observation of behaviour is valuable, regardless of whether this is done by formally commissioned ethnographic studies or less empirical investigation. Spending an afternoon in a shop, office or cafeteria watching people can offer a new point of view. New technology gives us new means for observation as well as formally conducted research; for example, chat-room discussions or bulletin-board postings can provide useful information on unmet needs and desires and "real" customer language.

It is important to map the experiences customers desire when making purchasing decisions and using products and services, and then compare these desired or "ideal" experiences with the ones that exist now.

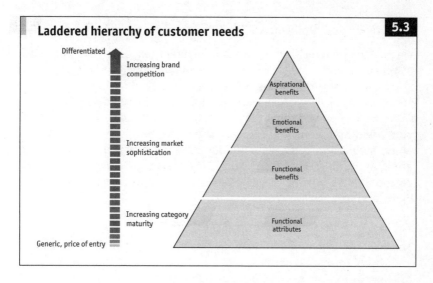

**Laddered hierarchy of customer needs**  5.3

Doing so provides an understanding of how existing and potential customers define "reality" and thereby identify the perceptions and symbols they assign to their relationships with brands. This "experiential mapping" involves five primary areas of questioning.

- What is the customer's connection with the category today? What is their frame of reference or context?
- What defines ideal experience? How would this make the customer feel?
- How does this compare with what exists today? Do any brands come close to meeting the ideal today? Which ones are furthest? Which sit in between?
- What other associations does the customer have with key competitors? With your brand?
- What would your brand need to do to make customers believe it meets the criteria for the ideal?

In getting answers to these questions, it is essential that group or one-to-one interviews start as broadly as possible so as not to bias participants with fixed viewpoints on the marketplace. Asking people to define the ideal experience is a broader question than asking them about their perceptions of what is available today. Determining the best starting point can be quite tricky.

For example, if you were seeking to define a brand for a company that provides business software, you could begin a discussion in three ways, each of which would elicit a different response. You could ask people to describe their uses and perceptions of office tools today, and to explain where they think these tools are lacking. You could enquire about the tasks they do at work, the tools they have to help them perform these tasks and what they think will be available in the future. Or you could ask them what makes them feel engaged or confident at work. Similarly, if you were seeking to develop a brand for a yogurt drink you could begin by exploring the different products people drink, perceptions of yogurt, or perceptions and attitudes regarding healthy living and eating.

### Taking up a position: the brand platform

The underlying aim of a brand position should be to enable it to survive and thrive forever, regardless of how competitive dynamics and business needs evolve over time. The challenge, therefore, is to identify a core idea that frames an ambition or aspiration for the brand that will be relevant to target audiences over time. Focusing on an inherent human need or desire is the way to do this.

The marketplaces in which brands exist are evolving faster than ever before. The speed of innovation has increased competitors' ability to imitate one another, and the proliferation of media vehicles makes long-lasting differentiation on basic product grounds increasingly difficult.

Articulating a core idea as a longer-term ambition or aspiration is the essence of developing a brand strategy that will last for more than 3–5 years. Vision, mission and values are the terms most often used to define the central building blocks for the brand, and they form the "brand platform". The vision gives the brand a reason for being; the mission provides it with specific strategic objectives to accomplish; and values underpin all actions taken concerning the brand and the perception of it among different stakeholders. Overall, the brand platform is designed to:

- ◪ impart a common understanding of the brand throughout an organisation;
- ◪ influence behaviours that shape stakeholder perceptions over time;
- ◪ serve as the creative brief for visual and verbal identity development, as well as communications in the round.

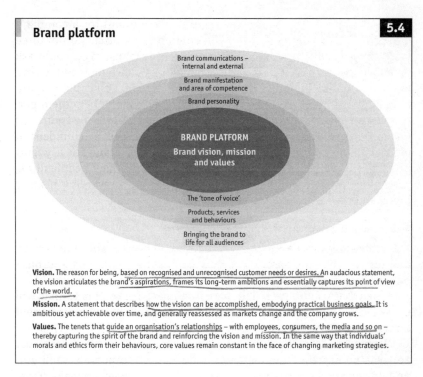

## Brand platform

Brand communications –
internal and external

Brand manifestation
and area of competence

Brand personality

**BRAND PLATFORM**
Brand vision, mission
and values

The 'tone of voice'

Products, services
and behaviours

Bringing the brand to
life for all audiences

**Vision.** The reason for being, based on recognised and unrecognised customer needs or desires. An audacious statement, the vision articulates the brand's aspirations, frames its long-term ambitions and essentially captures its point of view of the world.

**Mission.** A statement that describes how the vision can be accomplished, embodying practical business goals. It is ambitious yet achievable over time, and generally reassessed as markets change and the company grows.

**Values.** The tenets that guide an organisation's relationships – with employees, consumers, the media and so on – thereby capturing the spirit of the brand and reinforcing the vision and mission. In the same way that individuals' morals and ethics form their behaviours, core values remain constant in the face of changing marketing strategies.

## A working example

There are many examples of brands with strong brand platforms, such as Apple's "humanising computers" and Disney's "making people happy", which have been used to drive the companies' products, services, communications and indeed corporate behaviour over the years.

More recently, Marks & Spencer, a retailer that in the 1990s suffered a rapid decline after years as one of the UK's most admired companies, turned its business fortunes around by regenerating its brand platform. It did this after extensive customer, supplier and staff research and by taking into account the brand's history and likely consumer and market trends in future. The vision developed was "To be the standard against which all others are measured", with a mission "To make aspirational quality accessible to all". This brand platform was then the driving force behind new products and service and corporate behaviour, as well as a new visual and verbal style. It also provided a benchmark and filter for all new developments. All the business had to do then was live up to the promise of its brand platform.

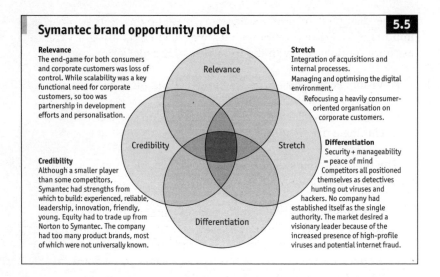

**Symantec brand opportunity model** `5.5`

**Relevance**
The end-game for both consumers and corporate customers was loss of control. While scalability was a key functional need for corporate customers, so too was partnership in development efforts and personalisation.

**Stretch**
Integration of acquisitions and internal processes.
Managing and optimising the digital environment.
Refocusing a heavily consumer-oriented organisation on corporate customers.

**Credibility**
Although a smaller player than some competitors, Symantec had strengths from which to build: experienced, reliable, leadership, innovation, friendly, young. Equity had to trade up from Norton to Symantec. The company had too many product brands, most of which were not universally known.

**Differentiation**
Security + manageability = peace of mind
Competitors all positioned themselves as detectives hunting out viruses and hackers. No company had established itself as the single authority. The market desired a visionary leader because of the increased presence of high-profile viruses and potential internet fraud.

When John Thompson left IBM in April 1999 to become CEO of Symantec, a network and security systems company whose products include Norton AntiVirus software, his goal was to be the leader in internet and security solutions for individuals and businesses both large and small. Internet usage was growing rapidly at the time among consumers and businesses were expanding into e-commerce. Thompson recognised that to be the leader in the field Symantec needed to broaden its range of products and services and become less dependent on Norton AntiVirus, and that it would need to invest in acquisitions and put more resources into R&D, product development and customer service. He believed a new brand positioning and identity would be the inspiration for the organisation to change.

A comprehensive "discovery" phase in the brand positioning process included interviews with management, analysis of the competition and competitive advantages, global customer research, discussions with industry and financial analysts, and working sessions with senior managers and the global operations committee. This culminated in some opportunity modelling, the highlights of which are summarised in Figure 5.5.

Based on the understanding that individuals take pride in being interconnected and networked but feel that their dependency on technology puts the flow of their work at risk, the insights from the opportunity model indicated that confidence – confidence that the work flow would not be disrupted by viruses, systems breakdowns and so on – was important. The core positioning idea was later summarised by the CEO as "pure confidence", with the following brand platform:

- ◪ Vision. People should be free to work and play in a connected world without interruptions.
- ◪ Mission. To collectively create products and services that eliminate distractions.

The defining pillars of the Symantec brand are its values, which its employees continuously strive to live up to.

- ◪ **Customer-driven.** "Every decision we make will be based on customer needs" (Thompson, CEO). Symantec's success depends on consistently providing value for its customers. Consequently, employees need to be attentive listeners able to respond passionately, quickly and decisively.
- ◪ **Trust.** "The greatest quality is to be considered dependable" (Anon). Trust is earned through the consistent display of attentive consideration and delivery of effective solutions. By listening to customers, employees demonstrate they care, and by responding to what they hear, they show they are dependable.
- ◪ **Innovation.** To be considered innovative, Symantec needs to be one step ahead of the high-tech revolution. Through an intuitive understanding of what is needed, the company anticipates new developments and problems before they arise.
- ◪ **Action.** Success flows from the effectiveness of products and services. Effectiveness stems from the provision of appropriate, intelligent, responsive, and proactive solutions.

This brand positioning work has enabled Symantec to think ambitiously about its current and future market, and about what it needs to provide for its audiences in the round, both practically and emotionally.

### Reflecting brand positioning in the name and broader identity
It is said that the first face of the brand is its name. With this in mind, it is not difficult to understand why name creation, especially for a brand that intends to cross geographic and cultural boundaries, is a challenge in itself. In the same way that parents choose a name for a child, a brand manager's choice of a name, even for a line extension, often becomes

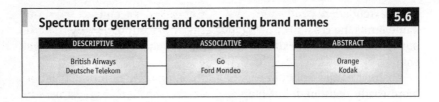

**Spectrum for generating and considering brand names** 5.6

| DESCRIPTIVE | ASSOCIATIVE | ABSTRACT |
|---|---|---|
| British Airways | Go | Orange |
| Deutsche Telekom | Ford Mondeo | Kodak |

personal. Complicating this further is the need not to grow overly fond of any particular name until legal and linguistic screenings are completed. Developing a name in close association with the brand platform helps to mitigate subjectivity, and provides the basis for objective evaluation. Since appealing names that meet their strategic objectives are difficult to come up with in today's cluttered product and service environment, it is important to recognise that although the name may be the first face of the brand, it works in tandem with the brand identity and broader communications.

In generating positioning ideas, it is helpful to consider a spectrum from what a brand does (for example, consumer champion), through the end benefit it provides (for example, "pure confidence"), to more lateral possibilities. Figure 5.6 illustrates a similar spectrum for generating and considering brand names.

The naming process will use the brand platform (see Figure 5.4), and the competitive and stakeholder insights within it, and will develop potential creative themes. Whether the name derives from the descriptive or the abstract end of the spectrum will depend on the history and culture of the organisation, the competitive situation (for example, what will give this brand name the most distinctive position, as with the core brand platform work) and future aspirations.

Descriptive names are the easiest to come up with and often the most defensible in media coverage and rational business discussions, but they can be constraining when it comes to future aspirations. For instance, Carphone Warehouse is no longer just about car phones, and the stores no longer look anything like warehouses. This does not matter in the UK, where the company has built a strong and broader set of service associations around the brand name, but it might have some explaining to do if expanding internationally. Equally, IBM was originally named International Business Machines. Although the company has established the initials IBM as the brand name property over time, names abbreviated to sets of initials risk losing personality and distinctiveness. However, many companies today use initials because they have extended beyond their core business and keeping to their full name limits the credibility of their offering. Interestingly, many that use initials in their letterhead still keep their original name as their legal entity.

Abstract names might be highly and immediately differentiated and more easily registered, but they also require substantial investment in communicating what they are about. Not surprisingly, many companies settle somewhere in the middle of this spectrum with a name that suggests the right associations (for example, Ford Mondeo with its associations of world, or Invensys or Zeneca with, respectively, their associations of invention and wisdom), but that goes beyond a straight description.

Abstract (and sometimes even associative) names can be the subject of criticism, even ridicule, when they are announced, and this can make an organisation fearful of going down this route. But unusual names are often more memorable than more predictable ones, and even those that are lampooned at first can become accepted and even admired in time. Diageo, Orange and Accenture are names that had their fair share of criticism when first launched but nevertheless have become familiar. Another reason for choosing an unusual name is that you are less likely to encounter the problem of someone having a claim to it in any of the countries where you want to register it.

### Brand architecture: organising to deliver value

Brand architecture orchestrates the relationship between the corporate brand and its businesses, product lines and product brands. Brand architecture creates value through clarifying all levels of branding based on:

- the needs and priorities of target audiences;
- expressing the breadth and depth of the offering;
- generating economic efficiencies;
- extending and transferring brand equity between corporate and product and sub-brands;
- making brand strategy credible.

Defining brand architecture begins by returning to the role a brand plays with different stakeholder audiences and, again, is based on an understanding of the ambitions for the brand. A comprehensive understanding of the organisation's lines of business (current and planned), purchase drivers by target audience and the

## Brand architecture structures 5.7

CORPORATE AND PRODUCT BRANDS WORKING

| Masterbrand | Overbrand | Endorsed brand | Freestanding brand |
|---|---|---|---|
| A single brand spans a set of offerings that operate only with descriptive offerings; continual product innovation, new releases, and so on. | Individual business unit or product brands operate under a strong family brand. Dual level of communications: individual offering establishes a unique position while leveraging credibility of the source. | "Source" brand provides the business or product with an aura of credibility. It may be difficult to understand in terms of the personal relevance to the endorsement brand. | An organisation consists of independent stand-alone brands, each maximising its impact on the market with little or no connection to its parent. There is a competitive need to develop distinct equities for line of business brands. Source brand does not fit or carries negative baggage. |

potential of customer relationships to run within and across product lines is often required. From this knowledge and an appreciation of strategic partnerships, it is possible to determine which existing brands (if any) are the best sources of credibility for communicating organisational competencies and the breadth of product offerings to target audiences. In "masterbrand" models (GE, Cisco, 3Com), the corporate brand is the primary source of credibility, and organisational competencies are identified by descriptive phrases. In "overbrand" models (Microsoft, Kellogg's) and other "endorsement" models (Viacom, Nabisco), the corporation is still the source of credibility, albeit to varying degrees. However, business units or product lines independently add something to the organisation and, as such, are branded with proprietary names (for example, Nabisco Ritz Crackers and Nabisco Oreo Cookies; Pratt & Whitney, a United Technologies Company and Otis, a United Technologies Company). Brand valuation and brand equity studies help this decision process.

Implementation of brand architecture systems should be sensitively managed throughout an organisation. Managers and employees strongly relate to the individual brand names that appear on their business cards or within their job titles, and these affiliations will be affected by the introduction of a new brand architecture system. Although brand architecture does not necessarily need to reflect organisational structure and processes (or vice versa), the two should support one another. For this reason, discussions regarding restructuring the R&D functions, customer services or sales processes often go hand in hand with a revised architecture. Even more than an identity change, new brand architecture systems may act as an impetus for a cultural shift.

Although there are various strategies for managing brand systems, many corporations are moving away from creating and supporting multiple abstract product brands, regardless of the nature of their business. This is not to imply that all organisations are moving towards developing the all-powerful masterbrand, but rather to indicate that overbrand and endorsement strategies are becoming stronger options. There are three reasons for this trend:

- **The communications environment.** There are no closed channels of communications today. All audiences, regardless of whether they are defined as business-to-business or business-to-consumer, can be exposed to all messages. Clearly, breaking through the clutter of messages and managing multiple free-standing sub-brands in such an environment is expensive and the companies that do it are usually among the top global media spenders. As you move up the ladder from an free-standing model to a masterbrand one, marketing costs generally diminish.
- **Technological advancement.** People expect the brands they purchase to evolve and remain relevant. Product life cycles are becoming shorter, so return on investment for a newly branded product launch is lower than in the past. It therefore makes sense for a corporate brand or its signature product and service brands to be seen as evolving. Furthermore, many financial analysts believe that, for companies with diverse or changing lines of business, the equity accrued from new business strategies branded under loosely endorsed or abstract names does not necessarily translate to sustainable financial value for the corporation.
- **Customer focused marketing.** If simplicity of decision-making is the aim, a brand architecture system that makes purchasing simpler is essential. Building on both the communications environment and the pace of innovation, there is a need to make new products readily identifiable to potential buyers. Consumer scepticism is high as the public grows ever more savvy about marketing tactics and wary of new, potentially fly-by-night brands. Research has shown that when purchasing products and services, consumers strongly consider the source brand – that is,

the manufacturer or product lineage – before deciding to
purchase a new product brand.

Hybrid brand architectures and the need to develop them are not
uncommon, since individual business lines often require different
levels of association with the corporation to establish credibility.
Nestlé is a classic example of this hybrid structure, with some businesses totally branded Nestlé (Nescafé, Nesquik), some endorsed (Kit
Kat, Crunch) and some free-standing (Buitoni, Perrier). However, even
hybrid structures must be carefully delineated and articulated to
accommodate new products and services appropriately and pay full
attention to existing businesses.

Many companies carefully delineate their corporate brand architecture but then fail to implement it through to product and service
naming. The value gained from a well-structured corporate brand architecture can be minimised or even destroyed when a mix of sub-brand
naming styles exists. Once such an architecture is decided, it is equally
important to move forward and determine "nomenclature conventions"
(better called naming architecture) for existing and future sub-identities.
Naming decision trees have historically been used, but more sophisticated web-based tools that combine naming issues with product life
stages, marketing expenditures and strategic opportunities are now
available.

Although the initial outlay for technology-based systems can be
more than desired, the return on investment for larger organisations is
high and fast, as IBM found to its financial and operating advantage. In
2001, the company comprehensively reviewed its naming architecture
in an effort to further reflect and strengthen the equities of the IBM masterbrand. Through strategic use of "family names" (such as WebSphere
and ThinkPad), it further enhanced associations with the IBM brand. It
also aided the sales process by supporting the corporate goal "IBM is
easy to do business with". Through the use of descriptors (such as Application Server) and identifiers (Version 4.1), it organised its vast portfolio
of products so that customers could appreciate the product range and
variety, and it established a cost-effective approach to manage name
development. The investment quickly paid back, saving the company
several millions of dollars in the first year on name development and
maintenance of trademarks. Not measured, but equally significant, were
the savings on marketing expenditure dedicated to supporting fewer
product lines.

## Long-term development and brand management

A well-thought-out brand positioning is as fundamental as a solid financial plan in creating long-term value for a business. It is the engine of sustainable brand value. This is particularly important as a result of the growth of intangible assets in business and the ability of competitors to mimic product developments more quickly.

The long-term horizon of the brand platform provides direction for interactions with all stakeholder audiences and is thus the engine behind brand positioning. Brand architecture and nomenclature systems present practical guidance to ensure business strategies and brand planning work in support of one another. Together, these essential elements of brand strategy can be used as the framework for long-term brand management and the basis on which a company is organised and rewarded. The discipline of brand strategy also generates the leadership, distinction and trust necessary to build long-term relationships with customers, investors, employees and the marketplace as a whole.

## References

1  Ries, A. and Trout, J., *Positioning: The Battle for Your Mind*, McGraw-Hill, 1981.
2  Cowley, D. (ed.), *Understanding Brands: By 10 People Who Do*, Kogan Page, 1996.

# 6 Brand experience

*Shaun Smith*

Part 1 of this book argued for making the brand the central organising principle of an organisation. Why, then, do so few companies do this? In *Uncommon Practice: People who deliver a great brand experience,*[1] it is found that although the notion of organising around the brand is gaining acceptance and becoming a strategic aim for many companies, it remains uncommon in practice because it is so hard to implement without a guiding framework. It requires leaders to take a holistic view of the brand that transcends the marketing function and makes it the rallying cry for the whole organisation. More importantly, it requires the organisation to align its people, processes and products with its proposition in order to deliver the promise it makes to customers every day.

Delivering the promise your brand makes may not be easy but it is very satisfying. In late 2002 researchers at Satmetrix Systems conducted a study to determine if there was a link between improved customer satisfaction and higher price/earnings ratios. They discovered that the P/E ratios of companies with above-average brand loyalty scores were almost double the ratios of their competitors.

So what is it that drives customer loyalty? For many years we have been told that a brand's success is a result of skilfully applying the "4 P's" of the marketing mix: product, price, promotion and place. Gallup, a research company, conducted a poll of 6,000 consumers between November 1999 and January 2000 and found that the fifth "p", people, is by far the most important driver of brand loyalty. In motor vehicle retailing, Gallup found that customers who feel their dealer representative "stands out from all others" were 10–15 times more likely to choose the same brand for their next purchase. The same ratio holds true for the airline industry, and in the banking sector the influence of people on the brand is even greater, with customers saying they were 10–20 times more likely to repurchase from those organisations with outstanding employees.[2]

Stelios Haji-Ioannou, chairman of easyGroup and founder of easyJet, makes this clear by saying:

*You can spend £15m on advertising, go bankrupt and your
name can still mean nothing to people. Your brand is created
out of customer contact and the experience your customers
have of you.*

Taking a broad view of branding has important and far-reaching
implications for organisations. It places the responsibility squarely on
the shoulders of the whole executive team, particularly the CEO, and it
means that the "product" cannot simply be mass-produced, quality-
assured and packaged. Customers experience the brand in many ways
– through the people who sell it, the product itself, the people who provide after-sales service, the reactions to it of friends and colleagues and
so on – and customers are sometimes irrational, inconsistent and difficult to manage.

### The holistic view of brands

Brands traditionally have been the province of the marketing department. The main focus has been on communicating a brand in a distinctive way to target customers and managing their expectations. The result
of a brand positioning exercise was often a thick book that carefully
specified a number of design rules that had to be adhered to, such as
pantone numbers and type faces. Soon, company vehicles would be
seen sporting the new logo and signage would appear on office buildings and warehouses announcing the new tag line.

In the case of an airline, the rebranding process can take years as
aircraft wait for their turn to be repainted in the new livery. But for
customers and employees not much else changes: the service levels are
no better, the planes are delayed as often, and management is as
remote from customers and employees as it was before. In other
words, the experience of the brand does not change. The exercise is
often cosmetic and fails to deliver any lasting benefit. The UK's nationally owned Post Office spent millions of pounds rebranding itself as
Consignia, yet failed to tackle the underlying performance problems
that were driving customers away. The result was public derision over
the choice of name, public criticism over the expense involved and
widespread scepticism that the rebranding would make any difference. The organisation is now rebranding itself as the Royal Mail
Group.

This is just as true for fast-moving consumer goods. A case in point
was Pepsi's Project Blue some years ago. In an effort to combat Coca-

Cola, Pepsi rebranded its cola with a new blue identity. To promote this it launched its "Pepsi blue" day, which involved printing a blue banner on the front pages of national newspapers, repainting the supersonic Concorde with a blue livery and extensive media advertising. Despite costing millions of dollars, the campaign failed to achieve its objectives. Advertising and promotional stunts are unlikely to have a lasting impact on brand loyalty.

No wonder consumers and employees have seen branding exercises as the corporate equivalent of rearranging deck chairs on the *Titanic*. This analogy is particularly apt as traditional branding exercises concentrate on the tip of the iceberg, changing what is visible, while below the surface the organisation functions much as before.

The attraction of consumers to a brand is much more fundamental than a simple marketing exercise. The Carlson Marketing Group conducted a survey in 2003 that quantifies the quality of the relationship between a consumer (or employee or channel partner) and the brand.[3] Their survey of 16,000 UK consumers found a direct relationship between the strength of the relationship and profitability. Customer spend, retention and their willingness to recommend the brand to others were all influenced by the strength of the relationship. Those organisations in the lower quartile had retention levels of just 32% compared with 87% for those brands with the strongest relationship scores. The brand rated highest was First Direct. So what is relationship strength? The researchers defined this as:

- **Trust.** Consumers believe that the brand will deliver its promise, respect them, and be open and honest with them
- **Commitment.** Consumers feel some longer term emotional attachment to their relationship with the brand
- **Alignment and mutuality.** A two-way affinity between consumers and the brand, with mutual respect, shared values and expectations met – which results in a continually rewarding experience.

Tom Lacki, Carlson's Senior Director for Knowledge Management, sums it up this way: "The consistency of the customer experience is key, because consistency enables trust, and trust is a fundamental enabling condition for the development of productive and authentic relationships."[4]

A holistic view of brands carries the implication that the brand is, or should be, no less than the DNA of the organisation, the fundamental building block and expression of its existence. In an ideal world, the customer should be able to experience any customer process, talk to any employee, examine any product and the essence of the brand should shine through. ANA, a Japanese airline, understands this. A recent ANA advertisement read:

> Attention to detail isn't written in our training manuals, it's in our DNA.

Amazon.com, the Carphone Warehouse, Harley-Davidson, First Direct and Starbucks all have the same clarity of purpose and holistic approach to managing their brand, even though they are all in very different markets. What they have in common is a leading position, enthusiastic customers and exceptional growth rates.

## The brand management iceberg

Subsequent chapters look at how to position and create brands. This chapter focuses on the management of brands according to a holistic approach that requires aligning the traditional marketing activities that lie "above the water" with the organisational capabilities that lie "below the water", as in the brand management iceberg illustrated in Figure 6.1.

### Clear proposition

Successful brands begin with a clear proposition. Unless a brand has a clear idea of the value it brings and to whom, it will have difficulty in ever making the brand stand for anything distinctive.

First Direct is a UK telephone and internet bank that is part of the HSBC group. If you visit its website, www.firstdirect.com/whyjoinus, you will find the following statement:

> The real difference about First Direct is simple, most banks are about money. First Direct is about people. Simple but revolutionary.

Unlike most retail banks First Direct then proceeds to deliver this simple proposition every day. No wonder it has the highest customer satisfaction ratings of any bank, with 82% of customers being willing to recommend the bank to others. In this way it attracts a new customer every

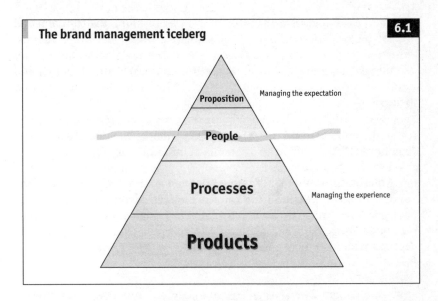

**The brand management iceberg**　　6.1

Proposition — Managing the expectation

People

Processes — Managing the experience

Products

four seconds through direct referral. Peter Simpson, the bank's commercial director, describes it thus:

> *What First Direct did was to realise that people were changing their habits and would want to bank 24 hours a day, seven days a week.*

As a result, the brand conceived the idea of centralised telephone banking built around an intimate knowledge of the customer backed up by simple processes and exceptionally friendly people. Paradoxically, First Direct is able to provide better customer service on the telephone than its competitors are providing face-to-face in branches.

So why is it that some organisations are able to deliver on their brand promise and others fall short? The answer lies in having a rigorous process for designing a customer experience that consistently delivers the brand promise.

The Forum Corporation, a training consultancy, undertook an employee survey with leading American companies in 2002 and identified that the dimension which most closely correlated with differentiating the brand from the employees' perspective was the extent to which the "leaders deliver a branded customer experience".[5] In other words, it starts at the top. As Simpson says:

> *You can't pretend to be one style of brand to your consumers*
> *if you're a different style of brand to your people.*

This takes us to the first element that lies at the brand waterline: people.

## People

People are at the waterline level because, for most companies, they represent the point at which customers finally interact with the brand. Customers have seen the advertisements or promotional activity and are interested – they have an expectation – now it is all about the experience. It is at this point that the brand delivers or not. Employees are the conduit through which all the careful product design, manufacturing, packaging and processes are finally delivered to customers; they are the means to bring the brand alive. In *Managing the Customer Experience: Turning customers into advocates*,[6] four steps are suggested to bring brands alive through people:

- Hire people with competencies to satisfy customer expectations.
- Train employees to deliver experiences that uniquely fit your brand promise.
- Reward them for the right behaviours.
- Most importantly, drive the behaviours from the very top of the organisation.

Take, for example, the Carphone Warehouse. This chain of mobile phone stores was once again voted the UK's best retailer in April 2003. The brand started out with the simple proposition of offering "simple, impartial advice" to consumers wishing to navigate the minefield of cellular phone contracts. The company is now offering value-added services and will be competing against BT, among others. Its new brand proposition "for a better mobile life" reflects this shift. However, what has not changed is its focus on differentiating the brand on the basis of the customer experience. Fundamental to the brand is the performance of its people. The company philosophy is summed up in five simple operating principles:

- If we don't look after the customer, someone else will.
- Nothing is gained by winning an argument but losing a customer.
- Always deliver what we promise. If in doubt, underpromise and overdeliver.

- Always treat customers as we ourselves would like to be treated.
- The reputation of the whole company is in the hands of each individual.

These principles are unusual in that they focus people on behaviours rather than high-level values like "trustworthy, valued or responsive". The way in which the Carphone Warehouse applies them also sets it apart. For example, it invests four times the industry average in training. New employees must undergo two weeks of intensive training and a rigorous assessment before they are allowed in front of a customer. The message here is that successful brands focus less on brand image and more on brand action.

There is probably not a large organisation in the UK that does not train its staff or have recognition systems of some kind, yet the fact remains that for most brands the experience that their customers have is largely undifferentiated. The reason for this is simple: companies' training and recognition schemes are generic, that is, they are much the same as their competitors' schemes and insufficiently tied to their brand proposition. This is particularly true when companies go to the same large consultancies for essentially repackaged service training or reward systems. The answer is to provide a learning experience designed to bring the brand to life for employees.

J. Sainsbury, a UK supermarket group, recently trained all 130,000 "colleagues" using a series of three-hour modules built into the rhythm of the operation and delivered by departmental managers. Each of the modules focused on one element of Sainsbury's brand promise and the behaviours necessary to bring it alive for customers. The desired behaviour was reinforced by aligning its mystery shopper survey with the new customer experience. The company has recently recruited 10,000 new employees to work in its stores to make the checkout experience easy for customers (one of the elements of its brand promise). At the same time, it has reduced its head-office staff by 25% in order to speed up decision-making and improve support for the stores. There is no doubt that the company is trying hard to differentiate itself from its closest competitors.

Recruitment also needs to be "on-brand". Most organisations use the same generic interview processes for hiring staff, yet their brands may require very different interpersonal qualities. Contrast this with Southwest Airlines, one of the few consistently profitable airlines in the United States. The company has won an enviable reputation for its fun-loving, friendly cabin attendants. The airline does not recruit; it holds auditions where would-be employees are encouraged to sing, act or anything else they choose. The process is designed to allow candidates to demonstrate their ability to bring their personalities to work. Would this recruitment process be appropriate for anyone else? Probably not, which is exactly the point.

Pret a Manger, a fast-growing UK sandwich chain, takes a very different approach. Prospective employees are asked to work in a store for a day, at the end of which the store's employees are asked to vote on whether they should be hired or not. Only 5% of the people who apply for jobs at Pret are accepted. The reason for this unusual recruitment method is that the company believes that "one of the biggest responsibilities of management is to look after the corporate DNA"[7].

For a brand to mean something different to customers it must behave differently internally, and that includes its processes.

### Process

One recurring fad is the attention that organisations give to their processes. We have seen total quality management (TQM), BPR (business process re-engineering), customer relationship management (CRM), customer managed relationships (CMR) and the re-emergence of the Six-Sigma Way. There is nothing inherently wrong with any of these concepts (which always seem to have three initials) as they encourage companies to focus on improving those processes that create the most value. Unfortunately, all too often these approaches are used simply as a means to take cost (or rather frontline people) out of the system without really examining whether the revised process is adding value to the brand and delivering the promise to customers. So UK high-street banks now have impersonal processing centres and customers can no longer phone their friendly bank manager directly. The banks may argue that this is to improve service, but their customers know that the main reason for the change is to cut costs.

CRM has been said to be the management tool that most often fails to meet management expectations. This is because it is essentially a "dumb" technology that is used to capture more and more information about customers without thinking about how it can be used to create value for customers or how it will improve customers' experience of the brand. Lengthy voice-activated response systems and more targeted direct mailshots are a poor substitute for processes that truly add value to the customer.

Amazon.com is one of the most widely recognised and respected brands in the world today. Jeff Bezos, the company's CEO, has said:

> It has always seemed to me that your brand is formed,
> primarily, not by what your company says about itself, but by
> what the company does.

An example is Amazon's "One-Click" ordering process. The Amazon brand promises reliability and simplicity, and to demonstrate these values the ordering process was reviewed. Amazon's web designers came up with the idea of One-Click, a system which remembers customers' payment and shipping details so that subsequent items can be purchased with literally one mouse click. When it was tested, customers were sceptical because of concerns about security and confidentiality. However, Bezos insisted on introducing One-Click because he felt that the simplified process was on-brand for Amazon and that his customers' trust in the Amazon brand would overcome their reservations. He was right and it has proved extremely successful.

Likewise, First Direct has helped turn its brand promise into reality through simple processes. Switching banks used to involve a lot of hassle so that customers who were dissatisfied with their bank could rarely be bothered to move their accounts. First Direct tells its prospective customers:

> We can now transfer your standing orders and direct debits
> for you – so transferring bank accounts has never been easier.

And it does. With one simple click on the "I agree" button, it swings into action and contacts your current bank to arrange everything on your behalf.

These examples raise another interesting question about this notion of holistic branding. What is the product? It used to be easy: it was the can of cola or the airline seat or perhaps the pair of jeans. But the expanded definition of brand means that the product is now much broader. It is the totality of the experience.

### Product

It used to be said that the difference between a product and a service is that customers are actively engaged in experiencing a service but they acquire and use a product. Customers experience a restaurant but cannot take it home; they buy a doughnut and consume it, but the doughnut does not provide a service. If this is true, what is the Starbucks product? Is it the coffee or the service experience? Howard Schultz, the company's chairman, believes that the advantage Starbucks has over traditional brands is that "our customers see themselves inside our company, inside our brand, because they're part of the Starbucks experience". Starbucks' customers seem happy to pay a premium for that privilege.

This is true too for many other sectors, including professional services. Clifford Chance, one of the world's largest law firms, sees the legal expertise that it provides as vital but expected and that the true differentiator for its brand is the relationship it builds with its clients. Clifford Chance is investing in training to help its lawyers deliver a more seamless and client-focused experience.

Some years ago the Greater China division of Leo Burnett, an advertising agency, was under threat from other agencies and was losing clients and employees. By taking a holistic view of the brand and working on improving the creative processes and upgrading the skills of its people, the division's products steadily improved. Leo Burnett cut employee turnover by 40%, raised new account profitability by 63% and rose from sixth to first place in total billings. Two years later it was voted Agency of the Year.[8]

Brands are now emerging that create experiences connected to the purchase or the use of a product, but they offer value to the customer that goes beyond the product alone and becomes synonymous with the brand.

The brand promise of Harley-Davidson, an American motorcycle-maker, is "We Fulfil Dreams". As it says in the company's 1999 annual report:

> *Fulfilling dreams for people from all walks of life who cherish the common values of freedom, adventure and individual expression, involves much more than building and selling motorcycles. The secret to our enduring brand lies in delivering an experience rather than just a collection of products and services.*

If you think that this is just PR spin, Harley-Davidson has over 750,000 active members in its Harley Owners Group (HOG) and these enthusiasts typically spend 30% more than Harley owners who are nonmembers. This increased expenditure is on clothing, holidays and events – in other words the experience.

Harley's bundling of customer experiences with product and direct involvement with customers has led to 17 straight years of financial growth and a 50% share of the big bike market. A shareholder who invested $10,000 when the organisation went public in 1986 would now be a millionaire.

### Redefine

When you think of Harley-Davidson, do you think of grizzly, tattooed middle-aged Hells Angels? Think again. Harley recently launched its "Riders Edge" programme, a motorcycling safety course designed to attract new riders. Of the 4,000 people who went through the programme in 2002, nearly 45% were female and half of these were aged under 35. J.D. Power and Associates, a global marketing information services firm, puts the median income of American motorcyclists at US$67,000. The reality is that a Harley-Davidson is more likely to be ridden by a professional female than by a middle-aged tearaway. Harley has redefined itself.

At a weekend rally in Austria in mid-2001, 25,000 people showed up including all the company's senior managers. Harley-Davidson management refers to these events as "super-engagement" because the leaders are all active participants in HOG activities. In this way the leaders keep tuned in to the changing needs of their customers and combat competitive threats. This has meant new processes and new products, including the V-Rod motorcycle that embodies all the traditional Harley-Davidson brand values in a state-of- the-art bike for which customers were clamouring.

Perhaps this is why Harley-Davidson celebrates its centenary in 2003 when so many other motorcycle brands have died.

Contrast this with another icon that has even higher brand recognition: McDonald's. Although it is one of the best-known brands in the world, it has recently declared its first loss and is currently shutting stores around the world. It came last in a 2002 *Wall Street Journal* customer satisfaction survey and achieved a lower customer satisfaction index than the US Inland Revenue Service in a survey conducted by the University of Michigan.[9]

Pick up any management textbook published during the last decade and the chances are that you will find a reference to McDonald's and its promise to provide consistent quality, service and value. These values are still there, but the problem is that consistency is now the entry price for any brand that wants to do business. Consumers now want brands to offer products and experiences that complement their lifestyles. Pret A Manger, in which McDonald's has acquired a stake, is consistent but also offers wholesome food with great service. Its proposition "Passionate about food" is evident in every detail. The brand has responded to customers who are now looking for fast food that is healthy and served in a pleasant environment by friendly employees. The message here is that tastes change, and unless brands can be dynamic and move quickly to meet emerging and changing needs they will decline. Mounting a new advertising or promotional campaign, launching a revised logo or even changing the brand promise is not enough. The response can and should include these activities, but unless it is accompanied by fundamental changes to the processes, upgraded products, and employees who are briefed and trained to be able to deliver the revised proposition, the marketing effort will be worthless.

A consequence of this concept is that the marketing department may still lead but no longer wholly own the brand. It has to be jointly owned by marketing, human resources and operations because each has a vital role to play in delivering the brand to consumers. The role of the chief executive is crucial in setting this agenda and ensuring that the three functions work together. This kind of alignment is called "Triad Power" and it will define how organisations will function in the future. What is needed now is a simple framework or tool for facilitating this alignment. The brand management process (see Figure 6.2) answers this need.

### Using the brand management iceberg

Although the process will vary according to the nature and needs of the brand, Figure 6.2 represents a logical framework for managing the activities that align both the expectation and the experience that customers have of the brand.

#### Customer experience audit

Begin by measuring the current experience of the brand. What is the total experience customers have of the organisation and the brand in terms of the following?

- **Proposition.** How clear is the offer and what does the brand promise? Is this valuable to target customers?
- **People.** To what extent do people behave in a way that meets customer expectations and delivers the brand promise?

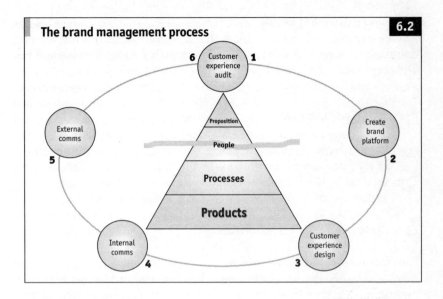

**The brand management process** 6.2

- **Processes.** Do processes create value for customers and deliver the brand promise?
- **Products.** Are products differentiated and valuable to target customers?

### Creating the brand platform

Some of this work is usually already in place, but make sure that it is absolutely clear and fully effective, as without clarity around the brand platform the following phases cannot be undertaken. It involves the following:

- **Brand positioning.** How can you position your brand with clarity and precision?
- **Brand naming.** Choosing a name for the brand that is distinctive and creates the right emotional associations.
- **Brand architecture.** How should the brand or sub-brands work together to communicate the proposition?
- **Brand identity.** How best can the brand be portrayed visually and verbally?

## Customer experience design

Having audited the current situation and created clarity around the
brand positioning and values, you can design the new experience that
will consistently deliver the brand to target customers. Attention should
be given to the same dimensions as for the customer experience audit.

- **Proposition.** What can the brand promise in specific terms to
  target customers that will create competitive advantage?
- **People.** How must people behave to bring this promise to life at
  every point where the organisation interacts with the customer?
- **Processes.** What processes need to be improved, eliminated or
  added to enable employees to behave in this way?
- **Products.** How can products be improved to highlight or
  demonstrate the brand values?

## Communicating the brand internally

Having designed the new experience, you are ready to communicate it
internally. At this point, many organisations rush out a new advertising
campaign and end up overpromising and underdelivering because their
people are not fully prepared. As much effort must go into marketing
internally as into marketing externally.

- **Communication.** Make sure everyone knows who the target
  customers are, what they expect, what the brand stands for and
  what it promises.
- **Leadership.** Prepare managers to lead the brand and demonstrate
  their own commitment to the promise.
- **Training.** Develop "on-brand" training that will emotionally
  engage managers and employees and equip them with the
  knowledge, attitude and skills to deliver the brand promise.
- **Measurement.** Align measurement systems so that everyone is
  aware of the extent to which the organisation is meeting
  customer needs and is rewarded for delivering the promise.

## Communicating the brand externally

Now, and only now, are you ready to communicate the proposition
externally. Much of this work may have been done in preparation, but
you will want to make sure the organisation is ready to deliver the experience before you raise the expectation by going live. The focus needs to
be on:

◪ **Brand communication.** How best can the brand be communicated to its intended audience? This includes advertising, promotion, packaging, and so on.

*Continuing management, audits and redefinition*
Lastly, the brand must be protected and refreshed over time to keep it current with target customer needs and competitively strong. This requires the following:

◪ **Management.** Cross-functional sponsorship and leadership to ensure all the activities that support the brand are aligned and managed.
◪ **Audits.** Regular measurement of brand image, reputation and the customer experience against the desired proposition.
◪ **Redefinition.** Periodic refreshing and upgrades to ensure that the offer stays current with target customer expectations and combats competitive threats.

Using the brand management iceberg allows senior managers to align an organisation's people, processes and products with the brand proposition to create value for target customers. As was said at the start of this chapter, this is common sense but still uncommon practice.

## Notes and references

1 Smith, S. and Milligan, A., *Uncommon Practice: People who deliver a great brand experience*, Financial Times Prentice Hall, 2002.
2 McEwen, B., "All Brands are the same", www.gallup.com.
3 Carlson Marketing Group Relationship Builder Survey 2003.
4 Lacki, Thomas D. (2003), 'Achieving the Promise of CRM', *Interactive Marketing*, Vol. 4, No. 4, pp. 355–375.
5 Smith, S. and Wheeler, J., *Managing the Customer Experience: Turning customers into advocates*, Financial Times Prentice Hall, 2002.
6 Smith and Wheeler, *Managing the Customer Experience*.
7 Andrew Rolfe, former CEO.
8 1995 Asian Ad Awards.
9 *Sunday Times*, April 6th 2003.

# 7 Visual and verbal identity

*Tony Allen and John Simmons*

In 1955, the president of IBM asked the following question:

> *Do you think it's possible that IBM could look like the kind of company it really is?*

The president was Thomas J. Watson Jr, son of IBM's founder. The man who answered the question in the affirmative – and then did something about it – was Eliot Noyes, IBM's industrial design consultant. Watson and Noyes realised that IBM was about to be eclipsed by Olivetti. That was the conclusion you would have reached if you had looked at the two companies side by side. Both of them were vying to be recognised as "leader of the modern world", but IBM looked more like the leader of Caxton's world. So a programme was born to introduce the discipline of corporate identity to IBM, spurred on by the man described by *Fortune* magazine as "the greatest capitalist who ever lived".

"Visual identity" is a recent term that was probably coined to avoid lengthy arguments about the meaning of "brand" versus "corporate identity". In the 1980s, the term brand migrated from soap powders and came to mean virtually anything on the planet with an ability to sustain an attraction or influence among people. Politics, countries, movements, artists, celebrities and educational establishments as well as companies and chocolate bars all became brands. So brand came to mean more or less what had been described as corporate identity: the total experience offered by a company to its staff, customers and others, a heady and distinctive concoction of intangible promises and tangible attributes and benefits.

Visual identity is a component in branding – the part you see, obviously. As such it is an important part because what you see is more likely to influence you than what you are told or what you comprehend from an 80-deck slide presentation.

## Visual identity

Visual identity comprises the graphic components that together provide a system for identifying and representing a brand. The "basic elements" of a brand's visual identity might comprise distinctive versions of the following:

- Logotypes
- Symbols
- Colours
- Typefaces

Think of the way IBM consistently reproduces its name in its logotype; the McDonald's arches symbol; the Royal Mail's use of pillar-box red; the Johnson typeface created exclusively for London Underground. These basic elements are often supplemented by other graphic elements such as patterns, approaches to illustration and photography, and a range of icons.

BMW uses the visual design and styling of its cars, key-rings, graphics, showrooms and communications to express its now powerful and easily recognised global brand identity. BMW's visual expression is clear, attractive, distinctive and noticeably consistent wherever you see it. Each part of a customer's journey to purchase or experience owning or driving a BMW is carefully orchestrated to send the same messages about the brand. The BMW brand is an often-quoted example of an exceptionally high standard in visual identity expression.

By contrast, despite being a truly mighty automotive brand, Ford made visual and verbal errors with the Edsel in 1957. A car whose visual quirkiness might work well now, the Edsel had an unpopular "horse-collar" grille, designed to stand out from other cars but described by one customer as looking like "a vagina with teeth". Moreover, the name (after Edsel Ford, son of Henry Ford and a former company president) lacked appeal as the public thought it sounded odd, and, indeed, the Ford family is thought to have disapproved of the use of it. These two factors were not the only ones to bring the Edsel to an early end, but they were crucial in sealing the unpopularity of the car and the brand, leading to discontinued production after 1960.

This chapter is also about verbal identity. This is another recent term that was coined to make it clear that identity is also expressed through words and language, whether we mean it to be or not. Some organisations have changed their language to be more "customer friendly" (tax offices, government agencies and charities). Some organisations still cling to powerfully bad verbal identities, so bad on occasion that you can only navigate them with a professional guide. For example, IT firms often still befuddle their audiences with technical terms, jargon and bad English, and many lawyers continue to intimidate their clients with arcane phrases and technical (sometimes Latin) terms.

### Verbal identity

Verbal identity's "basic elements" aim to make a brand's language distinctive. These might comprise the following:

- The name
- A naming system for products, sub-brands and groups
- A strapline
- Tone of voice principles
- The use of stories

Combining the visual and the verbal provides the means to make brands that really work. Ben & Jerry's ice creams, for example, have self-indulgent and tasty names like Phish Food, Chunky Monkey and Cherry Garcia, an edible tribute to the late Jerry Garcia of the Grateful Dead, a famous American rock band. Such carefully orchestrated naivety takes more effort to do well than, say, achieving the gleaming polish of Haagen Dazs (a made-up name). It is strange that the "soul" of Ben & Jerry's was thought to be at risk when it was bought by one of the most careful consumer branding companies of all – Unilever – which understands that brands need to have souls.

Any company, product, service or anything else will make little progress if it cannot show what it is about and why it is different. Showing this means having a purpose behind the way names are created and used, the creation of logos and symbols, the uses of colours and typography, illustration and photography, pattern, style and the use of language.

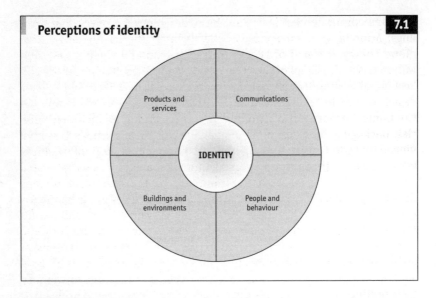

**Perceptions of identity**  7.1

This chapter examines the tactics and strategy of identity using examples of well-known companies and brands, several of which are featured in the colour plate section which appears in the book. But in order to put the subject in context, where does the idea of identity come from?

## From *brandr* to today

As explained in Chapter 1, the word brand comes from the Old Norse *brandr*, meaning to burn, and mass branding existed in the ancient civilisations of Etruria, Greece and Rome, where potters made their marks on the pots they made. Today in Texas there are some 230,000 registered cattle brands, many of them showing a fusion between the visual and the verbal – see the symbol, read the name and vice versa – in the same way as the brands of organisations such as the Red Cross, Shell, Penguin Books and "3", a mobile telecommunications company. Since the 1930s there have been certain identifiable trends relating to the creation of brand identities.

## Designer-driven identity

In the 1950s and 1960s, especially in the United States, corporate bosses put their faith in the creative skills of a number of unusually talented designers. These included, among others, Paul Rand, designer of the IBM and UPS corporate identities; Saul Bass, designer of AT&T, United Airlines, Minolta, General Foods, Rockwell International identities; Raymond Loewy, designer of "Lucky Strike" in 1940 and Shell in 1967; and Milton Glaser, designer of the "I love New York" logo. But one of the earliest notable grand-scale visual projects was Egbert Jacobsen's 1930s design of nearly "every surface" of Walter P. Paepcke's company, the Container Corporation of America (CCA), including its factories, vehicles, packaging, invoices, brochures and advertising. Paepcke was convinced that good design was an integral component of corporate culture, taking the view that just as national culture is shaped by its use of visual symbols and icons, so too are corporations by the symbols and icons they use. Jacobsen's work for CCA, William Golden's famous late-1940s "eye" identity for the Columbia Broadcasting System (CBS) and Rand's original design for UPS played an important role in establishing the importance of design in creating powerful visual logos and brand ownership symbols. It is also at this time that we see the beginnings of associations between corporations and the colours they used to identify their products and services, for instance yellow belonging to Kodak, red to Coca-Cola, green to BP, brown to UPS and blue to IBM and AT&T.

American corporations were largely responsible for establishing the professional role of corporate design, but the nature of the work often owed more to a relationship between the company owner and the designer than the intervention of the marketing department. This was partly because "marketing" was seen as more or less interchangeable with "sales" and therefore had a lower status. Similarly, the notion of corporate identity as a strategic tool was in its infancy.

One of the most famous examples of an owner-designer relationship is that of Thomas J. Watson Jr, son of the founder of IBM. In 1955, Watson recognised, partly as a result of prompts from a colleague in Europe, that IBM's designs and buildings were substantially "off the pace" for a company then entering the electronic era. In fact, at that time it was Olivetti, not IBM, that had an ultra-contemporary New York City showroom. Watson visited Adriano Olivetti in Milan and saw at first hand the extent and ingenuity of the identity programme which had been started by Olivetti and which included buildings, offices, employee housing, products, brochures and advertisements. Olivetti was even involved in bringing new functional and aesthetic designs to the urban planning. Watson wrote that it was then that he decided to "improve IBM design, not only in architecture and typography, but colour, interiors, the whole spectrum". The experience of seeing

Olivetti's work in Milan resulted in one of the most succinct quotations on the subject of identity and its meaning, which is included in the first sentence of this chapter.

The landmarks that followed included a series of changes to the famous IBM logotype masterminded by Rand, who had been brought into IBM and had quietly got on with redesigning the company's brochures and printed material. Rand was also responsible for building up IBM's design capacity, bringing new talent into the monolithic business and helping to spark a golden era of expressive identity design, matched by a vast array of building and architectural projects, notably IBM's pavilion at the New York World Fair in 1964.

IBM's story is an impressive illustration of visual identity. More recently, while remaining true to the principles of a consistent visual identity, the company has negotiated a transition from stolid and solid hardware manufacturer to cerebral "creative" solutions provider. Its visual identity has evolved seamlessly. Its verbal identity has changed subtly too, perhaps exemplified by the advertising line "I think therefore IBM". IBM's language has become less technologically obsessed, less to do with bits and bytes and more to do with having an interesting way of thinking. Indeed, in terms of verbal identity, it drew the response from Apple "Think different", which was a blow aimed at IBM's supposed weak spot: its association with "blue suit" conformity.

## Strategy-driven identity

In the 1970s, as a result of the boom in marketing, particularly market and customer research, and the vogue for change management initiatives, the ownership of corporate identity was transferred to the marketing department as one of an armoury of tools to be used and linked to other tools. Identity had to mature and be measured and accountable. It was not enough to say that the logo was the signature of the company. Was the logo the right logo for the customer?

Arguably, this was a time when designers, who formerly had free rein to work with corporate bosses on anything they wanted, looked for new creative opportunities in the growing non-mainstream areas, such as publishing, music and entertainment, where graphic design enjoyed boom times, especially with punk towards the end of the 1970s. Visual identity moved into a different kind of creative period as designers and marketers began to understand and play with new possibilities. Having established that the logo itself was the basis for a consistent visual identity, questions started to be asked about the memorability or recognisability of the mark. If this was to represent the company's business strategy, could it really be achieved by a "dynamic typographic rendition"? Or would more creative visual symbols help companies to express their strategies with a clearer sense of energy and novelty?

In this context, some visual identities stand out as landmarks. The Bovis identity, with its use of the humming bird as a symbol, was a breakthrough in the early 1970s. The humming bird itself was, from the advantage of hindsight, easy to justify as "nimble" and "industrious". But, more importantly, in the context of its time, it made a statement about the company's belief in aesthetic principles and its focus on the customer. After all, Bovis was aiming not to be just any old construction company; it was carefully creating the modern environments in which people would live and work.

From the 1970s until the mid-1980s, a new benchmark became apparent. It was about creating a visual symbol that had "artistic" quality while representing a clear commercial articulation of business strategy. This strand of visual identity continues today, but perhaps reached its pinnacle in Michael Wolff's work for 3i in the early to mid-1980s. Here the mark itself was a thing of beauty – a watercolour painting of the numeral 3 with an eye – but the logo became almost irrelevant in the overall scheme of the company's new identity.

First, it was a bold piece of renaming. The Industrial and Commercial Finance Corporation became Investors in Industry, known as 3i. This set the tone for a radical approach to marketing financial services and venture capital. Using illustrations by Jeff Fisher, the new 3i advertising burst out of the pages of business magazines, proclaiming through its visual and verbal style "we are different and we will support ventures that are different too". The challenge then was to maintain this sense of difference. The annual 3i calendar, using cartoons, helped to do this. Poetry by Christopher Logue, for example, reinforced the effect. But "being different" is a hard act to sustain, even if it is the goal of every identity programme. 3i survives, and prospers, with the basics of its 1980s identity intact, even if nowadays nobody speaks of it in quite the same hushed tones as they did then. Its market positioning, as well as its identity, is no longer as pioneering as it once was.

At the same time as being both strategic and creative, companies became more proficient at running identity programmes, which presented fresh problems.

## Controlling and category identity: the "CI manual" and the lookalikes

During the 1970s, 1980s and 1990s a vast number of powerful international identities were launched for companies such as Akzo Nobel, BT, ICI, BP and Unisys; and with them came weighty corporate identity manuals. These valuable management tools or "dead-hands", according to your point of view, were often to be found propping open a door instead of being pored over for their timely and topical advice.

Interestingly, this "professionalising" of visual identity probably did more to reduce differentiation between companies than at any other time. Professional standards were rapidly shared and copied, and many companies started to share similar visual cues. But in its way, the lookalike factor helped spur the rapid expansion of branding and identity in the past 30 years. This is because there has been a tendency to react in two ways to new breakthrough identities within a particular business category. The first is to acknowledge a rival's success in differentiation through identity by creating a completely different approach to the task. The second is to recognise success by saying "we'll have some of the same". So, for example, the 3i identity led to a plethora of illustration-based visual identities. Not all of them were bad, and because they found something new to say, they were not purely imitative. But, as ever, there were fashionable trends in design and identity, and sometimes these trends became more entrenched than the one-off, copycat, flash-in-the-pan reactions. In many cases, companies from one sector or category of business ended up "borrowing" ideas and learning from others; and often the borrowing was creative and catalytic for a different sector of business.

Commercialisation of the public sector in the UK has created many branding opportunities. One category could be called the lookalike higher education sector. In the late 1980s, polytechnics were able to re-brand as universities but to succeed they had to look like a university. Dozens of former polytechnics marched into corporate identity programmes to emerge looking the same. Category identity had taken off by the late 1980s, but it reached its zenith during the late 1990s as dotcom companies raced to portray the ethereal nature of their services and excited possibly the biggest spate of lookalike identities ever seen. There were endless flowing, single-line "swooshes" usually accompanied by a mad name and intended to convey a sense of energy and dynamism. But Nike's swoosh design mark has stayed the course, perhaps because of its sheer omnipresence.

But lookalike strategies may have a kind of "flocking" advantage. In a test with pharmacists during the Pharmacia and Upjohn merger in 1995, logos of famous drug companies were jumbled up, with the symbol of one paired with the logo of the other, and so on. Boards with these on were rotated to reveal the correct and incorrect versions. In six out of ten cases, pharmacists asked to identify the correct board got it wrong. In the second question, they were shown another board where the drug companies' logos had been redesigned to look like other well-known brands (Hoecsht made up as Heineken, for example). This time no one was in any doubt about which company was supposed to be represented. Maybe this illustrated that pharmacists do not care about drug company logos. Perhaps they simply recognised the category and that was enough for them to be able to do their job properly. After all, pharmacists are more likely to recognise a particular drug than the company responsible for it. So perhaps there is an advantage in adopting the clothes of the category to which you belong. By looking like a pharmaceuticals company, or a law firm, or a university, or a high-tech company, you can benefit from the legitimacy of the category. You may even be able to channel more funds into product sales as your corporate credentials will be confirmed by the category identity itself. This was particularly true of the bigger accountancy and management consultancy firms prior to 1998 and is largely true of banking and law firms today.

But a category identity will not be enough in a merger or acquisition where the idea of the new company has to be sold as offering something "truly new and better". In 2000, at the peak of the merger boom, the total value of announced mergers and acquisitions globally was $3.5 trillion, roughly equal to 10% of world GDP. A merger brings substantial challenges in terms of identity: what to call the new company; whether there should be elements of the legacy identities; how to communicate the sense of "new vision"; how to be the first to establish a "new category".

Novartis broke new ground on two levels. It was formed from the merger between Sandoz and Ciba in 1996 and was among the first highly visible pharmaceuticals companies to move away from its legacy elements, Ciba and Sandoz, and create a non-pharmaceutical or conceptual name (what has "Novartis" to do with pharmaceuticals?). Novartis also devised a new category title, life sciences (to replace simply "pharmaceuticals" or even "drugs company"), which has since been adopted as the buzz definition for the total category.

The merger boom of the 1990s brought experimentation. Identities had to be created faster than ever before. Huge sums were spent getting messages out quickly to a global workforce. And great attention was paid to combating the negative effects of a merger, including anti-climax and that "meaningless feeling" among the workforce, and even the disaffection felt towards a new partner who up till then had been an arch rival.

This internet-speed period in identity created a new approach, that of diversifying identities.

## Diversifying identities

The history of corporate identity is littered with examples of powerful structural identities that labelled every department and every function in the same way. By the 1990s, such an approach was considered to be overcontrolling and was even compared by some to the identities of Hitler's national socialism and Russia's communism. For many, the corporate identity manual, intended to be a vibrant source of inspiration for company-to-customer communication, became associated with negative regulation or a police-state environment. The unofficial job title "logo cop" came into being.

The explosive nature of the digital age, the recognition that a job was no longer for life and the concept that quality of work was more important than financial reward, promoted by magazines such as *Fast Company*, *Wired* and even *Fortune*, meant that identity, if it was going to succeed, had to be tackled differently, more intelligently and creatively than before.

In 1997, British Airways launched a new identity that took the idea of diversity to a height not seen before, at least not in the airline world. The reaction to it was mixed and often critical. The old BA identity had been classically "British", heraldic and sober, and the image-tracking studies carried out by the company in the mid-1990s had picked this up. Certainly, BA had an image of being global but hardly caring. The Britishness exemplified by the silver-grey crest on the tailfin said more about a cool and possibly unforgiving attitude to customer service than it did about a top-notch travelling experience for millions of economy-class passengers.

To combat this, the new identity was designed to make a highly visible display of the company's real interest in serving customers from all over the world. This was symbolised through a ground-breaking project: artists from different world communities were invited to display their work as an integral part of BA's visual identity, including placing art-works on the tailfins themselves, the traditional branding space reserved for only the most formal of identifiers.

What might have appeared as a surface treatment, possibly even a shock tactic, had serious ambitions in the area of employee retraining and behaviour. BA rightly observed that a change in perception in the minds of its customers would come only through a change in the experience they enjoyed from the beginning to the end of their encounter with the airline. The identity, with its obvious message of diversity, was a catalyst in significant internal change, and, perhaps, a reflection of internal change that was already taking place and becoming visible. As a result, BA people would master more languages in the future; they would be encouraged to be themselves with passengers; they would strive for the highest standards in service; and they would make this a self-fulfilling prophecy.

Interestingly, the reaction to the new identity included as much oppo-sition to the loss of British uniformity as praise for the globally diverse perspective taken by a British company. The visual identity, itself an expression of a radical change of business direction, became an easy target for those, internally and externally, who were unhappy about the company's new direction. This was exacerbated by the fact that airlines are, inevitably, partly representatives of national identities. Those who attacked the new BA identity most bitterly were also those who defended most stoutly the established view of the British national iden-tity. Other airlines, in other parts of the world, have found themselves in a similar position to BA when considering their identity. A changing iden-tity reflects a company, organisation or even a nation in a state of flux and forces the question: "Are you comfortable with the way you are going?" Inevitably, in some cases, the answer has been "No". BA back-tracked on the diversity of the new identity and the chief executive stood down not long after. The basic elements of the visual identity remained but the tailfins used the version of the Union Jack flag originally intended for use only on Concorde. A diverse identity had become monolithic.

Some of the issues touched on above, particularly the growing ambitions for identities to influence the behaviour of customers and employees, brought language into the identity mix more prominently. Perhaps for the first time language, or tone of voice, was identified as a "basic element" of identity. As such it was seen as a way to differ-entiate a brand and to reach out to audiences with a message about its diversity. Orange, a UK mobile telecommunications company, was much admired in the 1990s for doing this. So the logic of visual and verbal identity supporting each other to create a more engaging, rounded identity became accepted.

Like its visual companion, verbal identity has a number of possible elements that can be used separately or in isolation. Its equivalents to logo, colours, typography and photographic or illustrative style include name(s), straplines, stories and tone of voice. The identity mix becomes richer, while allowing individual elements of it to stand out. Arguably, the line "Just do it" became an identity element for Nike that was just as important as its swoosh design mark.

As with visual identity, corporations are keen to own and control their verbal identity. McDonald's has gone to the trouble and expense of registering ownership of more than 100 phrases. It is as if to say "this is our linguistic territory, no one else can enter it". Such a legalistic approach, though, is limited and limiting, because it also means that a brand's own language does not stray far outside those narrow borders. Brands such as Guinness have discovered that by being expansive rather than restrictive, by telling stories, they can connect more emotionally with audiences (see the example in the colour section). This might be with customers and potential customers, particularly through advertising, or with their own employees, suppliers and partners through a range of communications, including books, videos and e-mails. In doing so, they establish a storytelling approach that is verbally and emotionally rich.

### Innocent Drinks

From Innocent's *Company Rule Book*

*Always ask an expert*

What's the answer? We don't know. Most of the time we don't even know the question. But there's always someone we can turn to. And that's you, dear reader. We couldn't have done it without you …

In the summer of '98, we bought £500 worth of fruit, turned it into smoothies and sold them from a stall at a little music festival in London. We put up a big sign saying "Do you think we should give up our jobs to make these smoothies?" and put out a bin saying "YES" and a bin saying "NO". At the end of the weekend the "YES" bin was full so we went in the next day and resigned.

It is this desire for emotional connection that is encouraging brands to be more creative and adventurous with the words they use to express their personalities. Increasingly, humour can be employed as a deliberate strategy rather than a one-off campaign tactic. Brands like Innocent Drinks in the UK and Tazo in the United States take risks with humour and language that would have been unimaginable by serious marketers a few years ago. The logo cops would be making wholesale arrests. But if your brand name is Innocent, which expresses an innocent personality and approach to life, then that personality should be expressed consistently through an innocent visual and verbal identity.

So what next? What are the conclusions that can be made about visual and verbal identity and their relationship to brands in the future?

There are a few easy pointers:

- Verbal identity will for a while become a more important tool for brand expression. Totally "new" visual identities will be limited as long as merger activity remains suppressed by market conditions.
- Management of an existing visual identity will become a real concern. Brand owners will increasingly look for better integration between the languages of identity and advertising.
- Naming will undergo a regenerative period following years of cynical jibes from the media. Names will be sensible or extreme, but "manufactured" Latinate names (such as Consignia) have had their heyday.
- Photography and illustration will also go through a period of rethinking. Whereas the last ten years have been dominated by a noticeable style to show "real people in real situations", this will reach saturation point. Even the image banks will start to balk at the trend. Illustration with all its magical self-gratifying and artistic qualities will make a long overdue comeback.
- Controlling identities will reappear, not in the same way as in the 1970s and 1980s but in a practical, no-nonsense way. They will be implemented using simple automating technology so that the mechanics are swept out of the way of people's daily lives.
- The economies of Asia, Russia, China and Africa will leapfrog the branding learning curve. They will spark a new wave of identities combining "native" elements with familiar European or American visual cues. The result will be a heady mix to challenge the most staid patterns of our established markets, raising issues

of intellectual property, trademark protection and ethics between the developing and developed worlds.

☑ There will be a renewed emphasis on honesty, practicality and cost of implementation. But alongside this, perhaps, will be the realisation that brands and branding have not had the best deal recently and now is time to fly a flag for originality and freshness.

Visual identity and verbal identity are part and parcel of brands and branding. They exist and will make a statement even if brand owners choose to ignore them. When not controlled they can do damage, so it is better to lock them firmly into the brand management of a business.

An identity should be reviewed frequently and maintained like any other asset. Unlike pure science, identity is a triumph of opinion backed up by assertion. Its subjectivity is the very property that allows you to be bold and get away with it. The world's greatest identities are irrational, just like brands. Create them in this way and you will not go far wrong. Indeed, you might find the whole world casting admiring glances at you and hanging on your every word.

## Recommended reading

If you would like to read further around the subject of this chapter, you may find the following books interesting and useful.

Fletcher, A., The Art of Looking Sideways, Phaidon Press, 2001.

Haig, M., Brand Failures, Kogan Page, 2003.

Heller, S., Paul Rand, Phaidon Press, 1999.

McKenzie, G., Orbiting the Giant Hairball, Penguin Putnam, 1998.

Ogilvy, D., Ogilvy on Advertising, Orbis, 1983.

Olins, W., Corporate Identity, Thames & Hudson, 1989.

Pentagram, Ideas on Design, Faber and Faber, 1986.

Simmons, J., We, Me, Them & It: The Power of Words in Business, Texere, 2000.

Simmons, J., The Invisible Grail: In Search of the True Language of Brands, Texere, 2003.

Vincent, L., Legendary Brands: Unleashing the Power of Storytelling to Create a Winning Market Strategy, Dearborn, 2002.

Whyte, D., Crossing the Unknown Sea: Work and the Shaping of Identity, Penguin Books, 2002.

# 8 Brand communications

*Paul Feldwick*

Everything a brand does is communication. As Paul Watzlawick, a communications theorist, wrote: "It is impossible not to communicate."[1] The way the packs are designed, the words used, the way phones are answered (or not), the products the name is put to, the shops in which these are sold: all these can say powerful things about a brand. (Other messages about the brand are not under the control of the brand manager, such as the things that people who use the brand or others say or write about it.)

Some important aspects of brand communication are already well covered elsewhere in this book, especially in the chapter on verbal and visual identity. But as well as managing the brand's design and language, most brand managers also invest money in communicating directly to the brand's various stakeholders through direct mail and PR, telemarketing and website design, events and sponsorship programmes, and, not least, through the various advertising media of TV, print, cinema and radio.

From their beginnings as mass phenomena in the 19th century, brands and advertising (in the broadest sense of that word) have evolved together. Early mass-market brands, from Pears Soap to Kodak to Coca-Cola, built their business on heavy advertising investments; by 1912, Coca-Cola was spending over $1m a year on advertising. Right up to the present day, it is exceptional to find a large or successful brand that does not continue to invest heavily in communications.

Traditionally, brand communications have been segregated into categories known as "above the line" and "below the line". These names were originally connected with agency accounting procedures. The media paid commission for activities above the line but not for those below the line (an advertising agency's clients did not pay directly for its services; the agency made its money as sales agent for the media). Press, TV, outdoor, radio and cinema were above the line; direct mail, PR, sales promotions of various sorts, events and sponsorships were generally below.

Originally, advertising agencies would offer all these services and could subsidise the below-the-line activities with the commissions from the others. Over time, below-the-line activities became more specialised and separate agencies grew up to deal with them, and as advertisers negotiated to have rebates on commissions or to switch to fee payment, the economics of the old-style full service became unsustainable. Today a wide range of communications agencies offer specialised services, so that a brand's communications are normally fragmented among a number of different suppliers. The expressions above and below the line linger on, but there is now much talk about the importance of "integrated marketing", or "through the line", which is about how best to bring back together the fragmented pattern of activities in the better interests of the client.

It is fashionable at present to predict the "death of advertising", meaning the classic above-the-line media. This is unlikely to happen. Certainly things have changed in the advertising business. It is no longer easy to obtain the huge, monolithic mass-market audiences that UK or American network television delivered until the 1970s; the VCR, the remote control, and now TIVO and the PVR (personal video recorder) make it easier for audiences to avoid commercials. Meanwhile, advances in computing power have made individual targeting of consumers appear more practical, and the direct-mail industry has sold itself hard on this basis.

However, it is probable that all types of paid-for brand communication will continue to play an important role in building brands in the future, much as they have in the past. TV, despite the prophets of doom, is still one of the world's fastest-growing media, with the worldwide number of TV homes trebling in the past 20 years (one-quarter of them are now in China). And it still seems to work. Many advertisers who thought that they could get more efficient results by shifting their TV money into sponsorship or direct mail have found the results disappointing. This is not to say that sponsorship or direct mail are not valuable, but few brands have created or maintained strong brand identities using these channels alone.

### How do communications build brands?

Certain types of brand communication give information, or are aimed at leading directly to a transaction: brochures, coupons, mailshots, direct-response advertisements, and certain uses of websites and of most other media. But taking brand communications as a whole, through all channels, past and present, a great deal cannot be explained in either way.

BMW has one of the
world's most immaculate
and consistently powerful
visual identities which is
a benchmark not just for
automotive companies.

Ben Cohen and Jerry Green created a living identity for their ice-cream brand by apparently not trying. Names of flavours were sensical and non-sensical at the same time.

Who could possibly miss the lead guitarist of the *Grateful Dead* as the inspiration for Ben & Jerry's cherry concoction?

Woody Jackson cows are an integral part of Ben & Jerry's visual identity – you can buy t-shirts of the cows as an indirect tribute to the ice cream makers themselves.

Branding irons started the brand ball rolling. There are 260,000 registered variations of simple shapes like these in Texas today.

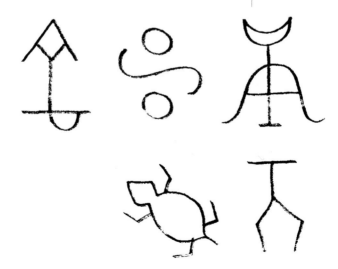

See the symbol, read the name:
Penguin Books.

3, Shell and Red Cross.

The Penguin logo is a registered trademark of Penguin Books Limited    Shell trade mark reproduced with the permission of Shell International Petroleum Company Limited

Some brands associated with colours.

Artist Haddon Sundblom created the universally recognised image of Santa Claus for Coca-Cola's advertising in 1931, dressed for the first time in red to match the company's corporate colours.

UPS and BP both retained strong colour associations when they rebranded.

You can't think of Kodak without visualising yellow and red.

bp

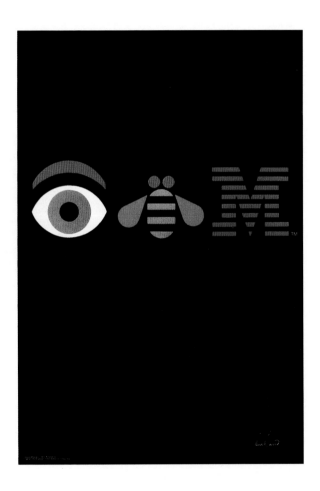

The Bovis Hummingbird,
a beautiful escape from the
predictability of company
logos in the 1970s.

The 3i logo inspired
countless tributes during
the 1980s and was restyled
in 2003. 3i calendar cartoon
by Charles Barsotti.

Lumino, also in the 1980s,
shows new possibilities
with the illustration style
made famous by 3i.

LUMINO

" YOU DAMN STUPID DUCK, EVERY
MORNING IT'S A BRAND-NEW
WORLD FOR YOU, ISN'T IT ? "

London fashion shop Jones
followed suit.

London's Natural History
Museum logo (1989) rounds off
a great ten-year era in soft,
communicative identity styles.

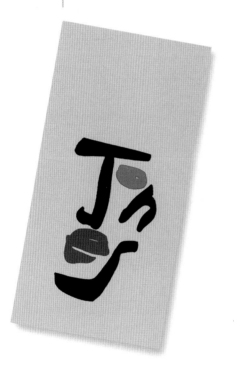

Around 60% of BA's customers live outside the UK. An important aspect of the controversial 1997 identity was to project the airline's global reach through tailfins decorated with artists' work from around the world. But departing from the convention of using a national flag met with disapproval from the country's former prime minister, Margaret Thatcher, who is seen here trying to cover up the new design with her handkerchief.

The labels on the smoothie bottles have a distinctive verbal style that could only be described as innocent.

Opposite is an example of how Guinness uses storytelling to build understanding of its brand.

Thou shalt not commit adultery.
You said it big guy. That's one guideline we follow religiously; our smoothies are 100% pure fruit. We call them innocent because we refuse to adulterate them in anyway.

Wherever you see the dude ☺ you have got our cross-your-heart-hope-to-die promise that the drink will be completely pure, natural and delicious. If it isn't, you can ring us on the banana phone and make us beg for forgiveness.

Amen.

**Why not say hello?**
Drop a line or pop around to Fruit Towers, 6 The Buspace, Conlan Street, London W10 5AP

Call the banana phone on **020 8969 7080** or visit our online gym at **www.beinnocent.co.uk**

® = Religious-experience

The story starts with

## the expletives deleted

We don't need to sanctify the memory of our founder

but no one ever recorded the swear words Arthur Guinness

flung across the barricades at the gentlemen

from the Dublin Corporation in 1775

**But fling them he did**

The temptation is to describe Arthur Guinness as a stout gentleman. Well, we make no point about his girth but we do know that Arthur Guinness took his time before he came around to brewing porter. When he finally did it, it was worth waiting for.

But it was water that did it. The whole history of Guinness is built on water.

Think of that the next time you sink a pint. If Arthur hadn't made his first stand against the bureaucrats and stood up for his commercial rights we wouldn't be here now thinking of new ways to fight the Guinness cause.

I did a deal **dammit** so let's stick to it!

Arthur Guinness stuck to it. It took him twelve years to win his fight for the Dublin water rights, but he won. And that was the first crucial turning point in the story of Guinness.

It takes strength to do it. Not necessarily the girder-lifting strength of a strongman, but the commitment that comes with an inner certainty.

Think about it

## Savour it

And lift your glass to Arthur

We owe it to him

The Edsel's curious visual extravagances raised more than one eyebrow. The grill was described by one commentator as looking like a "vagina with teeth".

Both globally recognised –
the Nike strapline and the
Swoosh Design Mark.

# JUST DO IT.

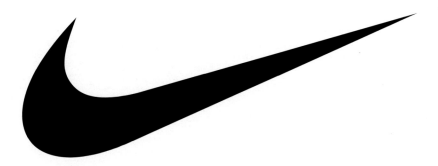

"Identity creation
remains a triumph
of opinion backed
by assertion.

The best identities
are irrational,
just like the best
brands.

So it is therefore subjectivity that saves
the day, which is refreshing to know".

(Tony Allen and John Simmons. Chapter 7: Visual and Verbal Identity).

Sponsoring a Rolling Stones tour, or the large proportion of advertising that contains no actual information about the brand: what exactly are these doing? How do they work, and how do they justify the large shares of profits that successful brand owners often invest in them? Some marketers may believe that any communication not directly involved in selling must be an indulgence, but history shows that, with few exceptions, strong brands are not built on this kind of thinking.

Communications with an immediate selling aim may appear more productive. Their direct results may be more easily measurable, but in terms of the long-term health of the brand it may be others that create more competitive advantage. Brand strength, although it involves sales, is also about more than sales. It is about the ability of a brand to resist competition, to support a premium price, to weather negative publicity and thus to offer to shareholders a more reliable promise of future cash flows.[2] Brand owners will want to ensure that their communications not only stimulate sales, but also enhance the underlying strength of the brand.

### Evaluating brand communications

Broadly, there are two types of measurable outcomes of brand communications: effects on sales or business and consumer responses. Both are important.

It used to be thought that sales effects of advertising could never be satisfactorily separated from other factors affecting the business. However, the problem is not such a great one, as long as reliable data exists, especially with the use of modern modelling techniques.

Consumer responses include reactions to the advertising itself – recall, liking – and attitudes to the brand. Of these, brand responses are ultimately the more important.

Longer-term effects of brand communications on the strength of a brand may be seen through attitudinal questions and by the brand's marketplace performance, such as its ability to command a price premium or resist competitive pressures.

Source: Feldwick, P., *What is Brand Equity, Anyway?*, WARC Publications, 2002

### *Stimulating short-term behaviour*

Single-source panels are research sources that record both individual buying behaviour and individual exposure to specific advertisements.

Analyses of these have shown repeatedly that in about 45–50% of cases, exposure to even one advertisement in a short period before buying measurably increases the probability of buying the advertised brand, sometimes by a very considerable degree. Thus advertising gives a real short-term nudge towards increased choice of the brand. Interestingly, one such analysis shows that the most effective communications are not only biased towards information, but also seek to play on emotions and to entertain.[3]

### Longer-term effects on brand behaviour

However, the short-term effects of advertising in themselves are rarely economic; profits on most brands would increase in the short term if spending on communications were cut. But the return on these investments lies in the long-term economic value of advertised brands. Brands that are supported with effective communications are more profitable, can command a premium price and are resilient to competitive activity. There is evidence for this in many specific case histories and in multi-brand studies such as the PIMS database, as well as the continued behaviour of most big brand marketers.[4]

### How do brand communications influence behaviour?

Any attempt to explain mental processes inevitably oversimplifies, but three common strands of thinking can be used to explain the process by which communications about brands have an influence on people's behaviour. These are loosely based on a 1990 study by Mike Hall and Doug Maclay, two British researchers.

### By communicating information

Claude Hopkins, an early and influential theorist, claimed that this was what really mattered. "Give people facts ... the more you tell, the more you sell," he thundered in 1922. In Hopkins's view, humour, unusual visuals, even white space, were all wasteful or counterproductive.

Within the limits of his own experience, Hopkins was more right than wrong. His experience was writing what were then called "mail order" advertisements, those with a coupon for the reader to close a sale, or at least send for more information. By careful measurement of responses, Hopkins and his contemporaries learnt from experience exactly what worked most efficiently.

Hopkins's rules are still good ones for most direct-response advertising, and for any situation when, in Hopkins's words, you want to "hail a few people only" and give them information that will be of interest to them. However, not all brand communications work this way.

Hopkins wrote:

> *The sole purpose of advertising is to sell ... it is not to keep your name before the public. It is not to help your other salesmen.*

But why not? Much advertising, perhaps most, does precisely these things. To say that the purpose of advertising is to sell is as helpful as saying that the purpose of a football team is to score goals. In one sense, this is absolutely correct, but it is misleading in so far as actual shots at the goal form a tiny part of what footballers actually do on the pitch (and indeed, off it) which is necessary to make those goals possible. In the words of Stephen King, the founder of account planning at the J Walter Thompson agency in the 1960s, the most important role of advertising is not to sell, but to create "sale-ability". This begins to explain why much effective advertising not only contains no factual information, but also can break any or all of Hopkins's other rules.

### By creating awareness, fame, familiarity or "salience"

This cluster of ideas is based on the fact that we have a general tendency, other things being equal, to choose things we are more familiar with, recognise or think of first.

We know this works at the individual level, from both advertising examples and psychological experiments. There is a social dimension to it as well. If a brand is famous, people generally assume it is popular and has the endorsement of others. DDB's Brand Capital survey has shown the power of this "contagious demand", in that brands with more "friends" almost invariably have a higher proportion of those friends as "lovers"; in other words, they have a stronger average attachment to the brand. In view of these findings it is important to think of brand communications not just as one-to-one messages from the brand to an individual, but also as public rituals creating shared meanings. Not only do I see an ad, but I know everyone else sees it too, and in many cases I am aware of how they react to it.[5]

There is such strong evidence to support the importance of this "salience" model (in Hall and Maclay's term) that some theorists believe this is all that is necessary to explain communication effects. Andrew Ehrenberg, a professor at South Bank Business School in London, argues that this is all that advertising does. The role that creativity or distinct brand properties play in the process is simply to enhance the salience effect, rather than to attach distinct meanings to brands. This may be an extreme view, but there is no doubt that the role that fame and publicity play in advertising effect, quite independently of advertising content, is often underestimated.

### The Bud Light Institute

To promote Bud Light beer in Canada, Anheuser Busch's agency DDB invented the (fictitious) Bud Light Institute. Its purpose is to help men spend more time with their male friends, preferably drinking Bud Light, by creating elaborate strategies to help them escape from their wives or girlfriends.

TV commercials launched the institute by showing how, for instance, they could provide a horde of Vikings to break up a family barbecue, or create the first 48-hour romantic movie that would keep women occupied for an entire weekend. Another commercial was a spoof advertisement for a compilation of romantic songs with titles such as *I love you because you let me go out with my friends on a weekly basis*. (The interest in this was so great that a real CD called *Ulterior Emotions* was made available through the Bud Light Institute website, and at one point this became the second best selling CD in Canada.)

Bud Light also covered a new office building in Vancouver with a huge hoarding announcing that this was to be the headquarters of the Bud Light Institute. It advertised for a director, held interviews and eventually announced the "appointment" of a real applicant.

In these and other ways the idea originally created for TV was developed into an elaborate joke through many different channels and devices. (As jokes are by their nature analogic, this digital summary totally fails to reflect the fact that the campaign is also very funny.)

The content of this campaign says nothing about the product, and indeed beer is featured only peripherally or not at all. The campaign works by a witty sharing of men's feelings about women, creating a sense of complicity and a friendly relationship with the brand.

Although one-to-one communications (website, promotions, direct mail) work well as part of this campaign, its overall effect depends entirely on the public, shared nature of the joke.

### By creating involvement

As well as these simple ideas, which could be called facts and fame, there is also a third strand, often recognised but more difficult to put into words. Hall and Maclay christened this involvement. James Webb Young of J Walter Thompson, writing in 1960, talked of how advertising "creates a value not in the product". Ernest Dichter and other Freud-influenced advertising psychologists of the 1960s wrote about motivation, and stressed the importance of symbol and metaphor in communication. Others have used the words enhancement and transformation. If you look at any selection of successful campaigns you will probably agree that there is an element of persuasive communication which is not based just on information or salience. Can we get closer to defining what this is?

This would be useful because this third strand is the one most likely to be overruled in practice. As the hardest to define and analyse, and therefore hardest to measure, it often has least force in the world of corporate decision-making. It is often subsumed under such unbusinesslike terms as emotion, intuition or artistry, resulting in frequent dialogues of the deaf between those who demand clarity and proof and those who "just know what feels right" (often, but not always, the client and the creative department respectively).

By drawing together some different ideas from neuroscience and communications theory, we can do something to legitimise this area. Some of the following ideas are recent, some less so, but generally they have not been applied enough to thinking about brand communications.

### By creating associations that will influence behaviour

One idea that may help dates back exactly 100 years to the first serious academic study of how advertising works: *The Psychology of Advertising* by Walter Dill Scott of Northwestern University published in 1903. Scott's theory, formulated long before Hopkins's model of information transfer had achieved its hegemony, was based on the simple and long established idea of associations. As a psychological theory this goes back to Aristotle, and it was a key concept for 18th century philosophers such as David Hume and John Locke. It states that any idea or sense experience automatically triggers connections in the mind to other ideas and feelings, and that although these connections may not always be conscious ones, they can be powerful enough to influence our behaviour.

Scott thought that advertising works by creating the right kind of associations for the brand. This process does not have to be conscious or verbal. He writes about the effects of pictures in advertisements, criticising a picture of a frog in a coffee advertisement because coffee should not be associated with a "disgusting, slimy reptile". He also quotes examples of how advertising can influence people's attitudes to brands without them being able to consciously recall seeing the advertising itself:

> One young lady asserted that she had never looked at any of the cards in the [street]cars in which she had been riding for years. When questioned further, it appeared that she knew by heart every advertisement appearing on the line ... and that the goods advertised won her highest esteem. She was not aware of the fact that she had been studying the advertisements, and flatly resented the suggestion that she had been influenced by them.

These ideas, which were subsequently sidelined in most advertising thinking for almost a century, are now strengthened by some recent findings in the study of the brain. Antonio Damasio in his book *Descartes' Error*[6] writes of neural connections called "engrams" and links between thoughts and feelings which he calls "somatic markers", thus founding our whole decision-making process not in reason but in our emotions and unconscious memories. Daniel Schacter in *Searching for Memory*[7] confirms Scott's observation (one that, incidentally, most advertising researchers have been inclined to ignore or deny):

> You may think that because you pay little attention to commercials on television or newspapers, your judgements about products are unaffected by them. But a recent experiment showed that people tend to prefer products featured in ads they barely glanced at several minutes earlier – even when they had no explicit memory for having seen the ad.

The topics of the emotive nature of brand decisions, and the power of implicit or low involvement processing, have been well reviewed by Robert Heath in his book *The Hidden Power of Advertising.*[8]

We can develop this third model, then, by arguing with Scott that advertising works by creating associations that will influence behaviour. These associations may well be non-verbal and also non-conscious. We now understand from recent research that such implicit learning, far from being weak, can be extremely powerful.

### Integration

Effective brand communications can be integrated in three different ways:

- Functional integration
- Brand integration
- Thematic integration

**Functional integration** means thinking about how the brand's different actions relate in real time and space to each other and to (for instance) the purchase decision process. So to encourage employees to sign up for a health care plan, they might need to go through a process of:

- recognising their need for health care;
- being aware of a particular brand;
- requesting information;
- reading the brochure;
- making an appointment for a sales meeting;
- keeping the appointment;
- concluding the agreement.

Moreover, the general effect of the brand's mass communications on "sale-ability" is likely to have a significant effect on conversion at each step of the process (though measuring response rates to each communication separately is unlikely to show this).

This level of planning requires a good understanding of the prospect's "road to purchase", and the practical or mental barriers at each step. It should acknowledge that creating sale-ability may be as important as closing a sale.

**Brand integration** means ensuring that everything the brand does in some way reflects and contributes to its unique identity as a brand: its values, its tone of voice, the kind of relationship it aspires to have with others. This is broader and deeper than a visual identity manual, although at a practical level this would also reflect the brand's identity in a tangible way.

If a brand's sense of identity is strong, this may be enough to ensure that any of its communications will be unmistakably linked to the brand. (Early Volkswagen advertisements were unlike other American car advertising, with simple black and white photographs of the car in white space, when everyone else was using coloured drawings, propped with glamorous people and surroundings.) The use of visual or other brand cues – the Dulux dog, the Pillsbury doughboy, the colours of Mastercard – is another common and more tangible way of linking a brand's communications together, without necessarily going quite as far as thematic integration.

**Thematic integration**, unlike the first two, should be regarded as optional but nevertheless has powerful effects. This is when a specific creative idea is developed through multiple channels or multiple messages: TV, outdoor, direct mail, internet promotions. The Bud Light Institute is a good example of this.

Theoretically, the creative idea that links this kind of campaign together could originate in any communication channel, from sponsorship to direct mail. In reality, however, it is hard to find examples of such big ideas that did not start in TV or print. This suggests that the greater creative freedom of these channels, when they are used fully, will continue to be a crucial ingredient in effective brand communications.

### Digital and analog communications

We need to realise, however, that if communication is non-verbal or non-conscious, it is a very different type of communication from the conscious, verbal sort that we find so comfortable to analyse. Indeed, at this point some readers may be worrying about the spectre of the hidden persuaders and sinister brainwashing techniques. But non-verbal, non-conscious communication is not something dreamt up by evil scientists or advertising people: it is simply the way we communicate most of the time in all our lives. In everyday interactions between people, it has been shown that between 55% and 95% of communication is non-verbal. We respond to gestures, tone of voice, physical appearance, clothes and context rather more than to what may be being said, and most of the time we do this without being consciously aware of it. Brands are no different.

We also interpret this non-verbal communication in a different way. Watzlawick makes an important distinction between what he called "digital" and "analog" communications (using an analogy between different types of computers). Other terms for the same idea are "denotative/connotative", or even "explicit/implicit". Digital communication aims to be precise; a word or symbol stands for one, unambiguous idea, almost as in a code. In analog communication, meanings are not fixed; they may vary from one recipient to the next, or in context, or simply show a multiplicity of possible interpretations. (John Hartley Williams, a poet, has written about "one dimensional and three dimensional language", the latter including poetry.)

In business we have been conditioned to believe that digital (precision) is good and that analog (ambiguity or vagueness) is bad. Yet all non-verbal communication, according to Watzlawick, is essentially analogic. This explains both the powerful effect that images, gestures or music can have and the unease that they can create in a business environment.

What is more, the function of analog communication is often different. For Watzlawick, every act of communication is about two things: the actual content, and the relationship between the parties communicating. If we stop to think about much of our everyday conversation, for instance (to say nothing of body language), small talk about weather, sports or fashion has more to do with our relationships with each other than with its ostensible content.

This applies to brand communications too. If an advert, event or mailshot is entertaining, shocking or informative, these choices of intended effect, quite independent of content, say something important about the brand and the relationship it proposes to have with the viewer. Looked at through this lens, many advertisements that seem pointless when considered in terms of content take on a whole new level of meaning, one which the audience has no difficulty intuitively responding to. (Max Blackston, a researcher, has argued that a person's relationship with a brand depends not just on what they think about the brand, but what they think the brand thinks of them.)

### The case of Degree

Degree antiperspirant was launched in 1990 in the United States, and by 2000 it enjoyed high consumer awareness for its body-heat activated positioning. Then new research uncovered an emotional concern among men about perspiration, that sweating was a sign of weakness or failure: "If you sweat, you're toast."

This insight created an opportunity to take body-heat activated to the next level with male consumers, and an integrated marketing programme was built around a new male-targeted product differentiator: "Kicks-In In the Clutch." Cartoon-style advertisements featuring action heroes in dramatic situations appeared in print and TV programming.

Building on the "Clutch Time" campaign, in 2003 Degree became the exclusive antiperspirant licensee of the Ironman Triathlon, a brand that brought to life Degree's endurance and high-performance credentials. A complete integrated programme featured creation of a Degree Ironman Team of athletes, brand-sponsored TV programming, advertising and publicity, and even a new product, Degree Ironman Protection.

Since the "Kicks-In In the Clutch" campaign was launched, the brand has gained 4% share, and independent testing revealed that Degree's brand communications received from men the highest awareness scores in its category in 2002.

This is a good example of "thematic integration". It also illustrates some other points made in this chapter:

■ basing brand communications on consumer insight;
■ understanding the emotional basis for consumer decisions, not just product features;
■ creating strong brand cues (in this case mainly visual) that strongly differentiate the brand and stand for its distinct values;
■ the leap from a strategic insight to artistry and imagination (from digital to analog).

With acknowledgements to Unilever

Watzlawick makes one further point of great relevance: it is extremely difficult to translate analog communication into digital. We need only to discuss any successful advertisement with a group of people to see this in action. Ask a simple question such as "What makes this advertisement work?" and you will get a multiplicity of answers. Many will contain some truthful element, but none will be the truth. Yet marketers continually struggle to translate the visual or audio visual language of advertisements and brands into a digital, verbal language of analysis. We look at Budweiser's well-known TV commercial "Whas-sup" and say it is about camaraderie; we look at the Michelin baby and say it is about trust. But in the process we have lost everything that made those campaigns successful.

This is why Scott was not necessarily right when he complained about the disgusting slimy frog in a coffee ad. That was only one possible reading of the image. It might equally have been seen as, for instance, playful, friendly, natural, organic, lively, jumping or fresh. Yet these too are just words, none of which fully does justice to the image. Images like this are powerful precisely because they are volatile and multifaceted, so their interpretation in decision-making is never simple. Many people might have wondered why chimpanzees were an appropriate vehicle to promote tea, as in the UK PG Tips campaign that ran for 35 years, or why frogs and lizards are an effective way to sell Budweiser. One answer in both these cases is that because the creatures were strongly anthropomorphised, their human characteristics predominated over what might have been negative animal associations. But such rational analysis has its limitations when talking about successful brand communications.

Businesses that dream of certainty will always be uncomfortable with the analog side of brand communications. But it would be a mistake to think that brands can do without this high-octane fuel, and equally wrong to think that the same results can be obtained by acknowledging only those aspects of communication that can be safely digitised and analysed. This does not mean we are powerless to make good decisions about creative work. We are all capable of making intuitive judgments as long as we are allowed to, and as long as we develop our intuition rather than suppress it. We also have a useful, if not infallible, guide in the voices of the target audience, as long as we know what kind of questions to ask them and how to make sense of their responses.

But if we acknowledge that this level of communication is important in advertising, it also explains why much that is important defies simple analysis. Bill Bernbach, voted the most influential person in the advertising business in the 20th century by *Ad Age*, once said:

> Logic and overanalysis can immobilise and sterilise an idea. It's like love – the more you analyse it, the more it disappears.

He also said:

> Is creativity some obscure, esoteric art form? Not on your life. It's the most practical thing a businessman can employ.

Referring to a famous and successful mail-order advertisement for a correspondence course, which ran for years from the 1920s onwards under the headline "They laughed when I sat down at the piano ...", Bernbach remarked:

> *What if this ad had been written in different language? Would it have been as effective? What if it had said, "They admired my piano playing", which also plays to the instinct of being admired? Would that have been enough? Or was it the talented, imaginative expression of the thought that did the job? That wonderful feeling of revenge.*
>
> *Suppose Winston Churchill had said "We owe a lot to the RAF" instead of "Never was so much owed by so many to so few". Do you think the impact would have been the same?*

## Conclusion

Brand communications may do three things for a brand. They can:

- provide information about the brand;
- make a brand famous and familiar;
- create distinctive patterns of associations and meanings that make the brand more attractive and saleable.

These associations and meanings may be non-verbal and non-conscious. The communication will be analog as well as digital and its purpose is about creating a relationship with the brand as well as about its actual content.

This may all sound theoretical, but is simply trying to find words to bring into consciousness things that we all experience every day in all types of communication. These ideas may not be ones we could ever objectively call right or wrong, but they may be more useful in conceptualising the ways in which communications build brands. Certainly, these ideas help make sense of many aspects of successful advertising which are poorly explained by the models of information/persuasion or simple saliency.

They also have big implications in practice:

- The return on communications budgets should not be measured only in the short term or in sales responses that can be directly linked to specific activities. For many brands, investment in communications, at a level comparable with competitors, should be regarded as a continuing cost of doing business and ensuring the future cash flows of the brand.

◪ Not all effective brand communications can be intellectualised in terms of content. Rational decision-making processes may destroy the analog communications that could become a major source of added value.

◪ Research techniques for evaluating advertising or other communications, whether before or after exposure, can easily become biased towards things that are easy to measure, such as verbal understanding of information or conscious memory. These do not necessarily reflect the effectiveness of communications.

Lastly, there are two caveats:

◪ To be clear, this chapter does not mean to argue that analog is good and digital is bad. Human beings communicate in both ways. Sometimes precise information is the most persuasive thing to offer, and offering information in itself creates a certain kind of relationship. With the current decline of the "'long copy" ad, there are undoubtedly many missed opportunities in such categories as IT and finance for brands to differentiate themselves positively by having an intelligent dialogue with their customers, rather than paying for yet another full page in a broadsheet newspaper containing a picture of a flower and a portentous phrase like "inventing the future".

◪ Effective communication frequently defies simple analysis, but this does not mean that the process of planning brand communications should be without any discipline. Important questions should always be asked, such as what is the objective of the communication, who are the target audience, what action does the communication seek to influence? And they should always be answered on the basis of the best and most sensitive understanding of the people you are seeking to communicate with. Consumer understanding and insight are an essential starting point, but effective communication at some point needs to take a leap into the realm of intuition and artistry. To quote Bill Bernbach again:

> There are two attitudes you can wear: that of cold arithmetic or that of warm human persuasion. I will urge the latter on you. For there is evidence that in the field of

*communications the more intellectual you grow, the
more you lose the great intuitive skills that make for the
greatest persuasion – the things that really touch and
move people.*

## Notes and references

1 Watzlawick, P., *Pragmatics of Human Communication*, W. W. Norton, 1967.
2 See Chapter 2.
3 Jones, J.P., *When Ads Work*, Lexington Books, 1994.
4 Doyle, P., *Value Based Marketing*, John Wiley & Sons, 2000.
5 Crimmins, J. and Anschuetz, N., "Contagious Demand", Market Research Society Conference, 2003.
6 Damasio, A., *Descartes' Error: Emotion, Reason, and the Human Brain*, Putnam, 1994.
7 Schacter, D., *Searching for Memory: The Brain, The Mind, and The Past*, Basic Books, 1997.
8 Heath, R., *The Hidden Power of Advertising*, WARC, 2002.

# 9 The public relations perspective on branding

*Deborah Bowker*

Perceptions, accurate or not, are the basis of decision-making. The power to shape perceptions is contingent on credibility, which only too quickly disappears when corporations or their managers are seen to be behaving in a way that undermines trust in their standards and motives. Public relations is increasingly about communicating credibly with key audiences who affect business results, such as media analysts, policymakers and policy influencers, customers and shareholders. It is an important element in supporting the power and value of an organisation's brand to all stakeholders.

All the elements of a corporate brand, from tone and personality, functional and emotional benefits, core message and end goal, to its reputation – if fully leveraged with internal and external audiences – can help raise performance and credibility. Enhancing the awareness, understanding and commitment to a brand through a PR/communications strategy is usually an essential part of any overall strategy aimed at sustaining and raising standards of performance and credibility.

## Putting the brand in context

A brand is far more than a visual symbol and memorable tag line; it anchors the mission and vision, operating principles and tactics of an organisation. Internally, the brand is central to all decisions, actions and values, thus enabling employees to deliver the brand promise. The internal and external messages about the brand must tell the same story and be seen as part of the same narrative, and they should relate to the following:

- Values – the organisation's core beliefs; what it and the brand stands for.
- Behaviours – how the organisation interacts with internal and external stakeholders.
- Positioning – what the organisation wants stakeholders to think about a brand.
- Identity – names, logos, visual standards, verbal themes.

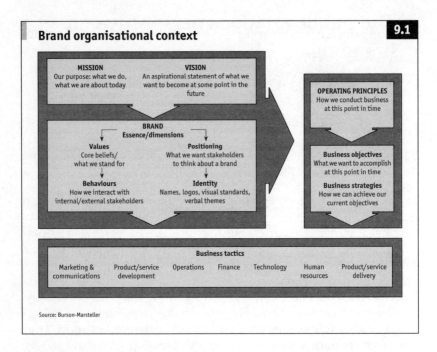

## Brand organisational context

**9.1**

**MISSION**
Our purpose: what we do, what we are about today

**VISION**
An aspirational statement of what we want to become at some point in the future

**BRAND**
**Essence/dimensions**

**Values**
Core beliefs/ what we stand for

**Positioning**
What we want stakeholders to think about a brand

**Behaviours**
How we interact with internal/external stakeholders

**Identity**
Names, logos, visual standards, verbal themes

**OPERATING PRINCIPLES**
How we conduct business at this point in time

**Business objectives**
What we want to accomplish at this point in time

**Business strategies**
How we can achieve our current objectives

**Business tactics**

| Marketing & communications | Product/service development | Operations | Finance | Technology | Human resources | Product/service delivery |

Source: Burson-Marsteller

A brand's value can be judged by an organisation's performance and that depends on interconnections. Recognising and reinforcing a brand's interconnections with an organisation's culture and performance through a communications campaign focused on employee alignment with business results and reputation can have powerful effects.

Brand identity must be built from within, across geographies, levels and functions. The notion of a winning culture is reinforced over time through recruitment, training, structure, reward and recognition aligned with the brand dimensions of values, employee behaviours, external positioning and symbols.

Brand-based values rather than vacuous slogans help people to "walk the talk", and defined behaviours, relevant to individual employees' day-to-day life, bring these brand-based values to life. Creating a community of employees who share an understanding of these values and behaviours brings a vibrancy and momentum to an organisation and helps focus people on the need for consistently high standards of performance. This is the source of customer satisfaction and corporate reputation.

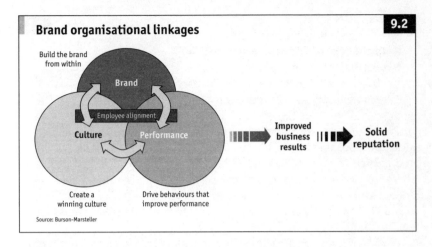

**Brand organisational linkages** 9.2

Build the brand from within

Brand

Employee alignment

Culture    Performance

Create a winning culture    Drive behaviours that improve performance

Improved business results → Solid reputation

Source: Burson-Marsteller

## The linkage with performance and reputation

High-performance organisations share certain characteristics at every location and level:

- Focus – a few key measures of success are clearly understood.
- Unity of purpose – a "one company" mentality with everyone pulling together.
- Energy – a sense of urgency, often emanating from the desire to fulfil a customer need.
- Agility – an ability to adapt to a changing business environment.
- Learning –a desire to share knowledge and the organisational infrastructure to enable knowledge to be shared.
- Identity – an individual and collective identification with an organisation's mission, values, business strategy and brand promise.

If all the above characteristics are fostered, high standards of performance can be sustained even in the face of fierce competition.

High-reputation organisations share certain robust drivers of reputation. For example, companies on *Fortune*'s Most Admired Companies list are rated by surveying perceptions of their reputation drivers among industry analysts, directors and managers. These drivers include:

- quality of management;
- quality of products and services;

◪ innovativeness;
◪ value as a long-term investment;
◪ soundness of financial position;
◪ wise use of corporate assets;
◪ ability to attract, develop and keep talented people;
◪ responsibility to the community and/or environment.

These drivers are given different weight and priority in different industries. But it is fair to say that they are perceived as strong or weak in a particular corporation based not only on actual financial performance, but also on perceptions of management reputation and credibility, and commitment to human assets and community relationships. A brand that is consistently perceived as representing high standards of quality and integrity is a strong and valuable brand.

Brand-owning organisations that are highly regarded share certain things:

◪ Leadership – a recognition that the brand is personified by the CEO and the whole senior management team.
◪ Pride – an appreciation that individual employee pride leads to collective quality.
◪ Innovation – evidence that sharing of ideas and the responsibility for taking risks is encouraged and rewarded.
◪ Long-term view – a focus on what is right in the longer term rather than what is expedient in the short term.
◪ Citizenship – an organisational commitment to acting as a good citizen.
◪ Talent – a recognition that talent must be valued and nurtured.

A brand can embody all of the above if there is a conscious choice to broaden its meaning beyond product benefits in order to connect with stakeholders in a holistic way. Public relations can help make that connection though a wide range of activities, as the following examples demonstrate.

### Brand and performance: Unilever

Unilever, a global company based in London and Rotterdam, owns many famous brands, ranging from Dove soap to Lipton tea to Birds Eye frozen foods. The company believes that agility, innovation and a focus on sustainable growth are keys to success.

In addition to product advertising and promotion, in recent years a significant emphasis has been placed on communicating the Unilever values and behaviours that drive growth. A multimedia internal communication programme has been implemented at all levels from the plant floor to the CEO. Shared values have been identified and desired behaviours defined, and rewards and recognition have been aligned around those behaviours. In an organisation that has traditionally functioned as separate units, all employees now focus on a consistent set of measures of success, with an eye on creating a winning culture. The focus on values and growth at every level is working well. In 2002, Unilever's leading brands in the home and personal care division surged with sales growth of 6.7%, while overall sales increased by 5.2%. This was in line with Unilever's *Path to Growth* strategy that is being implemented globally.

In Unilever's 2002 annual report, the letter from the chairman states:

> We can only meet and sustain the objectives of our Path to Growth strategy if our people have passion for winning and a culture that encourages and rewards enterprise. The development of Leaders into Action programmes, and the days we spend with our young leaders of tomorrow, are part of an overall programme to drive change. The results are evident in the enthusiasm to win we see throughout the business and examples of innovation that are driving fast growth and improved results.

### Brand and reputation: Coca-Cola

Coca-Cola, a global beverages company which owns one of the world's most famous brands, faces a number of challenges to its reputation as a result of increased antagonism to global brands, especially those so strongly identified with the United States.

Coca-Cola has taken several steps to recover any loss of reputation it has suffered. On obesity, which some have attempted to link to soft drinks, the company and its bottling partners have emphasised the choice of "diet" and other drinks. Its guidelines say that there should be no overt marketing of soft drinks to children who are 12 or under, vending machines offer a "portfolio" of beverages (soft drinks, water, fruit juice), and sponsored programmes in schools reinforce an active lifestyle.

As far as anti-Americanism is concerned, Coca-Cola may be an American brand, but its philosophy and the way it operates are international.

Outside the United States it has local managers and employees and takes care to demonstrate good local citizenship.

Doug Daft, Coca-Cola's CEO, states in the company's 2002 annual report:

> The values that underpin our success are integrity, quality, accountability, diversity, relationships based on our respect for each other, for the communities where we do business and for the environment. People know what to expect from the Coca-Cola Company precisely because we have always lived by our values. When a consumer enjoys a bottle of Coke, when people invest in us, when partners do business with us, or when we operate in a community, we keep our promise to benefit and refresh them. We create value – economic and social – reliably and predictably.

## The brand is the corporation

Ken Chenault, CEO of American Express, said recently:

> Our brand is, in essence, the litmus test for every business decision we make, and for the way we conduct those businesses. Because of this, our brand values and our corporate values must be consistent.

A survey of 137 American companies' executives, included in the April 2001 Conference Board report, *Engaging Employees through your Brand*, states:

> Executives told us their brand was being used as a rallying point for employees in a time of extensive change. Moreover, they expected employees to exemplify the promises the brand makes to the firm's customers.

From academia, Don Schultz, a professor at Northwestern University, offers:[1]

> A key to success appears to be the ability to develop appropriate internal systems to support the brand or brands and foster a unified, co-ordinated and cohesive execution of the brand promise in all its many dimensions, from communication to product development to customer service.

A robust corporate brand should:

◾ inform public policy and corporate positioning;
◾ support change initiatives;
◾ stand for credibility in difficult times;
◾ underscore employee values and guide behaviours.

This should happen if the corporate communications function assumes its responsibilities in championing the brand, protecting its reputation and demonstrating its values.

If a financial services organisation's goal is to be positioned as trusted adviser, then questions of corporate transparency must be weighed from many different viewpoints. What will be the short- and longer-term impact on the organisation's financial position, assets, values, and so on?

If a technology company is moving from selling boxes to selling solutions, then the brand needs to take into account and adapt according to how the change enhances core assets, strengthens functional benefits and aligns with evolved values.

As companies contemplate choices confronting them – for example, executive remuneration packages, sponsorships, reaction to a newsworthy issue – focusing on the core brand values can help them make the right decisions. It is often the vice-president for corporate communications or a PR consultant who will be the "conscience" in the debate.

Employees need to live according to the values of the brand and the behaviours that support those values. Southwest Airlines, US Postal Service and Four Seasons Hotels, for example, place customer-focused brand promise at the forefront of their new employee orientation, training, and reward and recognition programmes.

Herb Kelleher, a former CEO of Southwest Airlines, says:

> [Our people] know what needs to be done and they do it. Our culture is our true competitive advantage.

In quantifying the difference the engagement of employees can make to a business, in an article in the *Harvard Business Review* Anthony Rucci *et al.* stated:[2]

> A 5 point improvement in employee attitudes will drive a 1.3

*point improvement in customer satisfaction, which in turn will drive a 0.5% improvement in revenue growth.*

To get the most value out of a brand, it must be:

◪ defined by behaviours that will bring the brand to life;
◪ interconnected with elements driving organisational performance;
◪ recognised by leadership as a source of strategic focus;
◪ launched internally with a sustaining plan;
◪ reinforced by PR efforts in times of crisis or celebration.

To leverage the value of their brands, organisations need to recognise and communicate with the full range of stakeholders. Public relations can play a crucial role in this.

PR is not simply about making statements and issuing press releases. Today's best corporate communications functions recognise that accurately assessing and strategically shaping corporate perceptions must take account of the full array of influencers who drive issues, shape perceptions and have an impact on media coverage, and ultimately corporate reputation.

An affirmation of "who this corporation is and what we promise our customers, our shareholders, our employees, our communities" serves any organisation in times of crisis or celebration.

### US Postal Service: in crisis

The US Postal Service as a brand has been tested over time, from "going postal", referring to violence in the workplace, to "the mail moment", representing the anticipation and value of the mix of mail in a mailbox. The "We Deliver" tag line neatly encapsulates both the delivery of the mail and the brand promise.

Measures of the USPS brand reveal that it has enduring relevance and value to consumers, despite negative images of "snail mail" that attach to the medium itself. The brand attributes of traditional, reliable, trustworthy, and "cares about customers" served it particularly well throughout the anthrax crisis that followed the terrorist attacks of September 11th 2001.

Letters containing the deadly anthrax virus were delivered through the mail to the US Senate in Washington, DC, and to news media offices in New York and Florida. Some 800,000 employees were potentially at

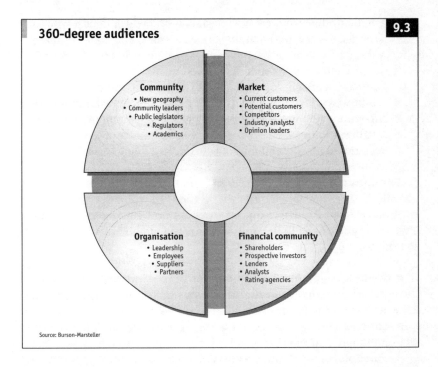

**360-degree audiences**                                                    9.3

**Community**
- New geography
- Community leaders
- Public legislators
- Regulators
- Academics

**Market**
- Current customers
- Potential customers
- Competitors
- Industry analysts
- Opinion leaders

**Organisation**
- Leadership
- Employees
- Suppliers
- Partners

**Financial community**
- Shareholders
- Prospective investors
- Lenders
- Analysts
- Rating agencies

Source: Burson–Marsteller

risk and 28,000 facilities were potentially contaminated. The safety of the mail was in question.

The challenge was to restore confidence and trust in the postal system among employees, who were handling and delivering the mail; major businesses and other organisational users of the mail system; and the public, who were continuing to receive their mail each day. Every stakeholder had to be reassured.

Tactically, the USPS managed the crisis in innovative ways, including:

- A special mailing for every American household with safety guidelines for mail handling.
- A redesigned internet site, created in just days, with a dedicated section on "keeping the mail safe and moving" with audience-tailored facts, videos, questions and answers, posters and mail service updates.
- A daily or twice daily facts update posted on the website and sent via e-mail and fax, eliminating thousands of customer and media calls.

- A daily update for local postmasters with facts and messages for their discussions with employees, customers, and communities.
- A three-tiered spokesperson cadre and daily press briefings with major media when needed.
- Mandatory all-employee meetings for the 800,000-person workforce with supervisors using crisis discussions and toolkits.
- An employee hotline for illness reports and general information.
- A summit with executives of major customers to discuss ways to keep the mail safe and moving.

The USPS moved through the crisis with its credibility intact and even enhanced. It demonstrated a communications function that was capable of more effectively managing information and stakeholder relations. Two surveys carried out in late 2001 showed that the brand's reputation was intact:

- A public opinion poll indicated 97% of respondents approved of its overall handling of the crisis; 96% said it was doing everything within reason to protect against future terrorism.
- Of the 90,000 employee respondents to a "Voice of the Employee" survey, 71% responded favourably to the statement: "I am proud to work for the Postal Service."

The strength of the USPS brand had given it a reservoir of public trust. The decision to provide continuously updated, reliable information reinforced that trust. By continuously providing reporters with facts and the public with consistent advice, ill-founded rumours were quickly quashed. Competence, caring and common sense prevailed.

### Coca-Cola: in celebration of a promise
Pure celebration is one of Coca-Cola's everyday brand messages. The task of PR is not to echo the marketing message, but to build on it through a range of stories that might involve local relationships, marketplace innovations, corporate responsibility and business results. PR should connect the dots between the product and citizenship, bottlers and community relationships.

Doug Daft, the CEO, explains:

> Some people would say our business is selling soft drinks.
> Others would say that our business is creating a special

*moment of refreshment, an experience. After more than 30
years of working in this great company, I would say our
business is building relationships. These relationships must be
based on mutual benefit, trust and shared values. This is the
essence of the Coca-Cola promise.*

*Ensuring that we operate as a good corporate citizen is
essential – to the strength of our brands, to the value we build
for our share owners and to our success as a company.
Building a bright future for our business rightfully includes a
commitment to helping build healthy, sustainable
communities.*

Ways that Coca-Cola builds its relationships and reputation include:

- Associations with a world of sports. Coca-Cola is the longest continuous sponsor of the Olympic Games, starting in 1928. Coca-Cola and its bottling partners support more than 50 sports in 200 countries, from grassroots soccer clinics in the Philippines to international competitions such as the World Cup.
- Through PR, highlighting innovation in connection with new products, techniques and technologies. In Asia alone, 21 new products were introduced in 2001, including fruit juices, waters, energy drinks, teas and coffees.
- Forming alliances with those who seek solutions to environmental challenges, such as the World Wildlife Federation and the National Geographic Society.

Managing the array of PR opportunities requires a disciplined approach:

- A worldwide team of corporate communications professionals linked through technology who are all fully aware of what Coca-Cola's position and message are on scores of issues.
- Constant multinational dialogue and examination of "local" issues which can become "global" issues.
- A clear understanding of worldwide, major media perceptions and relationships.
- An increasingly tighter linkage between marketing and PR objectives.
- Consistent image and messages wherever they are to appear,

from the annual report to a report on citizenship to regional employee publications.
- A redesigned intranet site highlighting continuously updated facts and corporate points of view on complex issues.
- The credibility and value of the corporate communications function underscored by reporting of results.

Clearly, Coca-Cola manages all the challenges to its reputation successfully as the company consistently stands at the top of worldwide lists of corporate brands ranked by value. It also leads in its industry on measures of long-term value.

## Conclusion

PR gives "legs" and life to brand attributes and the essential brand promise by telling credible stories and providing support for the truth of a brand's advertising images. This is all the more important in an evolving media and business environment.

Information sources have multiplied and consumers have become increasingly sceptical and weighed down by information overload. A National Quorum telephone survey of 1,007 American residents, conducted in February 1999 by Wirthlin Worldwide, a research and strategic consulting company, and published in The Wirthlin Report,[3] indicated that four out of five respondents thought that news articles were more believable than advertising. Three out of four felt that ads stretched the truth about the products they advertise.

The proliferation of television channels and niche magazines, the easy availability of 24-hour news and the exponential growth of the internet mean that organisations have no place to hide. They have to be up to the mark, ready to rebut damaging stories, and they must always make sure that they get their message across. The reality is that, according to Thomas L. Harris research, companies in the top 200 of Fortune's Most Admired Companies list spent twice as much on PR as those in the bottom 200.

All this illustrates how important PR is to brand strategy and to building and sustaining corporate reputation. The development of a successful PR strategy involves four elements:

- Identification of the various attributes and characteristics of the brand; for example, its values and supporting behaviours, its positioning and identity. Once these have been identified an assessment must be made of their implications with regard to an organisation's culture and opportunities for motivating performance. Then a public relations platform can be built on the brand's attributes, characteristics and promise.

◪ The perceptions of all external stakeholders must be assessed. This should extend beyond perceptions about products to include such drivers of reputation as leadership, innovation, financial value, quality of management and corporate citizenship.

◪ The corporate communications function should use the brand's attributes and characteristics internally to inform employees of the company's positioning on different issues to support change initiatives, to underscore credibility in crisis and to guide behaviour.

◪ An annual, measurable PR plan should be created, anchored by the brand promise, with the objectives of shaping key audiences' perceptions of leadership, customer connections, marketplace innovation and corporate responsibility.

## Notes and references

1  *Ad Age*, October 30th 1998.
2  Rucci, A.J., Kirn, S.P. and Quinn, R.T., "The Employee-Customer-Profit Chain at Sears", *Harvard Business Review*, February 1998.
3  *The Wirthlin Report*, Vol. 9, No. 3, March 1999. National Quorum is a twice-monthly omnibus telephone survey; *The Wirthlin Report* is published bi-monthly.

# 10 Brand protection

*Allan Poulter*

How do we go about protecting this valuable yet intangible asset known as a brand? This chapter is not concerned with how the brand's values are retained and developed from a commercial perspective (which is more than adequately covered elsewhere), but rather how we can use the law to protect certain physical manifestations of the brand from misuse or unauthorised use by third parties. In other words how do we maintain the exclusivity in the use of the distinctive features of the brand?

The first task is to identify the features of a business that serve to distinguish that business from its competitors or, indeed, any other business. The most obvious example is the brand name. But there are many other features that make up or represent the brand: logos, slogans, colours, sounds, the shape of a product, the "get-up" of packaging or "trade dress", layout of retail outlets, and so on. Which of these features would a brand owner want to prevent a third party from adopting?

Then there is the question of the geographical extent or aspirations of a business (and any local variations of the distinctive features that have been identified). Once these decisions have been taken it should be possible to identify what protection may be available in each relevant country.

Lastly, there is the crucial question of cost. What budget is available to protect the features that have been identified as important? It is unlikely that the allotted funds will be sufficient to allow for all possible available protection to be sought in all the countries of interest. It will be necessary to prioritise and determine what gives the best value in terms of the extent of protection afforded.

The area of law that is most useful in providing protection to the brand owner is that of intellectual property rights. There has been a fair degree of harmonisation of intellectual property laws throughout the world, and many of the principles discussed below are of general application in many of the major commercial jurisdictions. The need for a consistent approach to the protection of intellectual property rights on an international scale has long been recognised through a number of international initiatives that have supported the concept of reciprocal protection for such rights between countries. Although there may be local variations (particularly in procedure), the principles of protection are broadly the same. The position is continually evolving, but the trend is certainly towards harmonisation. This chapter concentrates on the general principles that apply in common law jurisdictions like the UK and the United States, referring also to EU and international initiatives.

## Trade marks

By far the most important weapon in a brand owner's armoury is a comprehensive portfolio of trade mark registrations. Trade mark rights are territorial and it is now possible to file applications for registration in just about every country of the world. The first application filed in the UK for trade mark registration was in 1876 for the Bass "Red Triangle" label mark and it remains on the register today. Indeed, many trade marks still on the register have celebrated their centenary, including household names such as Kodak, Coca-Cola and Wedgwood, to name but a few.

The legislation relating to trade mark registration has attempted to keep pace with changes in commercial practices, and there has been a fair degree of harmonisation of trade mark law, particularly within the EU. For example, the UK Trade Marks Act 1994 reflects the European Trade Mark Harmonisation Directive. Its definition of trade mark is very broad:

> A trade mark is any sign which is both a) capable of being represented graphically; and b) capable of distinguishing goods or services of one undertaking from those of other undertakings (Section 1(1)).

It goes on to state – and this is not an exhaustive list – that a trade mark may consist of

> ... words (including personal names), designs, letters, numerals, or the shape of goods or their packaging.

This marks a significant change, because under the previous legislation (Trade Marks Act 1938) an application had been filed for registration of the shape of the Coca-Cola bottle as a trade mark. The application was refused and the decision was upheld on appeal at the highest level. The basis of the refusal was that what was being sought to be registered was the product itself rather than something that was applied to the product. Following the implementation of the 1994 act, a new application was filed for the shape of the  bottle and this went through without difficulty. Indeed, many shapes have now been registered as well as the colours, sounds and even smells that form part of the "get-up" of products.

The European Harmonisation Directive has served as a model for many other countries that have adopted new legislation governing trade mark rights in recent years.

### What should be registered?

When considering what should be the subject of trade mark protection, the first step is to identify the features of a business that serve to denote the origin of the goods produced and/or services provided by that business. For example, Nike has protected, among other things, its word mark Nike, the swoosh design mark and the strapline "Just do it".

The Intel Corporation has registered its name Intel and the distinctive jingle that features prominently in its advertising and promotional campaigns. Sounds are becoming increasingly more important in commerce, and sonic branding is an area where there are likely to be further developments. This is particularly the case in the area of mobile telephony, which certainly lends itself to such marks because the visual imaging on handsets is, of necessity, limited.

Orange Personal Communications has registered both the name Orange and the colour orange for telecommunications services and related goods.

There are also examples of smells being registered, including "the strong smell of bitter beer applied to flights for darts". However, a recent decision of the European Court of Justice has called into the question the registrability of smell marks having regard to the difficulty in representing such marks graphically with sufficient clarity to define the scope of the protection afforded. The US Patent Office has accepted smell mark registrations, including the smell of plumeria blossom applied to thread.

Registrations have been secured for the shape and get-up of products, holograms, animated marks, the distinctive layout of retail outlets and even gestures.

### Classification of goods and services

Once the relevant distinctive features have been identified, the next step is to decide on the range of goods and services for which protection is required. This is, predominantly, a commercial decision based on the nature of the business being conducted and any likely expansion of its commercial activities.

Most trade mark registries have adopted the Nice classification system, which divides the register into 45 classes. When the range of goods and services for which registration is to be sought have been identified, it is necessary to determine the specific classes within which these goods or services fall. In many countries it is possible to file a single application covering any number of classes, paying an additional fee for each class, whereas other countries still require separate applications to be filed for each class. This can be costly.

Different countries take different positions on what is an acceptable specification. For example, the United States requires specifications to be restricted to those goods or services for which use of the mark can be established. The UK, however, allows for broad specifications as long as the applicant has an intention to use the mark for the goods and services claimed. In many other countries it is possible to file for all goods and services.

To avoid registers becoming cluttered with registrations of marks that are not being used, there is usually provision within the local legislation providing for the possibility of a registration being attacked on the grounds of (usually five years) non-use.

### Where should registration be sought?

Having identified the mark or marks for which protection is required and the relevant goods and services to be covered, consideration has to be given to the geographical extent of protection that should be sought. This will normally be governed by a company's current activities and its short-to medium-term ambitions. Of course, it may be that different marks will be used in different jurisdictions and the range of goods or services provided may also differ. However, once a decision has been made as to what protection is required and where, the next step is to identify how best to obtain appropriate protection in the most cost-effective manner.

One possibility is to file applications in each of the countries of interest directly through the national registration system of that country. This would normally require the instruction of lawyers in each country to file the application. However, an international registration system (the Madrid Agreement and Madrid Protocol) allows for a single application to be filed at the World Intellectual Property Organisation (WIPO) in Geneva, nominating the member countries for which applications are required. Where this is possible it can result in significant savings, as local lawyers will only need to be instructed if there is opposition or an objection to the application. A list of member countries of both the agreement and protocol can be found at www.wipo.org/madrid/en/index.htm. A notable exception is the United States, although it is scheduled to join the protocol in November 2003.

Within the EU it is also now possible to file a single application for a Community trade mark registration through the Office for Harmonisation in the Internal Market (OHIM), which is based in Alicante, Spain (colloquially known as the Community Trade Mark Office). This is not merely a system for filing applications within the EU countries; it is also a unitary system resulting in a single registration that is enforceable throughout the EU, effectively recognising the EU as a single market. As well as being significantly cheaper than filing separate applications in each of the EU countries (either directly or through the international system), there are other significant substantive advantages of using the Community trade mark system. For example, it is possible to get an EU-wide injunction to stop anyone infringing the trade mark, and the genuine use of the mark in any of the EU countries should be sufficient to protect the registration from an attack on the grounds of non-use. This is particularly useful for companies that have no current trading activity in most EU countries but intend gradually to expand their commercial activities across the region.

### Why register?

A registered trade mark provides its owner with the right to prevent the unauthorised use of the mark by a third party in circumstances where such use is not justified. Again, in most countries, the rights conferred by registration extend beyond merely being able to prevent use of the mark in respect of the goods covered by the registration. In certain circumstances, they may allow the proprietor to prevent the use of "similar marks" being used in respect of "similar" goods or services and, in some cases, the use of the mark in respect of "dissimilar" goods. The remedies that are normally available include the grant of an injunction to prevent the continued use of the mark and an award of damages to compensate for the loss attributable to the unauthorised use.

A registration is also a property right which can be assigned and which can underpin any licensing activity. This is particularly important for businesses involved in merchandising or franchising activities.

## Maintaining a trade mark portfolio

The phrase "use it or lose it" is relevant to trade mark protection. If a mark is not used within a country for the goods or services covered by the registration, it is likely to become vulnerable to an attack. Furthermore, token use designed solely to maintain the validity of a registration will normally be disregarded. Only genuine use of the mark within the relevant territory is likely to be sufficient.

## Renewals

Trade mark registrations last for a defined period, usually ten years, and have to be renewed if they are to be retained. It is, therefore, imperative that effective mechanisms are put in place to ensure that renewal deadlines are not missed. One important advantage of registered trade mark protection over other intellectual property rights is its potentially perpetual nature.

## Watching services

It is, of course, only possible to take action against potential infringements if and when you become aware of them. It is important that employees, local distributors and other parties involved in the company's business are made aware of the need to report instances of potentially infringing activities, and that there is in place a reporting line that enables such information to reach the desk of the person or department within the organisation responsible for handling these issues. It is certainly worthwhile subscribing to a watching service so that notification is received of any attempt by a third party to register a mark that is similar to your mark. You can then take action to prevent registration and, if appropriate, to prevent the use of the mark by the applicant.

## Record keeping

It is essential to keep comprehensive records of the use of the mark in each country as well as copies of promotional and marketing materials and evidence of sales in each country. The first line of defence in an infringement action is for the defendant to attack the validity of the registration on the grounds of non-use. It is not uncommon for companies to have difficulty in obtaining evidence of their use of marks even where such use may have been extensive. This information will also be relevant in infringement proceedings or passing off (see below) or unfair competition actions where it is necessary to establish goodwill or reputation within a particular jurisdiction.

### Creating a new mark: searching

There is no point in selecting a new mark where, because of earlier conflicting rights, the use of the mark is likely to be prevented by the owner of such earlier rights. As well as ensuring that the new mark satisfies the commercial demands of the company and does not have any unfortunate linguistic or cultural connotations, sufficient legal clearance searches have to be conducted. Although the cost of these searches may seem daunting, they can represent a fraction of the cost of having to change the name or fight infringement proceedings following a rebranding project or the launch of a new product or service.

You can save money by allowing sufficient time in the name creation process for straightforward searches for identical (or almost identical) names and marks before embarking on the more comprehensive full-clearance searches that are required to enable legal advisers to make an informed decision about the availability of the chosen mark.

Searching is a form of risk assessment or insurance. The more comprehensive the searches conducted, the less likely it will be that significant problems will be faced. A properly conducted search programme will help to avoid both the embarrassment of launching a brand whose name you do not own in territories that matter and the cost of withdrawing it and rebranding.

The legal aspects of creating a new name should never be underestimated. There are more than 500,000 registrations on the UK register alone with over 35,000 new applications being filed each year. Since its launch in 1996, over 300,000 trade mark applications have been filed at the Community Trade Mark Office. The procedure is even more difficult in the United States, where there are well over 1m current trade mark registrations.

It is uncommon for any search report to conclude that there are no risks associated with the proposed adoption of a new mark. However, this does not necessarily mean that such a mark should be disregarded. Many options may be available to overcome any conflicting rights identified by the searches. Earlier trade mark registrations may no longer be in use for all or even any of the goods or services covered by the registration and may be open to a challenge on the grounds of non-use. In other circumstances, where there is a technical legal risk that has been identified, it may be that further investigations could establish that there is no commercial overlap with the activities of the proprietor of the earlier right and that a co-existence agreement can be negotiated to avoid or reduce any potential conflict between the parties. Earlier rights can also be purchased or licences negotiated. It has even been known for the proprietor company to be purchased in order to secure the rights in a name.

You should also be prepared to allow time and budget for any further investigations or negotiations that may be necessary.

In general, the less distinctive the chosen mark, the more likely it is to run into problems. Furthermore, rights conferred on marks that are of a descriptive nature are likely to be construed restrictively. Indeed, most registries refuse to register a mark that consists exclusively of words that are descriptive of the goods or services or their characteristics unless it can be established that the mark has become distinctive as a result of its use by its owner. The more descriptive the mark is, the harder it is to establish acquired distinctiveness.

The failure to conduct appropriate clearance researches can have expensive consequences. Although trade mark infringement claims following the launch of a new brand or company name do not often come to the public's attention (usually because any subsequent settlement agreement will include a confidentiality clause), it is not uncommon for such claims to be made. Substantial payments have been made within the context of a co-existence agreement to avoid the need to cancel a launch, remove a product or rebrand. There are examples of seven-figure sums being paid to avoid the possibility of a negative result within litigation even where the alleged infringement claim has had little prospect of success, thereby removing the slight risk of the additional expense, inconvenience and embarrassment associated with an aborted rebranding exercise.

### Trade mark portfolio audit

An audit of a company's existing portfolio of trade mark registrations will almost certainly reveal gaps in the protection, inaccuracies of details recorded on the register and possibly vulnerable, unnecessary or redundant registrations. As organisations become larger, particularly where growth has been by merger or acquisition, it is likely that these deficiencies will be even more significant. Multi-brand and international organisations are also more likely to have large and complex portfolios, which increases the likelihood of records being incomplete or containing inaccuracies.

The "clearing up" of such a portfolio should not be seen merely as an administrative problem but also as an essential process to ensure that the protection required to maintain the value of a brand is kept in place. Such an audit will also identify opportunities for cost savings.

### *Passing off and unfair competition*

In many jurisdictions, it is possible in certain circumstances to bring an action to prevent the unauthorised use of a mark even in the absence of a trade mark registration. The elements of such a cause of action vary from country to country, but common features include the necessity to establish goodwill in the mark within the country and the likelihood of confusion arising from the defendant's activities. Such "passing off", as it is called in the UK, allows the owner of goodwill in a mark to prevent another party from benefiting from or damaging that goodwill through misrepresenting that its business or goods are in some relevant commercial way connected.

As Lord Halsbury stated the principle in the case of Reddaway vs Banham (1896), "nobody has any right to represent his goods as the goods of somebody else".

Bringing proceedings for passing off can be expensive as it is usually necessary to establish not only that goodwill exists but also that there has been a relevant misrepresentation that is likely to cause confusion and lead to damage. It is not uncommon for survey evidence to have to be obtained to help substantiate such a charge.

### Copyright

The law of copyright is designed to protect original works (the most relevant to branding being artistic works and, in respect of sonic branding, musical works) from copying. Copyright arises automatically upon creation of the work and, with certain exceptions, copyright will initially belong to the creator of that work. The main exception is a work created by an employee in the course of his or her employment, in which case the copyright is normally vested in the employer.

There is no requirement to register copyright, although in the United States and some other countries it is possible to register it, which is important from an evidentiary viewpoint should there be any dispute about ownership of a copyright.

The obvious relevance of copyright to branding is where an original logo or get-up has been created specifically for a brand. The required level of "artistic" merit for copyright to exist is low, and the principal factor in establishing copyright in a work is that of originality.

The rights conferred by copyright are more limited than registered trade mark rights to the extent, as suggested by the term, that copyright provides the owner with the right to prevent copying of the work. If the alleged infringing work has been created quite independently, there will be no grounds for a breach of copyright action. However, unlike trade mark rights, a copyright in an artistic or musical work is not specific to any goods or services to which it is applied but extends to any copying, subject to certain defences.

Unlike registered trade mark rights, which, subject to certain conditions being met, can be renewed in perpetuity, copyright in an artistic or musical work is of a defined and limited duration, usually the life of the author plus a further 70 years. Where an artistic work has been applied commercially, this period may be reduced further.

Copyright should not be seen as a substitute for trade mark registration, but it can provide a useful additional basis for attacking unauthorised use of visual marks and sound marks. Where the "work" has been created by someone who is not an employee of the company, such as an independent design contractor, it is important to secure an assignment of the copyright. This requirement should be spelt out in the contract with the design contractor.

### Registered designs

As an intellectual property right, design rights have been considered something of a poor cousin to the other rights discussed above. However, recent changes in the legislation governing registered designs within the EU have raised their profile and their potential significance in the area of branding. Following the implementation of the EU's Design Harmonisation Directive and the introduction of a new European Registered Community Design right, the scope of what can be registered as a design has been extended significantly. It now includes such things as logos, get-up and packaging, which traditionally would have been protected through trade marks or copyright.

As with copyright, registered designs do not limit the scope of protection to specific goods, and the registration process is reasonably cheap and quick. The rights conferred by registration are also not restricted to the prevention of copying. However, the period of protection for registered designs is limited to an initial period of five years, which can be renewed for subsequent five-year periods up to a total of 25 years.

## Domain names and the internet

Although undoubtedly a valuable commercial asset, the ownership of a domain name does not of itself give any rights in the name (other than the fact that it will prevent a third party from obtaining the identical domain name). For example, the ability of Amazon.com to prevent third parties from using "Amazon" or any confusingly similar name for online retailing does not arise from its ownership of the top-level domain www.Amazon.com. It will be dependent upon its having secured appropriate trade mark registrations and goodwill in the Amazon name as a result of extensive use and promotional activities within the countries where protection is desired.

The internet has had a significant impact on trade mark legal practice as a result of the dichotomy between the territorial nature of trade mark protection and the unconstrained geographical boundaries of the internet. This has raised some interesting issues in terms of the location of the "use" of a mark within infringement proceedings. In countries where the question of use has been considered by the courts, there seems to be a degree of conformity in treating the internet merely as a medium for communication. This requires an analysis of the facts of each case to be considered to determine where use of the mark has actually taken place (notwithstanding that any website can be accessed from anywhere in the world).

There are other questions relating to trade mark law arising from the use of marks on the internet. For example, is it possible to infringe a trade mark registration where the alleged infringement is in the form of a meta-tag which can be picked up by a search engine but is not visible to potential customers? Courts in several jurisdictions have held that such use can constitute an infringement.

It has become clear that the ownership of relevant trade mark registrations has played a significant role in allowing the proprietors of such registrations to secure the removal or transfer of relevant domain names incorporating the registered mark through procedures operated by domain-name registries such as ICANN and Nominet.

## Conclusion

So what does the future hold for brand protection? From a trading perspective, the world is shrinking and brand owners are increasingly having to consider protecting their brands beyond their traditional geographic boundaries. Careful thought needs to be given to the appropriate nature and extent of protection sought.

Starting from the viewpoint that a brand is worth protecting, this exercise should not merely be treated as an administrative inconvenience. A company's legal advisers on brand protection should be actively involved in devising and implementing a strategy for securing, maintaining and enforcing appropriate intellectual property rights in a cost-effective manner. The protection secured should be reviewed on a regular basis to ensure that it retains its relevance to the business as it develops. Too much effort is expended in creating and developing a brand to risk jeopardising the value created through failure to secure adequate legal protection.

The following are some of the questions that should be addressed:

- What are the identifiable distinctive features of the brand?
- For what range of goods or services is brand protection required?
- In which countries does the brand have or is likely to have a commercial presence?
- Have appropriate trade mark registrations been secured?
- Has ownership of copyright been established in any artistic or musical work that underpins any element of the brand?
- If outside contractors are being used to create a mark, have they agreed in writing to assign any rights in it?
- Are the identified features of the brand covered by a watching service?
- Is there a mechanism in place to report instances of unauthorised use or misuse of the brand?
- Is there a mechanism in place for the central collection of evidence to establish use, goodwill and so on?
- How are renewals of registered rights dealt with?
- Has an audit of the portfolio of intellectual rights been conducted recently?

# 3
# THE FUTURE FOR BRANDS

# 11 Globalisation and brands

*Sameena Ahmad*

Globalisation has become a dirty word. Although the benefits of open markets, free trade and internationalisation are all around us, most people – in the West, at least – believe that globalisation is to blame for the inequalities they observe in developing countries and the loss of jobs they see at home. This has put brands, as the public face of companies in the dock – as easy scapegoats for the worst excesses of global capitalism. The arguments made by critics of globalisation and capitalism against brands and big business have moved off the streets of Seattle and Genoa and into the political and social mainstream. Brands and their creators are accused of manipulating our desires, exploiting our children, spoiling the landscape, using their financial and political clout to control us, homogenising our culture and taking advantage of the world's poorest to make the things we crave.[1] It has become so fashionable to decry brands that even those who promote labels for a living are eager to join in the assault. European marketing bosses at luxury icons Gucci, De Beers diamonds and Dunhill all confess to being worried that "branding has gone too far".[2]

That this argument has become so widely accepted makes it dangerous – all the more so because the guardians of brands, mostly large multinational corporations, have made such a poor fist of defending their case.

## The case for brands

Although in the West we increasingly bemoan consumerism,[3] brands are anything but superficial. They are an important indicator of economic health. At its most basic, a brand is a way for a product or service to distinguish itself from another. Like a string of would-be suitors, brands compete for our attention. To win it, they must offer us something better than what went before: a superior product, a lower price or some intangible attraction such as exclusivity. Either way, we as consumers stand to gain from higher quality, lower prices and product innovation. The more brands there are and the more ferociously they compete for our hearts and wallets, the more of those benefits we will garner. This competition leads to better, cheaper and cleverer things, and helps stimulate economic growth. Having lots of brands around tells us that the economies we live in are competitive and open. And as studies from institutions including the World Bank[4] and the Fraser Institute[5] show, economic openness is one of the best indicators of future prosperity.

This is important, because critics of brands like to claim that big brands stifle competition and reduce choice. To see how wrong that argument is we only have to look at the former Soviet Union. In communist Russia, brands did not need to exist because there was no competition. Everything was supplied by state-owned companies at set prices. Since there was no incentive for suppliers to improve quality or innovate, the result was economic stagnation and falling living standards. Compare this with Wal-Mart stores and Starbucks. The discount store giant[6] and coffee chain are frequently used to point to everything that seems wrong with big business: the relentless spread of ugly facias, boring sameness and standardisation, reduced choice, the destruction of small towns and small competitors in America and the exploitation of suppliers.

In reality, Starbucks can be said to have revived a dying industry, not destroyed a healthy existing one. In America, Starbucks has helped reverse a decline in coffee consumption outside the home, doubling consumption since the mid-1980s. The group's focus on quality and service has forced local operators to match or beat it to stay in business. The result is that independent coffee shops are both proliferating and thriving. Nationwide independents accounted for half of the industry's growth between 1996 and 2001 when, according to research published in January 2002 by Mintel Consumer Intelligence, the number of coffee houses in America doubled to 13,300, including Starbucks. Most of the large independents have survived in the past decade, and being near to Starbucks actually helps. Tully's Coffee Corp, a Seattle chain, says it deliberately opens outlets near to a Starbucks to benefit from the increased traffic. Starbucks, admit rivals, educates and expands the market. It also scares many chains into improving their service and quality: Kansas City's Broadway Cafe banned smoking and began roasting its own beans when Starbucks opened next door. Similarly, the arrival of additional Starbucks shops in Long Beach, California, prompted the five-store "It's a Grind" chain to spend thousands on cosmetic improvements as well as staff training, customer service and quality control. Sales have been rising by 8% to 15% since Starbucks arrived in 2003.[7]

Wal-Mart has had an even more profound impact on the American economy. A report by McKinsey, a management consultancy, in 2001[8] found that better management at the retail giant probably played a bigger role in America's productivity miracle of the late 1990s than the huge surge in investment in information technology. The report found that almost one-quarter of the productivity growth – from 1.4% a year between 1972 and 1995 to 2.5% between 1995 and 2000 – came from the retail sector and most of that was due to huge gains at Wal-Mart, whose emphasis on low prices and big stores increased its efficiency and sales and forced other companies to follow its lead. Wal-Mart has not only increased productivity, but also boosted ordinary people's spending power by saving them money. In his autobiography, Sam Walton, its founder, calculated that by operating efficiently, between 1982 and 1992 alone the company had saved its customers a "very conservative" $13 billion, or 10% of sales, over the decade. "Wal-Mart has been a powerful force for improving the standard of living in our mostly rural trade areas, and our customers recognise it," he wrote.[9] Wal-Mart's "productivity miracle" can be partly credited to the fact that, like Starbucks, its presence forced rivals to raise their game. Walton devoted a chapter in his book to describing how companies could compete: not by trying to beat it (Wal-Mart) on price (where the world's biggest retailer has a clear advantage), but by offering things it could not, such as specialist product know-how or a cosy store ambience. It is a lesson that Toys 'R Us, for one, has taken on board. After its decision to copy Wal-Mart's cheap prices and big box format proved disastrous, the company is now finding new ways to distinguish itself.[10]

### Who really holds the power?

The idea that big, established brands are all-powerful is simply wrong. As the troubles of McDonald's, Coca-Cola or Marks & Spencer show, being big often leads to complacency and the inability to respond nimbly to change. These companies suffered from the complacency of being dominant, from failing to respond quickly to new competition and ultimately to the changing tastes of their customers. At all three the reason was arrogance at the top. For years McDonald's failed to react to a proliferation of stylish "fast casual" chains that were serving better quality food in nicer surroundings and eating into its market share. McDonald's share price and profits became as soggy as its burgers. Only after Jack Greenberg, then its chief executive, stepped down in December 2002 did the world's biggest restaurant company fight back by improving service, sprucing up its menu and making sure that basic things like toilets and floors in its outlets were clean. Coca-Cola suffered similarly from complacency – failing to react with proper concern to a poisoning scare in Belgium – which cost its boss Doug Ivestor his job. And Marks & Spencer also basked for too long in its past successes, and did not see that its once loyal customers were deserting it for more stylish and cheaper chains.

In truth, what determines the power of a company is not its size, but the presence of competition. In the 1950s the three biggest companies in the media and automotive markets in America were much smaller in absolute size than they are today. However, they had considerably more power since competition was more or less fixed and they controlled some 90% of their markets. Today, companies relax at their peril. Competition can come from anywhere. Who would have thought that banks would have to consider supermarket chains as rivals? Yet Britain's Tesco and Japan's Seven-Eleven are competing with them in financial services. Or that a quintessentially British retailer like Marks & Spencer would have to compete with foreign clothing chains like Zara (Spanish), The Gap (American), Uniqlo (Japanese) and Hennes (Swedish).

Banks and airlines are still monopolies in many ways – banks because it is a hassle to move money around and airlines because their routes are limited. But even these sectors are being forced to improve as start-ups come in and offer cheaper prices and better service. Britain's First Direct telephone bank (part of HSBC) raised everyone's expectations about how good a bank can be if it tries. And the low-cost carrier jetBlue has become one of the few profitable airlines in America because it is getting the basics right – like treating passengers with respect and adding little comforts like leather seats.[11]

The truth is that brands don't control anyone – and consumers control everything. Brands are the ultimate guarantee, making companies accountable. In the West, if our Gap jeans fray or our Mercedes car breaks down, we know exactly where to go to complain. We may not get a perfect response, which may lead us to shop elsewhere next time, but if we are regular customers the best brands will fall over themselves to put the problem right. In the unbranded Soviet Union, customers had no recourse if something went wrong. Indeed, the quality of goods and services fell so much as a result that in the 1950s, Soviet planners in central office decided to artificially introduce brands on some goods to make their producers more accountable and force them to improve.

That companies are more powerful than governments is simply not the case. The financial resources of most companies are tiny compared with the GDP of most countries. Governments have the power to tax, imprison and change laws. Moreover, while companies use their size and importance to lobby governments, so do other groups like unions and non-governmental organisations (NGOs) and consumer groups. And financial resources are only one source of influence; media pressure and votes count too. Anyone worried about drug companies influencing academic research, or Coca-Cola influencing the curriculum of schools, should also note how effective America's huge steel and textile unions have been at persuading politicians to protect their domestic markets from cheap imports and the power of NGOs like Greenpeace and Oxfam (both well-funded brands; Oxfam even advertises in *Vogue*), whose political and media lobbying denied genetically modified maize to millions of starving people in Zaire. Lobbying is a sign of a healthy democracy, and in a healthy democracy, commercial interests will always be weighed against others.

## Goodness and guilt

A more fundamental misconception is that companies need to be moral entities in order to do good. The fact is that companies are neither good nor evil. They are simply structures designed to look after other people's money: that of their owners or shareholders – and through our mutual funds and pension plans we are all shareholders. It is exactly by looking after this money, by trying to grow their profits, that companies are able to use those profits to invest, create jobs and generate more growth. It is a good thing not a bad thing that companies put profits first. By giving them the freedom to focus on their long-term financial health, society can secure a long-term source of jobs, investments and tax revenue. That is the most exciting aspect of the free-market system. When firms, acting within the law and with a view to their reputation, pursue profits, the result is to advance social good, almost by accident. At this point, critics will cite the recent glut of corporate scandals and say that most businesses do not, in fact, act within the law. It is a naive argument. As non-moral entities, some companies will of course be tempted to break the law to boost their stock prices and profits, but they are a minority. And free markets governed by democratically elected politicians and underpinned by carefully crafted, relevant corporate regulation are the best methods for swiftly rooting out bad behaviour and punishing it.

That critics of brands, of companies, of free trade and even of capitalism have lost sight of these truths reflects a western middle class increasingly ill at ease with its own success. People in developed countries are mostly long-lived, leisured and comfortable. They also are inclined to romanticise the past and take relatively recent innovations like computers, cell phones and cancer drugs for granted. Rather than trying to understand the complicated and exciting reasons for our success – free trade and globalisation – we in the West will claim that world has got worse and that materialism has made us less caring. Yet there is no evidence for this. In fact concern – for people and the environment – is a feature of economically well-off societies. People who have enough food in their mouths can afford to think about others, to give their time to good causes or their money to charities.

Leisure to think about happiness is a by-product of our progress, impossible without our timesaving washing machines, microwaves, newspapers and convenience food. Our wealth pays for access to the internet and television channels, which remind us daily of how easy our lives are compared with those of people in the developing world. But as our grandparents could tell us, it would be hard to argue that saving up a year's wages to buy a bicycle, living without heating and expecting early illness and death were better.

Still, an increasing number of westerners feel some need to protect people in the developing world from becoming shallow consumerists, obsessed by brands, fascinated by American culture, mesmerised by television. In doing so, however, they are attempting to deny the vast majority of humanity the opportunities and material progress that will eventually allow them the time, as we have, to cultivate a guilty conscience. But meanwhile poor labourers in Africa and the aspiring middle classes in India and China have no time for such scruples: the Chinese open almost all their direct mail, an Indonesian farmer may find the taste of a Chicken McNugget exotic, and upwardly mobile Indians are hungry to acquire western brands. Westerners may be sated, but those still climbing the economic ladder want exactly the same sort of consumer culture that we already possess.

## What globalisation can do for you

In fighting globalisation, its high-minded critics are opposing the very mechanism that can deliver greater wealth to the less-developed parts of the globe. Globalisation is a stepping-stone to prosperity. Countries that open themselves up to trading their products and ideas freely with other countries raise everyone's standard of living. Rich countries are forced to shift out of manufacturing and build new, more productive, more advanced industries to make room for countries that can make goods more cheaply. Poor countries get a leg up out of poverty, moving their economies from farming to manufacturing and eventually services. It happened to Hong Kong. It is happening across Asia from China and Vietnam to Malaysia and South Korea. Developing countries that open their markets to foreign investment are seeing their income per head grow fast; at some 5%, even faster than western countries that are growing at some 2%. Those countries that are not globalising (mainly African and Arab countries) are slowing down.[12] Their economic malaise makes them dissatisfied and unstable.

One of the most effective tools for promoting globalisation is foreign direct investment (FDI). When established western multinationals move into the developing world, it is often assumed that they exploit workers who toil in sweatshop conditions. Yet exploitation happens far more at faceless, unbranded local companies, which can abuse their workers and pay derisory wages without fear of being noticed. Multinationals have their brands, their reputations and their share prices to worry about. That is exactly why they make such ready targets for activists. Yet it is those very multinationals that set the highest standards in pay, benefits and conditions. By attacking them, western activists are threatening some of the best jobs that foreign workers are likely to get.

Nike, a sports shoemaker that has been criticised for its operations in the developing world, is a case in point. A survey from the University of Minnesota, published in a World Bank report in December 2000, found that workers in Vietnam employed in foreign-owned companies were less likely to be living below the poverty line. The figures showed that although 37.4% of the population as a whole lived below the official poverty line, the percentage was just 8.4% for those working for wholly owned foreign companies and 21.4% for those working for companies managed as a joint venture (partly foreign, partly local). An Australian survey found that Nike factories in Indonesia paid its women factory workers 40% higher wages than local companies. Another report by the University of Michigan found that Nike paid above-average wages in its foreign-owned export factories in Vietnam (above five times the legal minimum wage) and Indonesia (about three times the legal minimum). In Vietnam, Nike is the country's second-largest exporter and has helped cut poverty in half in the past ten years. Since Nike set up a third-party-run factory in Samyang, near Ho Chi Minh City, employing 5,200 people in 1995, it has helped to create an economic hot spot, which has spread beyond its own factory as other local companies have been forced to compete for workers. Samyang currently pays three times the wages paid by state-owned factories and twice the local wage. Four times more residents in the area have telephones than when Nike moved in; two in three have motorbikes (compared with one in three before); 8% are earning less than $10 a month compared with 20% before; and 75% own televisions compared with 30% in 1995.[13]

In the Philippines, locals working at Nestlé's milk factory in Cabayo near Manila need no encouragement to explain how desirable jobs at multinationals are. Workers there are paid an average of $27 a day compared with the $8 legal minimum wage. Three-quarters are eligible for healthcare and receive benefits of food and housing loans. Juan Santos, aged 64, head of Nestlé Philippines, is proud that his daughters now live in America, possible because he was given an overseas posting with Nestlé. Patricio Garcia, manager of the Cabayo factory, has used his savings to put his children through medical school, something he says he could not have afforded to do had he worked in a local factory. He points to the 20,000 applications that he receives for every new job at the factory: "People know that we are fortunate and that Nestlé is an excellent employer." And Jovy Colcol, who at 28 has worked for Nestlé since she left school, is able to use her own money to pay for a new house, helped by a loan from Nestlé, rather than relying on her unemployed husband to support her and their two children. For her, Nestlé has meant economic independence.[14]

### Think about intentions

Certainly big international companies do not always behave well in emerging markets, particularly if they are operating in countries where corrupt politicians encourage and protect bad behaviour. However, as Daniel Litvin's account of multinationals in developing markets describes,[15] throughout history western observers, susceptible to manipulation by local activists, have exaggerated or misjudged the role that western corporations play in the problems of developing countries, with serious consequences for how those problems are subsequently dealt with. Shell in Nigeria is a case in point. The corruption endemic in Nigerian politics did far more damage to the lives of its people than Shell. Indeed, the government resisted attempts by Shell to share the profits of its oil exploration and now relies on the company, stung badly by criticism from the West of its role in Nigeria, to fund schools and hospitals: in other words, to do its job. As Mr Litvin makes clear, companies are more often just clumsy and incompetent when they enter a new market, rather than setting out with any intent to exploit. Their mistakes at least result in them trying to change, which cannot be said for most of the world's nastiest political regimes.

The case of Shell also illustrates the dangers of grafting western moral values on to countries at a different stage of economic development. The $40m a year that the oil group now spends on good causes in Nigeria might possibly have led to greater prosperity if Shell had been allowed to invest it in its core business, creating permanent jobs through long-term investment. Similarly, in Pakistan, the western campaign that urged consumers to boycott Nike products in the 1980s, because the sports firm was using children to stitch footballs, cost thousands of children jobs that their families depended on, forced them into more dangerous, more poorly paid employment and did nothing to change the fact that over 200m children in Pakistan work and probably will until the country becomes rich enough to afford to develop a moral conscience about the practice. The campaign had another unintended side effect: it cost many women their economic independence since the boycotts forced Nike to take the stitching work out of homes, where women could work, and into dedicated factories to which they were unable to travel because of strict societal rules.[16] Although branded multinationals are obviously easier targets than local organisations or governments, western activists do not always understand that their campaigns can have unintended consequences that may hurt the very poor people they are trying to help.

### Time for a new approach

Multinationals, however, have only themselves to blame for becoming so vulnerable. Brands and companies would not be under such fierce attack if they had not lost their connection with mainstream consumers. Fierce competition and increasingly fragmented media make it hard for brands to be heard. In the West, people are so saturated with brands that it is hard for them to see they have any value at all.

Westerners are exposed to over 3,000 messages a day: pop-up advertisements on computers, increasingly intrusive e-mail spam, billboards, television commercials, product placement in films. We take marketing classes in universities: around one-quarter of students in America learn about the art of marketing that way. We know the enemy and understand how big companies try to sell to us. We have access to books, which claim to expose how the marketing machines at companies like McDonald's[17] or Wal-Mart[18] manipulate us. These days, many of us find marketing a yawn. Only ten years ago, when there were fewer advertisements and fewer television channels, marketing campaigns could easily become embedded in our popular culture, remembered as fondly as pop songs or television hit shows of the time: Coca-Cola's "I'd like to teach the world to sing", for example. Today, advertisements aimed at western consumers have lost that status. We are less susceptible to being manipulated by advertisements than we used to be.

Yet the majority of marketers have been unable to respond quickly enough to change. A lot of advertising is still based on old ways of defining markets – for example by pigeonholing target audiences into stereotyped categories. The reason is the innate conservatism in big marketing departments and simply that human beings are complicated – it is hard to understand our desires and motivations especially with blunt tools like focus groups or software that can only crudely predict what we'll buy next from the mess of data routinely collected on our shopping habits. Meanwhile, while marketing remains a soft subject, finance directors increasingly want hard proof that the money spent is worthwhile. Planning, advertising and commissioning market research is no longer enough. Marketing must be linked closely with business strategy and able to prove its contribution to shareholder value.

### The need for honest answers

The marketing profession is in crisis. Books abound with gloomy titles like *The End of Advertising as We Know It*[19] and *Big Brands, Big Trouble*.[20] Most big branded consumer-goods companies, from Gillette, McDonald's and Disney in America to Unilever and Nestlé in Europe and Panasonic in Japan, are facing slowing growth, declining market share or worse. Brands are getting weaker not stronger. As well as being under attack from the anti-corporate brigade, a lack of global economic growth has put pressure on corporate profits and share prices. Marketers are under pressure to produce better results with fewer resources, to "do more with less". They have to demonstrate the true value of marketing to chief executives and the board or face further cuts. Company managements, meanwhile, are questioning the effectiveness of advertising and are busy streamlining marketing departments; the purge of layers of marketing management at Procter & Gamble in 2003 will surely not be the last such restructuring.

Many marketers are reacting to such pressures by focusing not on the nuts and bolts of building brands and margins with product improvements, high prices and ensuring their customer base remains loyal, but on desperately trying to hang on to the customers they have, tempting them with price cuts, free offers and loyalty programmes. Chasing short-term sales at the expense of brand building is a dangerous and short-sighted strategy.

In order to regain appeal for their brands, marketers will have to learn to adopt new tactics that are only gradually catching on, such as guerrilla marketing (one-off events designed to be startling enough that people talk about them), sponsoring events and product placement in hit shows like *Sex in the City*. BMW's series of series of mini-movies from famous directors and starring BMW cars are one example of how to do things differently. Companies will also have to face up to the fact that they need to overhaul their recruiting procedures, incentive programmes and career structures to improve the quality of people that choose marketing as a career.

At the same time, companies should be much more forthright about both the weaknesses and the strengths of their brands. An example is McDonald's, which currently denies any link between its fast food and obesity. The company is acting defensively, fighting in the law courts rather than the court of public opinion, not unlike the tobacco companies a few years ago. Would it not be wiser, perhaps, for McDonald's to admit that eating too many of its burgers and fries is unhealthy and that obesity is a real problem? The fast-food giant is introducing salads and putting the number of calories on its products in response to criticism. But it is doing little to engage openly in the debate or to persuade the public that these issues are not ones for the court but for parents.

Similarly, when it comes to facing their critics, companies should be robust enough to stress the enormous benefits of their branded products, in terms of lower prices, higher quality and innovation in the West and jobs and wealth created in the developing world. Rather than being the Achilles heel of globalisation, brands have the potential to become colourful, appealing motifs that could help the public understand the great benefits of globalisation and free trade. Brands could be used to turn people on to concepts that at the moment turn them off. Already a marketing consultant in San Francisco has composed an "American Brandstand" billboard of the most mentioned brand names in the pop music charts. They may be anathema to activists, but brands are becoming cool icons for musicians. For rap artists, it may be just that words like Mercedes, Burberry and Gucci lend themselves to interesting rhymes. But if consumers understand that buying Nike shoes is one of the most effective ways to provide people in Indonesia with a secure wage, wearing them should become cool even for those who waved placards on the streets of Seattle. They must relearn – and it is now the job of companies to help teach them – that brands are good for us.

## Notes and references

1 Klein, N., No Logo: Taking Aim at the Brand Bullies, Picador, 1999.
2 Interviews with the author, February 2003.
3 Frank, R.H., Luxury Fever: Why Money Fails to Satisfy in an Era of Excess, Free Press, 1999.
4 Dollar, D. and Kray, A., Trade, Growth, and Poverty, World Bank Working Paper, June 2001.
5 Gwartney, J. and Lawson, R., Economic Freedom of the World: 2002 Annual Report, The Fraser Institute, June 2002.
6 Ortega, R., In Sam We Trust. The Untold Story of Sam Walton and How Wal-Mart is Devouring America, Times Books, 1998.
7 Helliker, K. and Leung, S., "Despite Starbucks Jitters, Most Coffeehouses thrive", Wall Street Journal, September 24th 2002.
8 McKinsey Global Institute, U.S. Productivity Growth, 1995-2000, October 2001.
9 Walton, S. with Huey, J., Sam Walton. Made in America. My Story, Doubleday, 1992.
10 The Economist Annual Marketing Roundtable, "From brand champion to corporate star – recognising the value of marketing", March 2003.
11 The Economist Annual Marketing Roundtable, March 2003.
12 Dollar, D. and Collier, P., Globalization, Growth and Poverty: Building an Inclusive World Economy, World Bank Policy Research Report, December 2001.
13 Legrain, P., Open World: The Truth About Globalisation, Abacus, 2002.
14 Interviews with the author, September 2002.

15 Litvin, D., *Empires of Profit. Commerce, Conquest and Corporate Responsibility*, Texere, 2003.
16 Schlosser, E., *Fast Food Nation: The Dark Side of the All-American Meal*, HarperCollins, 2002.
17 Litvin, *Empires of Profit.*
18 Ortega, *In Sam We Trust.*
19 Zyman, S., *The End of Advertising as We Know It*, John Wiley & Sons, 2002.
20 Trout, J., *Big Brands, Big Trouble. Lessons Learned the Hard Way*, John Wiley & Sons, 2001.

# 12 An alternative perspective on brands: markets and morals

*Deborah Doane*

Naomi Klein's bestselling anti-brand book *No Logo*, which came out just after the protests against the World Trade Organisation in Seattle, was anathema to the business world and a call to arms for anti-globalisation protestors the world over. *No Logo* put the case for people to look more closely at both the good and bad sides of global corporations and to acknowledge the legitimate role of "activists" in seeking to keep global corporate power up to the socially responsible mark. So influential was it that *The Economist* felt the need for rebuttal and ran a "Pro Logo" special that it featured on the cover.

The anti-brand argument goes like this: brands are bullies; they commodify cultures and they are unaccountable. The pro-brand argument, however, holds that brands are accountable and transparent, and that they provide more value and economic benefits for people than ever before. The reality is probably somewhere in between.

In the world of branding things move fast and so, too, has the debate about brands in relation to globalisation. The main issue is still how corporations, both big and small, behave in a global marketplace. But the question is whether or not this behaviour is a cause or a consequence of the "branding" phenomenon. Here it is necessary to look at the conduct of markets themselves, which generally dictate the behaviour of the brand.

Nonetheless, corporate leaders and others have turned a blind eye to the reality of the marketplace, failing to acknowledge the limitations of questionable corporate social responsibility programmes. In an optimistic world, though, businesses will finally see not just that their actions are causing harm to the environment, but also that short-sighted approaches to our social future will eventually fail us all.

## No Logo or Pro Logo?

In the sparring between the No Logo and Pro Logo camps, who is right? The awareness of brands has held them up to more scrutiny than ever before. It is difficult for global corporations like Gap, Nike, Coca-Cola or McDonald's to evade criticism, even when they are doing more than their unbranded counterparts. Consumers can probably put more trust, for example, in a Nike shoe than a non-branded shoe from their local store, not just because of better quality, but also because of the knowledge that Nike has to ensure higher standards of working conditions for those who make its shoes because it is under the eye of the global watchdog.

At the same time, signs of the brand bully are everywhere. Big brands threaten local competition and buy up successful smaller brands. In places like India or South Africa, if you want coffee, you generally find that you can only get a "Nescafé".

A brand's purchasing power extends its ability to gain access on the shelves, squeezing out other, newer competition too. Supermarkets provide better shelf space for well-known brands, ensuring they have a better chance of being seen and bought by consumers. At the same time, high streets around the world are looking increasingly familiar, making it difficult to distinguish between a street in Munich, Tokyo or Toronto.

Brands also have a tendency to dilute cultural diversity. Branding demands immediate knowledge and recognition, ideally on a global basis. You can ensure that if you walk into a Gap in North America, Japan or Germany you will be getting the same thing. Michelle Lee, an American fashion writer, laments the "McFashion" era that the battle for the brand has created. She argues that, while the strengths of the fast-food approach to clothing give us affordability and reliability of style, "the consistency has bred a scary level of homogeneity". In the United States, 75% of men own a pair of Dockers Khakis, and 80% of Americans own at least one pair of Levi's jeans.[1] As styles from other countries become fashionable, such as the Chinese chemise or Indian-style dresses, they are also at risk of being devalued through the market. The originality that gives rise to their value as fashion items will fade and the styles will become little more than another commodity to buy, sell and replicate, eventually to their cultural detriment.

Is the brand accountable or not? Many think not, especially when it comes to social or environmental concerns. Over the past couple of decades brands have worked in chameleon-like ways. When they are challenged for poor ethical behaviour, they change names: so Altria emerged from Philip Morris, many argue as a misguided attempt to shield its non-tobacco business from the "drag" brought down by the negative reputation of tobacco and impending law claims. The *Ameri-*

can *Journal of Public Health* charged that the name change was the culmination of a long-term effort by the tobacco giant to manipulate consumers and policymakers.[2] In the last few years, victims of the Bhopal disaster in India have found it difficult to make claims against Union Carbide over the incident that took place in 1986 but has yet to be resolved. In 2001, Union Carbide was bought by Dow Chemical, which as recently as May 2003 denied any responsibility for the disaster.[3]

When you are buying a brand, whose brand are you really buying? Few consumers know that Kraft Foods is owned by a tobacco company, or that Ben & Jerry's ice cream is now part of Unilever. It makes it difficult for people to choose brands for their ethical stance when the brands themselves have been subsumed by large multinationals. Part of BP's strategy for demonstrating its green credentials has been to buy up existing producers of solar energy. It now owns about 17% of the global solar market without having had to add any new production in solar.[4] Social investment groups have argued that the problem with this approach is that the companies continue to have their main activity in a wholly unsustainable business, such as oil. In the case of BP, investment in solar is less than 0.1% of the business.

Brands may have the power and the resources to ensure that economic might wins over social good. But many would argue that in the main they do not, citing the rise of the corporate social responsibility movement over the last few years.

## Social responsibility and brand behaviour

Corporate social responsibility (also known as CSR) has been the business-led response to the No Logo critique. Post-Seattle, a CSR policy has become de rigueur for top companies, which make statements on everything from environmental performance to labour standards. Given the CSR hype, it would be easy to believe that things have moved much further along and that companies are taking the issue of their responsibility rather more seriously than a few years ago.

The corporate conference circuit is now dotted with monthly gatherings on "social responsibility" and "reputation management". Big accountancy and PR firms now have whole units dedicated to corporate social responsibility, with firms like Burson-Marsteller having co-opted the activists themselves. Lord Melchett, previously head of Greenpeace in the UK, has been on their roster of top-level consultants.

The mantra of the CSR world is that business can "do well" and "do good": the proverbial win-win. Pharmaceuticals companies such as

GlaxoSmithKIine (GSK) point to their programmes for improved access to medicines in developing countries and partnerships with non-governmental organisations (NGOs) such as Médecins sans Frontières, and even British American Tobacco is aiming to be the world's most socially responsible "tobacco company".

But is it really all so rosy? The "face" of a company's CSR programme is usually demonstrated through its corporate social and environmental report. From a few deep greens such as The Body Shop or Traidcraft, to "ethically challenged" companies such as Shell just a few years ago, companies as wide ranging as Cadbury's, Unilever and British Aerospace have prepared such a report. These are particularly popular in the UK. Just two years ago, fewer than 25 UK companies reported on their social performance alongside their annual report. Econtext, a consultancy group, now finds that 50% of FTSE 250 companies are reporting[5] on their social and environmental impacts on a voluntary basis, and SustainAbility, another consultancy, has found 234 companies reporting globally.[6]

However, the quantity of CSR-type reports says little about the quality of what really goes on. CSR, it seems, is now more about public relations than anything else. Repeated studies, including SustainAbility's *Global Reporters Survey* released in November 2002, confirm that there is little meaningful social and environmental reporting by companies to indicate that they are grappling with the great issues of our time, from climate change to tackling poverty.

GSK's drugs programme has come to fruition as the company has finally had to face critical competition from generic manufacturers and the threat of regulation by governments. Its temporary climb-down is a defensive move against losing critical intellectual property rights and to protect its reputation. It is certainly not a result of the moral impetus of tackling AIDS or malaria in sub-Saharan Africa. And most people would still argue that attempts such as GSK's are still inadequate to deal with the mammoth health challenges that developing countries face.

BP has had immense success with its social responsibility policies. Sir John Browne, its chief executive, has effectively been the poster child of the CSR movement. But NGOs are highly critical of BP's attempts to demonstrate social responsibility. In 2001, when it tried to rebrand itself as "beyond petroleum", activists pointed out that it was not actually moving away from hydrocarbon production. In the end, BP was forced into an embarrassing climb-down.[7] In the latest challenge by a consortium of NGOs, BP has found itself at the front end of a challenge to the

OECD *Guidelines on Multinational Enterprises* over its work in Azerbaijan. The group, which includes Friends of the Earth, claims that BP and its partners sought or accepted exemptions related to current social, labour, tax and environmental laws, while exerting undue influence over the government to free it of any future liabilities. BP's approach to managing its reputation has been effectively to ensure that it manages risk, which means passing off risk to governments that rely heavily on its foreign income.

Why are these the outcome of CSR, rather than anything more substantial? Because CSR is voluntary. Even codes of conduct, like the OECD *Guidelines for Multinational Enterprise*, are unenforceable. CSR managers have to ensure that the "business case" can be made to promote investment in social causes, especially where there is no regulatory requirement to do so. Other than through a few "eco-efficiency" arguments, which can see a pay-off over a shorter period of time, the case is made for pitching sustainability programmes under the headline of "brand reputation". Indeed, a recent issue of *Brand Strategy* magazine is dedicated to the subject of "branding success" and ways of communicating sustainability.[8]

This is the fundamental problem with CSR. It should come as no surprise that many CSR programmes are now staffed by people with marketing expertise, rather than those with an environmental background. As a result, we find prescriptions that are more about image than anything deeper.

One of the biggest crimes in CSR is cause-related marketing (CRM), which results in companies such as Cadbury's providing sports-equipment vouchers in exchange for consuming enough chocolate. Such superficial attempts to improve a company's reputation and contribute to a social good make a mockery of good intentions. Childhood obesity is now one of the leading causes of concern for health activists. McDonald's, purveyor of the ultimate in childhood indulgence, is now being sued because it is accused of making people fat.[9]

### The myth of the ethical consumer

Corporate social responsibility is driven in part by the expectation that consumers will ultimately reward those companies with a better social and environmental record.

To some extent this is true. The 2002 Ethical Purchasing index confirms that businesses that have a social aim, such as Café Direct, will be duly rewarded. The Fair Trade company is now the sixth-largest coffee brand in the UK, having grown at a rate of almost 20% in 2002, capturing 8% of the coffee market. There are a few other examples of fast-growing deep green ethical businesses out there, but by and large, these continue to capture less than 1% of their overall market share.[10]

But consumers, although conscious, are a fairly passive lot. The National Consumer Council notes that consumers are often unwilling to make changes in their habits. A poll by MORI shows that although 83% of us intend to act ethically, only 18% do so (and only occasionally), while less than 5% could be considered "global watchdogs".[11]

In spite of the perceived increase in anti-globalisation activism and demands for greener products, these trends appear to be worsening over time. The annual Roper Green Gauge study in the United States found that Americans are less concerned about the environment than they have been over the past ten years. The 2002 survey found that although 23% of consumers bought products made with recycled goods, this was 3% less than the year before; and almost half of consumers, 45%, thought it was the responsibility of businesses, not consumers, to do more.[12]

Much of this comes back to people's wallets. According to one American study, consumers would gladly make the greener choice if the product did not cost more or require a change in habits, if it could be purchased where they already shopped, and if it was at least as good as its competition.[13] This is echoed in the UK, where the Institute of Grocery Distributors found that consumers are more concerned with price, taste and sell-by date than ethics.[14]

Although there appears to be scope to encourage consumers to be more active and "ethical", the evidence to date suggests that if we rely on them to deliver social and environmental change, we will be waiting a very long time.

## Misguided intentions

CSR has ultimately failed to provide the answers to the No Logo critique. Business cannot always "do well" and "do good". What the mantra is missing is the caveat to the phrase: business can "do well and do good ... up to a point".

CSR strategies are part of the microcosm of the failure of markets themselves. They work only in so far as they help to protect the brand. But there is a wide chasm between what is good for a brand and what is good for society.

Fifty or 100 years ago, when many of the big multinationals started, the aim was to provide an affordable product or service to people and make a reasonable profit at the same time. It is doubtful that the founders of any major multinationals ever set out on a path aiming to subsume other cultures, cut down forests and exploit cheap labour halfway around the world. But the role of a company has, over the past century, taken on a life of its own, where its primary function is to return capital to the anonymous shareholder, not to serve the needs of society. In today's capital markets, companies need to grow, to find new markets in which to trade and to keep their costs down through anything from ensuring "affordable" labour to reducing tax liabilities.

When a company gives a "profits warning", the markets downgrade its share price. Consequently, investing in things like the environment or social causes, which promise longer-term and peripheral pay-offs rather than immediate pay-offs to the bottom line, becomes a luxury, and they are often placed on the sacrificial chopping block in a crisis. Littlewoods, a high-street retailer, recently backed out of the UK's ethical trading initiative, and the Dole Food Company in the United States slashed its entire CSR programme in 2001 as part of a cost-cutting exercise.

This is no different from how markets deliver value to shareholders outside of the ethics regime, even if it means sacrificing other parts of the business in the process, as in the value-destroying mergers and acquisitions frenzy of the late 1990s. In the most grotesque examples of market behaviour, the product itself becomes almost irrelevant. In the case of the now infamous Enron, the company changed from a middle-sized energy provider to a de facto Wall Street bank through its various energy trading schemes.[15] Its eventual collapse was the first in a series of corporate scandals that contributed to the worst economic downturn in over 30 years.

If there is a business case for brands to enshrine their value through social goods, then this should be done through voluntary means. Business has always had to innovate and try different things and seek new sources of competitive advantage. But pretending that these business intentions will always provide the best outcomes in the interests of the greater public good is simply naive, especially when shareholders' interests are part of the equation. Marjorie Kelly, publisher of the American-based *Business Ethics Magazine*, contends that our assumption that voluntary actions by progressive business people would transform capitalism was misguided. She writes in her book *The Divine Right of Capital* that "it is inaccurate to speak of stockholders as investors, for more truthfully they are extractors".

There is a significant risk in business assuming the role of the social-welfare provider through misguided CSR programmes. In the United States, Cisco Systems "adopts" schools that have inadequate funding. In parts of Africa, Unilever helps to distribute condoms through its distribution network to combat the AIDS crisis. Both are probably well-intentioned programmes to deal with immediate problems. Cisco needs an educated workforce; and most companies operating in Africa are feeling the impact of the AIDS crisis. But they represent a more worrying trend, about which both activists and businesses should be concerned: the increased blurring of the lines between public and private, and the abdication of state responsibility to uphold the public good.

Nike's and others' investment in labour-standards monitoring in developing-country factories is a laudable attempt to ensure at least that their workers are protected and that their brand values are upheld. But, as Daniel Litvin writes, the complexity of trying to monitor 700 factories employing 500,000 people around the world is immense.[16] It puts the brand itself at risk, as activists continue to seek out poor working conditions, whether in suppliers' factories or their suppliers' factories. So firms such as Nike are constantly on the defensive.

Nike can tackle labour standards, up to a point. But even with the constant onslaught from protestors and continuous improvement, it actually has limited power in the wider economy in developing countries that keeps wages low and, in some countries, means that a job in a Nike factory can be more desirable than being a doctor or a teacher because the wages are higher and workers' rights are protected.

In this sense especially, CSR is a false economy. Would it not be better to ensure that systems in these countries – laws, regulations and so on – are developed to strengthen institutions that protect a wider portion of the population? As Patrick Neyts, head of corporate responsibility in Europe at Levi-Strauss, notes, it is not unusual in a developing country to find a well-known product being manufactured in a pristine setting on one side of a wall in a factory, while on the other side people continue to be subject to unsafe conditions, longer working hours and poorer wages.

Business is, in part, to blame for contributing to the institutional vacuum in the first place. In the United States, there is no longer a school system that is adequately supported by the state because businesses, increasingly, fail to pay their share of common taxes. Corporate income taxes in the United States fell from 4.1% of GDP in 1960 to just 1.5% of GDP in 2001.[17] The OECD attributes this, in part, to countries wanting to reduce taxes in order to lure foreign investment or maintain inward investment. But this is having perverse effects, limiting governments' ability to invest in common assets, such as the environment or education. Nowhere is the issue more pressing than in developing countries, where states are already weak. The corporate sector, rather than looking for tax exemptions, should be finding ways to ensure adequate support for governments and the development of strong public services that would provide a healthy economic and social environment in which to operate.

These issues go well beyond traditional brand protection and reputation management. They are issues which owners of brands themselves should consider how best to respond to, if they want to protect their domain. Indeed, multinationals have the power, but currently lack the courage, to break ranks and call for another way forward.

### Redefining brand value?

It is difficult to dispute the economic importance of brands. According to Interbrand, a brand consultancy, 70% of the average FTSE company's value is based on "intangibles". But this heavy weighting of the brand makes many of us more vulnerable. As the values of companies on the stockmarket tumble, usually because of a lack of faith in the "brand", our savings and our pensions are at risk. In the latest economic downturn, even trusted brands like British Airways have lost their coveted place on the FTSE 100 index.

Right now, brand valuation methods such as Interbrand's focus solely on the economic use of the brand, with occasional considerations of things like staff training included in the equation. At least a partial way out of this quagmire is for us to make "brand value" far less dependent on traditional economic intangibles and more dependent on genuine measures of social and environmental performance.

Inroads are already being made in defining how to measure these things. The Global Reporting Initiative, an international multiparty endeavour aimed at providing common indicators for reporting on social and environmental performance, is something that brand valuation experts should look at.[18] In recent years, a number of organisations have made efforts to measure "social capital", but the methodologies for doing so are not shared with the public, so it is almost impossible to tell what is being measured, let alone compare the approaches to arrive at common standards. Social capital, as a form of trust, should be able to incorporate measures of real commitment to communities, such as using local labour. There is an added business benefit to this. Shokoya-Eleshin Construction, a fast-growing UK construction firm, reported that when it used local labour its buildings were not vandalised in an urban area traditionally experiencing high levels of crime.

There is a dual purpose in making the intangibles more tangible and basing them on social and environmental outcomes. Measurement will help policymakers ensure that companies pay for the real costs of their social and environmental impact (internalising externalities, in economists' terms). It will also help ensure that businesses do not make compromises in business practice that favour financial outcomes rather than non-financial ones, because all will eventually contribute to the bottom line.

## A case for leadership

No corporate brand is produced with the specific intention of doing harm. But corporate leaders often avoid looking at the wider complexity of the issue. As with CSR, a business generally does what it can rather than what it should within the confines of the market. This is where corporate leaders need to confront the dilemma head-on. The No Logo crew is not calling for a mere tampering at the margins, a small increase to a charity budget or a cause-related marketing attempt at improving brand image. It is calling for a revolution in the way that business is done.

Take, for example, companies that depend on commodities, such as Nestlé and Cadbury's. Although their work with the Biscuit, Cake, Chocolate and Confectionery Alliance aiming to eliminate the use of child labour in cocoa plantations is crucial, they do not confront the fundamental issue of how their products perpetuate poverty in the first place. The vulnerability of people who are dependent on commodities is not something that can be brushed aside. How can commodity markets be transformed so that fair trade is no longer needed? So that a quality product is still available to consumers, but producing it does not keep people in poverty unnecessarily? It is not just a matter of protecting the corporate brand and reputation through individual defensive means: it involves the entire system. All companies will be vulnerable to criticism and consumer backlash until we recognise that fact.

In the oil sector, companies such as BP and Shell should make bigger investments in renewable energy and stop using the facade of buying up small solar producers to add to their green credentials; investing less than 2% of profits in renewables is just a drop in the ocean. Why aren't

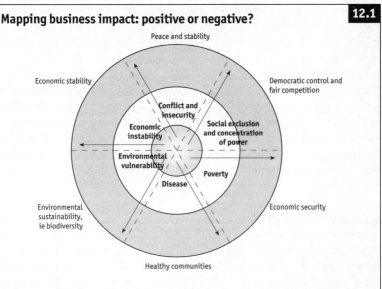

**Mapping business impact: positive or negative?** `12.1`

Businesses traditionally consider the impact of social and environmental issues on reputation and financial outcomes for the business; but turning this equation around provides a different perspective and potentially allows businesses to be far more proactive in defining future strategic directions. Within its sphere of influence, can a business play a more proactive role in sustainable development?

Source: New Economics Foundation and EIRIS

these corporate leaders aiming to have 50% of the business in renewable energy in ten or 15 years' time? How can these companies lobby governments more effectively to ensure that tax incentives and other forms of policy intervention make such goals ultimately profitable? It is traditional for the oil industry to fight regulation, not to ask for it.

The question that society should be asking is this: what businesses and institutions do we need to deliver sustainable development? Big business and, by extension, big brands have been intent on responding to the concerns of activists by trying to minimise their negative impact on society and the environment and marketing these interventions as having solved the world's problems. However, by promoting CSR as a "competitive advantage", big business is effectively holding people to ransom and inhibiting the bold changes that are really needed. CSR should have been about solving the big global problems without compromise, not about brand reputation management.

Ironically, at the moment, the more good a company does, the more

Table 12.1 **Global issues: can business really help?**

| Issue | Problems | What can business do? |
|---|---|---|
| **Poverty, exclusion and concentration of power** | ◪ Growing gap between rich and poor.<br>◪ Lack of participation in economic and political life.<br>◪ Huge influence of large corporations on national economies has led to loss of democratic control.<br>◪ Poor suffer from irresponsible business practice.<br>◪ Low investment in deprived areas.<br>◪ Poor-quality investment that fails to stimulate local economic activity. | ◪ Invest in deprived areas and measure the local impact of investment.<br>◪ Rely where possible on local procurement and employment.<br>◪ Involve stakeholders in corporate governance.<br>◪ Be aware of and apply things like the Global Reporting Initiative to improve transparency. |
| **Environmental vulnerability** | ◪ Over-consumption of resources, particularly fossil fuels.<br>◪ Global warming, rise in sea level and increased frequency of high-intensity storms and flooding.<br>◪ Increased risk to poor communities caused by effects of climate change. | ◪ Reduce consumption of fossil fuels.<br>◪ Ensure marketing does not become a tool for "greenwashing".<br>◪ Cease lobbying to maintain energy subsidies; call for fiscal incentives to increase investment in renewables.<br>◪ Transparent reporting on environmental impacts, including full-cost green accounts. |
| **Disease and access to medicine** | ◪ Lack of sanitation and health-care services in poor countries means many die of preventable diseases.<br>◪ Patents keep drugs out of reach to the poor.<br>◪ Spread of HIV virus, decimating populations in some poor countries. | ◪ Release patent rights on drugs<br>◪ Contribute to development and maintenance of community water and sanitation services.<br>◪ Contribute to public research funds for affordable drug treatments. |
| **Economic instability** | ◪ Short-term portfolio investment and currency speculation has destabilised national economies.<br>◪ Fall in commodity prices coupled with crippling debt has hit poor countries hard. | ◪ Support national economies by paying in local currency.<br>◪ Procure goods, services and employment locally.<br>◪ Undertake appropriate long-term investment.<br>◪ Limit lobbying on policy areas which can contribute to economic destabilisation. |
| **Conflict and insecurity** | ◪ Many regions are plagued by armed conflict.<br>◪ War economies undermine long-term social and economic development.<br>◪ This can inadvertently be fuelled by businesses operating in conflict zones. | ◪ Screen locations for investment.<br>◪ Transparent reporting of business activities in conflict areas.<br>◪ "Zero tolerance" policy on bribery and corruption, including facilitation payments. |

it is open to scrutiny by global activists. Never could there be a more compelling argument than this for companies to look at their role in society, and to call for appropriate levels of regulation by governments to level the playing field. Ed Crooks, economics editor of the *Financial Times*, says:

> *The balance between making money, protecting the environment and looking after individual rights affects all of us. We should all be able to take some responsibility for the big decisions – and that means not leaving it all to business.*[19]

Brands are unlikely to disappear any time soon; even smaller companies with an ethical aim, such as Café Direct, eventually succumb to the temptations of "growth" and need to achieve brand recognition for long-term success. But let us hope that the smaller, up-and-coming ethical brands do not compromise their morals and their methods in the process.

The issue is not brands as such. It is how big brands, often with near-monopoly power, have behaved. Brands do have the potential to be a force for good, so long as we consider the ways in which they are valued, and couple the natural instincts of the market with appropriate regulation.

## Notes and references

1  Lee, M., *Fashion Victim*, Broadway Books, NY, March 2003.
2  Smith, E.A. and Malone, R.E., "Altria means tobacco: Philip Morris's identity crisis", *American Journal of Public Health*, Vol. 93, No. 4, April 2003, pp. 553–6.
3  Vosters, H., "Partial Chronology of Union Carbide's Bhopal Disaster", CorpWatch, May 15th 2003.
4  Lean, G. and Anderson, A., "Does BP mean Burning the Planet?", *Independent*, September 3rd 2000.
5  SalterBaxter and EContext, 2002.
6  SustainAbility, *Trust Us: The Global Reporters 2002 Survey of Sustainability Reporting*.
7  Buchan, D., "BP Driven to the Back and Beyond", *Financial Times*, April 20th 2001.
8  *Brand Strategy*, Issue 165, November 2002.
9  Buckley, N., "Big Food's Big Problem", *Financial Times*, February 17th 2003.

10 Co-operative Bank and the New Economics Foundation, Ethical Purchasing Index 2002.

11 Co-operative Bank, *Who are the Ethical Consumers?*, London, 2000.

12 *Roper Green Gauge Report*, Roper-Strach Worldwide, New York, 2002.

13 Makower, J., *Consumer Power*, RAND, IP 203, 2001. www.rand.org/scitech/stpi/ourfuture

14 "Food shoppers appear to shun ethical goods", *Financial Times*, November 21st 2002.

15 Partnoy, F., *Infectious Greed: How Deceit and Risk Corrupted the Financial Markets*, Times Books, 2003, p. 299.

16 Litvin, D., *Empires of Profit: Commerce, Conquest and Corporate Responsibility*, Texere, 2003, p. 245.

17 Miller, J., "Double Taxation Double Speak", *Dollars and Sense Magazine*, March/April 2003.

18 www.GRI.org

19 Sustainable Development Commission, *Business @boo.m&bust*, 2001. www.sd-commission.gov.uk/pubs/ar2001/04.htm

# 13 Branding in South-East Asia

*Kim Faulkner*

The Asian tiger economies of the early 1990s are recovering after the severe setbacks they suffered during the economic crisis that hit them in 1997. Although the more recent global recession has slowed their recovery somewhat, countries such as Singapore, Malaysia, Thailand, the Philippines and Indonesia have recognised that there is much they can do to renew economic growth and investment interest in their markets.

According to the report on "Global Economic Prospects and the Developing Countries 2003" by the World Bank, developing countries will on average grow at 3.9%. However, this global average masks wide regional differences, with East Asia leading the pack at 6.1%, followed by South Asia at 5.4%.

Of the many important lessons learnt from the Asian financial crisis, good governance, sound institutions, as well as the development of stronger Asian brands, stood out as being key to economic recovery, the latter being one of the few means of helping local Asian companies diversify geographically, thus providing greater stability and reducing overdependence on the domestic market for growth. This coupled with the fact that Asian consumers are among the most brand conscious consumers in the world has made many Asian companies review their intangible assets.

This chapter focuses primarily on branding in South-East Asia, a region where a "West is Best" culture – in terms of lifestyle, entertainment and standard of living – and the aspirations of consumers have led to a pent-up demand for western brands. However, lower levels of disposable income as well as the Asian predilection for getting a "good deal" (that is, getting something of value at a much lower price) led to a counterfeiting culture that became prevalent in many developing countries of Asia. Thus counterfeit Rolex watches, Chanel perfumes and Gucci bags were sold on many street corners and snapped up by the locals (not to mention the western tourists). The lack of importance attached to protecting intellectual property and intangible capital is likely to change, however, with the creation and development of strong, internationally distributed Asian brands. Furthermore, higher levels of disposable income among the population will lead to a gradual preference for genuine brands rather than the cheap counterfeits.

So far, even though Asians are acknowledged to be some of the most "brand conscious" consumers in the world, this has not, outside of Japan, translated into Asian companies generating many powerful global brands. This is not to say that they have not generated any significant brands, but rather that few of these brands have achieved recognition as leaders in their respective categories outside their home markets. This could be partly explained by the fact that the focus has been on manufacturing and increasing productivity through greater production efficiencies, often at the expense of innovation, creativity and thus also branding.

Some markets in Asia have been insulated from international competition by their governments, with "strategic" sectors such as airlines, agriculture, shipping, financial services, the media and telecommunications controlled by the public sector. In countries such as Indonesia, it has been more important for firms to get access to distribution, which has been controlled by local conglomerates, than to create strong brands. These factors have lulled many Asian companies into thinking purely in terms of their home markets and national interests; there has been less compulsion to build brands for overseas markets. But with economic liberalisation, there are signs of new thinking.

## Asian brands hold their own

However, although there may be few Asian brands of international stature, it would be wrong to assume that there are no strong Asian brands. In many consumer-goods categories in Asia home-grown brands proliferate and hold their own against foreign competition. These brands are not only highly recognised in their home market, but also very much a part of the day-to-day lives of many people.

Traditional brands such as Rabbit milk sweets were well-loved treats for children, as were Bee Cheng Hiang Chinese barbecued sweetmeats during the Chinese Lunar New Year. If the Malaysian consumer woke up to a cup of tea, it had to be Boh Tea because "Boh ada Uumph!", and if they needed a bit more of a boost, they drank Yomeishu tonic because it was "trusted by generations". Many young women smothered Hazeline Snow on their faces to attain that smooth, fair complexion prized for centuries in Asia, long before the new whitening and anti-ageing formulas currently marketed by L'Oréal and other international cosmetic brands existed.

Tiga Kaki (literally "three legs" in Malay) headache pills stopped people's headaches and Darkie toothpaste (complete with a smiling black minstrel on the packaging) gave them gleaming teeth – political correctness was not an issue then. These were brands that their parents and grandparents trusted and used, and they were familiar names in many households.

There are five main categories of Asian brands:

- Traditionalists
- Revitalised
- New Asia
- Challengers
- Established

### Traditionalists

Traditionalist brands are, by definition, those that have held on to the traditions and heritage that made them so trusted and relied upon. They are brands that have been developed over decades, if not centuries, in their respective home markets. Before these markets were liberalised, traditionalist brands dominated the categories in which they operated, leveraging their wide domestic distribution network, heritage and high brand awareness in the marketplace.

However, as their home markets started to open up and international brands began competing in their territory, some of these brands came under pressure to evolve or risk extinction. One is Tiger Balm from Singapore, a topical, pain-relieving ointment used by generations of consumers throughout South-East Asia for their aches and pains. In the face of competition from international over-the-counter brands marketed by international pharmaceuticals firms, a number of new applications were developed for the brand.

The original Tiger Balm product was a thick, hard, waxy balm sold in tiny hexagonal glass jars which was used judiciously to relieve headaches and muscle aches. Haw Par, the company that manufactured and marketed the product, faced two main challenges:

- Only a tiny amount of the product was used in each application, which meant that repeat purchases by even the most ardent loyalists were few and far between.
- It was a product and brand associated with people who were old and ailing, and younger Asian consumers appeared to have little use for it. It was therefore operating in a shrinking market.

By the late 1980s the brand had expanded into new product formats, such as medicated plasters, muscle rubs, oils and liniments, targeting sportsmen and a new generation of fitness enthusiasts and joggers. This extension coincided with the brand's overseas expansion into western markets in the United States and Europe, where it sponsored and distributed free samples of its products at sporting events to gain awareness and to encourage people to try them. With its distinctive packaging and tiger trade mark design, and its new positioning and new product lines, the brand was able to tap new markets. It has since added more products to its portfolio including headache pills, bath salts and mosquito repellent. It is marketed in over 100 countries worldwide, and overseas sales account for almost 60% of Tiger Balm's total revenue.

### Revitalised brands

While some traditional brands faced the brave new world by extending the usage of and applications for their products, others, such as Brand's (essence of chicken) by Cerebos Pacific, decided that a radical revitalisation of the brand was necessary. The revitalisation meant not just extending the product format from the traditional tonic drink to the more portable and palatable caplets, but also reinventing the brand proposition and venturing out of the "essence of chicken" category into new health supplements which did not contain any "chicken essence".

Brand's, which is currently marketed in seven different markets across South-East Asia and Greater China (China, Hong Kong and Taiwan), owes its product formulation to the court of George IV, a British king. It was produced while he was convalescing from a serious illness. It arrived in Malaya in the 1920s, and because of its strong link with the Chinese belief in the restorative powers of double-boiled chicken soup it quickly became popular. It has a long history in Asia as a brand that students rely on to improve their mental stamina during the long hours spent studying for those all-important school exams.

Although the brand continued to dominate the "essence of chicken" category, with market shares of 85–90% in each of its Asian markets, sales started to decline in the mid-1990s. This set alarm bells ringing at Cerebos Pacific, by then owned by Suntory. By 1998 the company had embarked on an aggressive brand revitalisation exercise in all its seven markets. One of its main objectives was to win back the growing number of lapsed users: the students who did not return to the brand once they got through their exams, and the working population who turned to more modern health-supplement brands such as Kordels, GNC or Blackmores. Other objectives included attracting new and younger users to supplement its loyal but ageing customer base, leveraging the trust and heritage of the brand, enhancing its credibility and positioning it as a trusted health supplement for consumers throughout every stage of their lives.

This meant a number of changes, starting with the introduction of a new product format for the core range, the caplets, and then extending into other health-supplement products, such as glucosamine, and a new range of sesame-based products sub-branded Sesamin. The brand image was updated through a new brand identity, packaging and marketing communications aligned throughout all markets. Activities to build an understanding of the new brand proposition included a website offering tips on a balanced life, a personalised "Health Mate" health-management information programme and an enhanced global customer-loyalty programme.

The brand relaunch resulted in sales increases in key markets, tapping into the trend towards greater consciousness and management of their health as Asians grappled with the financial crisis, global recession and increasingly stressful urban lifestyles. The new product offerings have encouraged lapsed users to return to the brand and have been particularly successful in markets such as Singapore, Taiwan and Thailand where the health-supplement category has enjoyed double-digit growth since the late 1990s.

### New Asia brands

Even as the traditionalist and revitalised Asian brands have evolved or reinvented themselves to face the challenge of international brands entering their home market, a slew of "New Asia" brands have emerged in sectors traditionally dominated by international brands. These new brands leveraged the culture, history and identity of their homelands to create distinctive brand experiences that are internationally appealing and contemporary but also distinctively Asian in inspiration.

In the hospitality sector, for example, the once-dominant Hiltons and Hyatts are now challenged by Asian brands such as Shangri-La and Raffles International, as well as resort brands such as the Banyan Tree and Aman. In travel, Singapore Airlines and Cathay Pacific have gained international recognition and won accolades for in-flight service and innovation. What these brands have done is to capitalise on the innate warmth and graciousness of Asian hospitality and translated them into a seamless customer experience that encompasses design and aesthetics, with refreshing product and service innovations.

The Banyan Tree resorts, for instance, have departed from the reassuring consistency and sameness that was the basis of many hotel brands, whose goal was to make customers feel as if they had never left the United States even when they were on the other side of the world. Asian hospitality brands are determined that people should experience an authentic Asian experience but with all the creature comforts and luxury that modern technology offers. Banyan Tree resorts and others like it have created brand consistency around an experiential idea (in their case the idea of romance and intimacy). They also infuse subtle variations of the brand in each of the locations in which they operate, such that the individual experience remains true to the core proposition yet offers a refreshing difference in each interpretation.

For example, the resorts adopt the architectural styles and interior design finishes of the country or province in which they are located. So the Banyan Tree resort in Phuket has Thai architecture and uses Thai crafts in its interior furniture and fittings as well as in the resort merchandise; by contrast, the Bintan resort adopts an Indonesian style and uses local Indonesian crafts. The same applies to resorts in the Maldives and Seychelles. In all Banyan Tree resorts, the staff, who are locals, are proud to ensure guests have an experience that authentically reflects the nuances of Thai, Indonesian, Maldivian and Seychelles customs, culture and style of hospitality.

What characterises these New Asia brands is their pride in their provenance. This reflects the new confidence in their roots and sense of identity that many Asian companies now have. They have recognised that internationalism does not mean trying to be western in Asia. This is more obvious in countries such as Thailand and Indonesia, which have taken great pride in the richness and diversity of their cultural history and local crafts.

A good example of an Asian brand that has remained true to its cultural origins is Jim Thompson, a Thai silk manufacturer and retailer. This is a brand that has thrived under a shroud of myth and mystery. Its founder, a successful American businessman and well-known resident of Bangkok, disappeared on a trip to the Cameron Highlands in Malaysia. He went out for a walk one evening and never returned; his body was never found and to this day his fate remains unknown. His mysterious disappearance became the stuff of legend, but this businessman left behind more tangible legacies.

Thompson almost single-handedly revived the Thai silk industry. By the end of the second world war, there were only a handful of Lao-speaking villagers still weaving the fabric as cheaper and more efficient machine-made silk took over the market. Thompson was excited by the raw, shot-silk texture of this hand-woven fabric, which was so different from the smooth, almost featureless machine-made silks. He collected as many samples as he could and took them to the editors of *Vanity Fair* and *Vogue* in the United States. There, the story goes, Edna Woolman Chase, editor of *Vogue*, took one look at the lengths of Ban Krua silk spread across her desk and fell in love with them. The rest, as they say, is history.

Thompson went on to found the Thai Silk Company in 1948. But interestingly and to his credit, despite advice to centralise production and to set up a mechanised factory, he insisted that things be done the traditional way so that the Thai Silk Company would retain its individuality and unique appeal. It went on to supply the unique fabric around the world, making it available not just to the fashion industry but also to the furnishings and furniture industries. The company set up a chain of retail stores in Bangkok and other important tourism sites in Thailand, selling the fabric as well as finished items such as scarves, handbags, tote bags, wallets, cushion covers, tablecloths and other home accessories.

Today, the brand is sold throughout Asia. As well as the core merchandise, the range includes beautifully designed, modern, high-end furniture that is distinctively Asian in inspiration but crafted in a contemporary, minimalist style. The company has also recently introduced a Wedding and Gift Registry Service, which offers "Living with Jim Thompson" home interior gifts for couples as they embark on their new life.

In contrast to brands such as Jim Thompson that have retained many facets of their provenance but modernised their product ranges and retail strategies to suit changing demands, more cosmopolitan countries like Singapore have taken a different route to building indigenous New Asia brands. In fact the term "New Asia" was coined by the Singapore Tourism Board as it identified Singapore's niche in Asian tourism as being the "gateway to Asia", presenting the cultural diversity of Asia in a compact, contemporary context.

This island state has long striven to carve a unified identity from its multiracial, multicultural roots, but its desire to create cohesion and fusion out of multiple ethnicities presents challenges. Singapore has been accused of being "faceless" and "sterile". Yet out of its New Asia identity have emerged brands such as OSIM, a health-conscious, lifestyle brand offering customers a wide range of "healthstyle" products from massage chairs costing US$3,000 to smaller, more inexpensive gadgets such as hand-held massagers, eye massagers, blood-pressure monitors, water-based vacuum cleaners and water purifiers. Although the OSIM brand originates in Singapore, its core products, such as the high-end massage chairs, are made in Japan and its other gadgets are made all over the world.

OSIM's image is neither overtly Asian nor western. The brand identity, packaging and retail designs are international in style and the brand name is Asian, as is the brand's outlook and philosophy. The models and celebrities who advertise and endorse OSIM products are also proudly Asian. For instance, Gong Li, a Chinese (now Hollywood) actress, was recently signed up to promote the OSIM range of Mermaid vacuum cleaners. Although it may be stretching the imagination to believe that she still pushes a vacuum cleaner around her own home, Asian consumers identify her as someone who has earned international success while remaining true to her Asian roots, and in that context she is a role model for many.

### Challenger brands

Challenger brands are those that have attempted to impersonate their western counterparts with pseudo-European names such as Bonia or Fion in leather goods and handbags, and Riccino in shoes. They have made full use of their knowledge of the local market and local tastes, but offer western-styled products at a fraction of the price of imported brands.

These brands sought to inject a cosmopolitan appeal and sophistication to their products by projecting a western image, and who can blame them? After all, young men in Asia were shunning the Crocodile and Three Riffles t-shirts they had worn for years in favour of Lacoste and Ralph Lauren Polo t-shirts even though they cost ten times as much.

Challenger brands reflect the enterprising spirit and determination of Asia's small and medium-sized enterprises, which are flexible and responsive enough to tap into the latest trends and tastes in Asia. However, challenger brands are not limited to "copycat" brands seeking to exploit Asians' love for western designer labels.

BritishIndia, for instance, which originated in Malaysia, is a fashion and lifestyle brand that has created a style and look of its own. The style of the brand is the Asian "colonial look", with cottons and linens that will certainly give international brands like Gap or Ralph Lauren a run for their money when it makes its foray into western markets. British-India is evocative of the romance and gracious tropical living of the colonial era without being traditional, or overly Victorian. The colonialism in the brand, which extends to homeware and furniture, is best described as tropical, contemporary and "luxuriously utilitarian", a term coined by Patricia Liew, BritishIndia's founder.

The brand's origins can be traced to Metrojaya, a large department store chain in West Malaysia, where Liew was formerly the merchandise director. It was there that she became involved in brand development and created a number of successful in-house labels for the department store, among them East India Company. In 1997, a management change at Metrojaya prompted her to venture out on her own. She created BritishIndia, which clearly took its inspiration from her East India Company label, one of the most successful of Metrojaya's in-house labels.

Today the brand is available in seven countries in Asia and the Middle East, including Malaysia, Singapore, Thailand, Indonesia and Dubai. It appears to be going from strength to strength, despite difficult economic conditions, and has won a loyal following not just among Asians but also among the western expatriate community in these countries. Its sizing policy suits both the petite, small-boned Asians and their taller, bigger-boned western counterparts.

### Established brands
One of the most established brands in Asia is Singapore Airlines. In the early 1970s, the airline realised that to compete effectively against the big European and American airlines it had to offer a strong and meaningful differentiation, particularly as it did not have a huge domestic market to rely on. It identified a simple gap: quality of service. Planes were hollow steel tubes which transported people thousands of miles with minimum comfort, and it was only after they had landed that the passengers would begin to enjoy themselves. So Singapore Airlines decided to offer the experience of enjoying the magic of Asia from the moment passengers boarded the plane. The famous "Singapore Girl" was born, with her beautiful uniform, grace and charm symbolising the enchanting service that passengers would get. It is an approach that has gained the airline recognition around the world as a leader in the industry.

Table 13.1 **Top 50 Asian Brands, 1999**

| Rank | Brand | Category | Origin |
|---|---|---|---|
| 1 | Singapore Airlines | Airline | Singapore |
| 2 | Speedo | Apparel | Australia |
| 3 | Shangri-La Hotels | Hospitality | Singapore |
| 4 | Lee Kum Kee | Food & Beverage | Hong Kong |
| 5 | Foster's | Alcoholic Beverage | Australia |
| 6 | Qantas | Airline | Australia |
| 7 | Sound Blaster | IT | Singapore |
| 8 | Acer | IT | Taiwan |
| 9 | Star TV | Media | Hong Kong |
| 10 | Cathay Pacific | Airline | Hong Kong |
| 11 | Regent Hotel | Hospitality | Hong Kong |
| 12 | HongkongBank | Financial Services | Hong Kong |
| 13 | Mandarin Oriental | Hospitality | Hong Kong |
| 14 | Thai Airways | Airline | Thailand |
| 15 | San Miguel | Alcoholic Beverage | Philippines |
| 16 | Tiger Beer | Alcoholic Beverage | Singapore |
| 17 | Lonely Planet | Media | Australia |
| 18 | Banyan Tree | Hospitality | Singapore |
| 19 | Samsung Electronics | Electronics | Korea |
| 20 | Giordano | Apparel | Hong Kong |
| 21 | Sheridan | Home Furnishing | Australia |
| 22 | Watson's | Retail | Hong Kong |
| 23 | Brand's | Food & Beverage | Singapore |
| 24 | Anchor | Food & Beverage | New Zealand |
| 25 | Hyundai Motor | Automotive | Korea |
| 26 | Raffles Hotel | Hospitality | Singapore |
| 27 | Want Want | Food & Beverage | Taiwan |
| 28 | Tiger Balm | Consumer Products | Singapore |
| 29 | Royal Selangor | Home Furnishing | Malaysia |
| 30 | Far Eastern Economic Review | Media | Hong Kong |
| 31 | Aman Resorts | Hospitality | Hong Kong |
| 32 | Peninsula Hotel | Hospitality | Hong Kong |
| 33 | Arnott's | Food & Beverage | Australia |
| 34 | Amoy | Food & Beverage | Hong Kong |
| 35 | EVA Air | Airline | Taiwan |
| 36 | TVB | Media | Hong Kong |
| 37 | LG Electronics | Electronics | Korea |
| 38 | Jim Thompson | Home Furnishing | Thailand |
| 39 | Tsingtao Beer | Alcoholic Beverage | China |
| 40 | Vitasoy | Food & Beverage | Hong Kong |
| 41 | DFS | Retail | Hong Kong |
| 42 | Anlene | Food & Beverage | New Zealand |
| 43 | Malaysia Airlines | Airline | Malaysia |
| 44 | Channel V | Media | Hong Kong |
| 45 | Quick Silver | Apparel | Australia |
| 46 | Chesdale | Food & Beverage | New Zealand |
| 47 | Country Road | Apparel | Australia |
| 48 | G2000 | Apparel | Hong Kong |
| 49 | Hazeline | Consumer Products | Singapore |
| 50 | Star Cruise | Leisure | Singapore |

Source: Interbrand

Table 13.2 **Top Singapore brands, 2002**

| Rank | Brand | Brand value (S$m) | Market cap (S$m) | Brand value as % of market cap[a] |
|------|-------|-------------------|------------------|-----------------------------------|
| 1 | SingTel (fixed/mobile) | 3,000 | 31,373 | n/a |
| 2 | DBS | 1,000 | 19,966 | 5 |
| 3 | UOB | 950 | 19,953 | 5 |
| 4 | APB[b] | 820 | 1,165 | n/a |
| 5 | OCBC | 625 | 14,152 | 4 |
| 6 | Great Eastern | 400 | 4,689 | 9 |
| 7 | SIA (airline) | 380 | 13,400 | n/a |
| 8 | Tiger Balm | 110 | 146 | 75 |
| 9 | F&N (soft drinks)[b] | 95 | 2,247 | n/a |
| 10 | Creative | 90 | 1,079 | 8 |
| 11 | Informatics | 75 | 344 | n/a |
| 12 | Brand's | 75 | 650 | n/a |
| 13 | OSIM | 45 | 107 | 42 |
| 14 | Eu Yan Sang | 30 | 54 | 55 |
| 15 | Hour Glass | 20 | 51 | 39 |

a  n/a indicates that only a segment of the company's business was considered.
b  Valuation reflects all brands within their respective portfolios.
Source: Interbrand

## Where things stand

In 1999, Interbrand's survey of the Top 50 Asian Brands (see Table 13.1) showed that a significant number of the strongest brands were in the travel and hospitality sectors where service is crucial to the customer experience and therefore to brand distinctiveness and loyalty. In 2002, in a separate study commissioned by the Singapore government, Interbrand provided a "benchmark value" of the top Singaporean brands (see Table 13.2). There were three notable findings from the study:

- ◪ Despite the fairly low valuations themselves, the brand was becoming the most valuable single asset for the businesses surveyed.
- ◪ The brands that succeeded were not single-product brands, they were services or range brands.
- ◪ Many of the strongest brands were characterised by a focus on

customers' attitudes and lifestyle needs and not on image or functional benefit.

## Looking ahead

Economic and political upheaval in the late 1990s and the SARS outbreak in 2003 were body blows to the travel and tourism industry (and other sectors) of a number of South-East Asian countries. Yet despite these upheavals, local companies remain determined to survive and succeed, and to build and sustain strong brands.

It is true that outside of Japan (and more recently South Korea) there are few Asian brands that stand out in the global marketplace, but it may just be a matter of time before there are more. Since the economic shocks of the late 1990s, crony capitalism, where who you know matters more than what you do and how well you do it, is on the decline, and deregulation and economic liberalisation are gathering pace. Companies are discovering the need to focus on their core businesses and to develop their competencies.

They have also started to recognise that they need to become less dependent on their home markets and to develop strong brands that can compete internationally as well as at home. Name recognition alone, they have discovered, does not necessarily imply that they have a powerful brand, capable of securing consumer preference and loyalty. As a result, many local companies have embarked on branding programmes, driven by pure necessity, to meet the challenges of a more liberal and increasingly global economy. This combination of "push" and "pull" factors will result in many more Asian brands appearing on the global stage.

Gradually, the region will emerge from its mindset of having to play catch-up with the West. It will increasingly embrace and celebrate its own identity and build on what makes South-East Asia distinctive and unique to develop strong brands, as the Asia-originating brands described above have done. Singapore Airlines and Banyan Tree have made the most of the concept of Asian hospitality. OSIM, Tiger Balm and Brand's have positioned themselves around the Asian holistic approach to health management. Jim Thompson and BritishIndia have looked to the past to develop a modern Asian concept of style and fashion.

The can-do, never-say-die attitude of South-East Asian companies will stand them in good stead as they find their own voice and identity in the global marketplace. They have recognised that the factors that

Asian consumers are looking for in international brands – the focus on added value and unique experiences – are exactly the attributes that characterise the best of Asia and the best of Asian brands. Specifically, the growing demand among consumers around the world for authenticity, for diversity not sameness, for personalised service, for a holistic and alternative approach to health, and for new culinary experiences is something from which Asia can profit.

So although today consumers around the world may not feel comfortable with putting a "Rabbit" in their mouths, a "Tiger" on their aching muscles and a "Crocodile" on their backs, this probably will not apply forever in the western search for new experiences.

### Tips for brand builders in Asia

- **Be true to yourself.** Asian consumers are increasingly looking for authenticity not western clones.
- **Don't overpromise.** Asian consumers value good value and expect you to deliver what you have said or implied you will.
- **Appeal to universal needs.** Avoid cultural stereotyping; consumers the world over have similar human desires.
- **Don't be too culturally sensitive.** It is important to understand religious customs (for example, halal meat in McDonald's) but don't take at face value claims that certain colours, for instance, won't work.
- **Do be culturally literate.** Understand what the different cultural nuances are; for example, in a Chinese dominated country, make sure you understand *feng shui.*
- **Protect, protect, protect.** Make sure that all elements of the branded experience are properly protected through intellectual property law and pursue any counterfeiters, frauds or pirates as best you can.

# 14 Branding places and nations

*Simon Anholt*

Places have always been brands, in the truest sense of the word. Mentioning this fact invariably upsets people, yet countries have been branding themselves deliberately and systematically for centuries. The reputations of places have always been managed and occasionally invented by their leaders, who have often borrowed from others to augment their political skills: poets, orators, philosophers, film-makers, artists, writers. If nowadays governments use advertising or PR agencies, that does not seem like a particularly dramatic development, or an especially unpredictable one either. It is important to clarify, however, that the people who are upset by the idea of branding countries usually come from rich countries. The notion that a country can be actively marketed to the rest of the world – for growth, for tourism, for trade and for positive "image" generally – appears to cause none of this hand-wringing in most poor and developing countries, unless it is because not enough of it is being done.

Of course, branding places is different from branding products, and nobody in their right mind would claim that you can approach both tasks in exactly the same way. Most of the controversy, as Wally Olins points out,[1] is created simply by the use of the word "brand".

The fact is that most countries actively engage in the business of taking care of their good names, as they have always done, and an increasingly large number of cities and regions, both supranational and intranational, are beginning to do the same. They may not do it well, and almost none do it with anything like enough rigour, consistency, patience and single-mindedness, but most do it, and if they don't do it, they talk about doing it.

The marketing profession has been judged only quite recently to have something useful to contribute to the business of improving places. But marketing is coming of age in many ways. As the developed world has become organised more and more along commercial lines, it has become clear that a science which shows you how to persuade large numbers of people to change their minds about things or part with hard-earned income has various interesting applications.

So it is no longer merely businesses which recognise the usefulness of marketing. Political parties, governments, good causes, state bodies, even non-governmental organisations are turning to marketing as they begin to understand that profound truth about human endeavour which marketers always knew: that being in possession of the truth is not enough. The truth must be sold.

## Place branding

What is meant by branding a place is, at least in principle, quite simple. A place-brand strategy is a plan for defining the most realistic, most competitive and most compelling strategic vision for the country, region or city; this vision then has to be fulfilled and communicated. The better strategies recognise that the principal resource of most places, as well as a primary determinant of their "brand essence", is as much the people who live there as the things which are made and done in the place. They therefore concentrate on finding ways to direct some of the energies of the population towards better communication of its qualities and aspirations: it is the exact place-branding equivalent of "living the brand"[2] in the commercial field. In all cases, it is fundamental to ensure that the vision of the place is supported, reinforced and enriched by every act of communication with the rest of the world.

This coherence of communication is necessary because in the globalised world in which we now live, every place has to compete with every other place for share of mind, share of income, share of talent, share of voice. Unless a place can come to stand for something, it stands little chance of being remembered for long enough to compete for any of this precious attention. Most of us spend no more than a few seconds each year thinking about a country on the other side of the world or a city at the other end of the country. So unless that country or city *always seems exactly like itself* every time it crops up, there is little chance that those few seconds of attention will ever add up to a preference for its products, a desire to go and visit the place, an interest in its culture, or, if we were prejudiced against the place in some way beforehand, a change of heart.

The acts of communication in which places commonly engage may include:

- the brands which the country exports;
- the way the place promotes itself for trade, tourism, inward investment and inward recruitment;

## The place branding hexagon

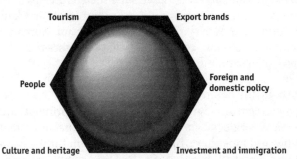

Tourism     Export brands

People     Foreign and domestic policy

Culture and heritage     Investment and immigration

### Tourism

Often the most visible aspect of place branding, tourism is usually also the biggest spender and the most competent marketing force. But it only presents a part of the picture, and needs careful alignment with the other channels of communication in order to achieve its full potential as "flagship" for branding the nation, city or region.

### Export brands

A powerful, distinctive, broad-based and appealing national brand is the most valuable gift which a country or region can give to its exporters: think what "Made in Japan" does for electronics, or "Made in Italy" for fashion. Today, branded exports form one of the most potent ways of building and sustaining national image.

### Foreign and domestic policy

Places are also judged by the part their leaders play in foreign and domestic affairs, and this activity, just like every other, needs to be performed with sensitivity to the strategic imperatives of the brand. When policy is in synergy with the other channels, there are few faster ways to establish a place's position in the global community.

Source: www.placebrands.net

### Investment and immigration

Many of the best examples of rapid growth during the last century have happened because certain places became magnets for talent, investment and business ventures. A powerful and consistent place brand can help create positive preference and get places on the right shortlists.

### Culture and heritage

Places which treat growth as a purely economic issue run the risk of developing a two-dimensional brand image, of interest only to investors, tax exiles and currency speculators. Culture, heritage and sport provide the third dimension, giving places richness, dignity, trust and respect abroad, and quality of life at home.

### People

One "channel of communication" which is fully equal to the huge task of communicating the complexities and contradictions of a place to the global marketplace is its people. When each ordinary citizen – not just diplomats, media stars and politicians – becomes a passionate ambassador for his or her home country or city, positive change can really happen.

---

◢ the way it behaves in acts of domestic and foreign policy, and the ways in which these acts are communicated;

◢ the way it promotes and represents and shares its culture with other places;

◢ the way its citizens behave when abroad and how they treat strangers at home;

◢ the built and natural environment it presents to the visitor;

◢ the way it features in the world's media;

◢ the bodies and organisations it belongs to;

◢ the other countries it associates with;

◪ the way it competes with other countries in sport and entertainment;
◪ what it gives to the world and what it takes back.

These and the other ways in which places express themselves usually fall under one or another of the six basic categories of communication which form the place branding hexagon (see Figure 14.1).

Place branding aligns as many of these "channels" as possible into accomplishing and communicating the development strategy of the city or country or region. If done well, such a strategy can make a big difference to both the internal confidence and the external performance of a place, as places like Ireland, New Zealand, Spain, Bilbao, Bangalore and Liverpool have shown in recent years. These countries and cities have completely changed, in a relatively short time, the way in which people think about them, and they have done it quite deliberately.

The best example of national rebranding from our own times is undoubtedly that of modern Japan. The effect of Japan's economic miracle on the image of the country itself was quite as dramatic as its effect on the country's output. Only 40, or even 30, years ago "Made in Japan" was a decidedly negative concept, as most western consumers had based their perception of "brand Japan" on their experience of shoddy, second-rate products flooding the market. The products were cheap, certainly, but they were basically worthless. In many respects, the perception of Japan was much as China's has been in more recent years.

Yet Japan has now become synonymous with advanced technology, manufacturing quality, competitive pricing, and even of style and status. Japan, indeed, passes the best branding test of all: whether consumers are prepared to pay more money for functionally identical products, simply because of where they come from. It's fair to say that in the 1950s and 1960s, most Europeans and Americans would only buy Japanese products because they were significantly *cheaper* than a western alternative. Now, in certain valuable market segments – such as consumer electronics, musical instruments and motor vehicles – western consumers will consistently pay *more* for products manufactured by previously unknown brands, purely on the basis that they are perceived to be Japanese. Little wonder that Dixons, a UK retailer of consumer electronics, gave its new house brand a mock-Japanese name, Matsui, in order to borrow a little of the "public domain" equity of brand Japan.

Image and progress unfailingly go hand in hand. Although it is usually true that a positive image is the consequence of progress, rather than vice versa, it is equally true that when both are carefully managed in tandem, they help each other along and create accelerated change.

Place branding gives equal prominence to perception and to reality. This is because the first lesson that marketing has to teach is that people are often more influenced by what they believe than by what is true. The second lesson is that other people are less interested in you than you are, so if you care about what they think, it is your responsibility to make yourself properly understood. Objectivity becomes a cardinal virtue when branding a place. It is hard enough for marketers to be dispassionate enough about a fizzy drink or a training shoe to really get under the skin of an indifferent consumer, let alone about a "product" in which they and their forefathers were born and raised.

Marketing also teaches that people cannot be deceived for long; that the higher you raise their expectations, the more completely they reject your offering when they are disappointed; and you can't make people buy a bad product more than once. So every good marketer knows that his or her primary responsibility is to ensure that the product matches up to the promise, because misleading marketing is ineffective marketing.

### The power of country of origin

Wherever you go in the world, the most desirable brands in the shops nearly always come – or appear to come – from the same places: America, England, France, Germany, Italy, Japan, Scandinavia, Scotland, Switzerland or South Korea. These places are the top ten as far as brand image is concerned. Tell people that a brand is made in one of these countries or regions, and they will immediately expect a certain kind of brand image and a certain level of quality, and will be prepared to pay a certain price for it.

If Coca-Cola or Marlboro or Nike were not American, if Ferrari or Gucci or Barilla were not Italian, if Chanel or Dior were not French, and if Burberry or Rolls-Royce were not (originally) English, they would truly be half the brands they are today.

The country images which so often guide our buying decisions are so familiar to us that we accept them pretty much without hesitation, along with the qualities with which we believe they endow their products and services. It is for this reason that a powerful and appealing national brand is the most valuable gift that any government can give to its exporters: it is their "unfair advantage" in the global marketplace.

There are fewer and fewer good reasons why developing countries should not also benefit from the synergy of a strong nation brand and branded goods and services. The Bangalore technology cluster, for example, spearheaded by companies like Wipro and Infosys, is rapidly updating the brand image of India as modern, innovative, entrepreneurial and global, just as the emergence of consumer brands like Samsung, Daewoo and LG have done in recent years for South Korea, and Sony, Toyota and others did for Japan in earlier decades. "Brand India" is clearly capable of embracing other values too, as several emerging Indian brands are beginning to demonstrate through their export success. Perhaps the most striking of these is Urvâshi, a perfume created by Deepak Kanegaonkar, a Mumbai industrialist, which is currently enjoying remarkable success in the department stores of Paris, and playing its own part in reaffirming India's more traditional brand qualities of exoticism, mystery, luxury and sensuality.

The importance of the country-brand/product-brand effect has not escaped the Chinese government. In a recent symposium on "China's Rising Famous Brand" in Beijing, Wu Bangguo, the vice premier, called on the Chinese nation "to make efforts to promote the development of China's brand commodities so as to benefit the world's people ... development of brand commodities concerns China's economic growth and social progress". A report published for the symposium noted that the top ten most valuable Chinese brands have shown an average increase of 30.9% in annual sales, and will be strong enough to challenge the world's top 500 on the global stage in 3–5 years' time. There are enough examples of thriving Chinese brands – such as Legend computers, which aims to become the world's leading PC manufacturer within ten years, and Haier, already the world's second-biggest refrigerator brand – to suggest that this may be more than idle boasting.[3]

There is more to a good place brand than boosting exports, however. If we pursue the thought to its logical conclusion, a country's brand image can profoundly shape its economic, cultural and political destiny, because global policymakers, just like the rest of us, are ruled by both their heads and their hearts.

What ultimately makes the European Commission decide which countries will be considered for membership of their elite club, and in which order? Consciously or not, their deliberations also relate to the brand image of each applicant state, and what it might or might not ultimately contribute to the brand image of the European Union. When complex wars erupt between countries, and even experts are hard-pressed to say which is truly the victim and which the aggressor, it is surely the brand image of each country that sways world opinion towards its customary black-and-white view. And world opinion, as we know, acquires a more and more pronounced influence on the outcomes of these matters as time goes by.

More than just a fashionable way to create "competitive edge" for the countries which are rich and smart enough to practise it, branding places is an absolute imperative in a globalised world. Ever since Adam Smith made the connection between a free-market economy and the wealth of the nation-state, the need to brand places has become clearer and clearer. More recently, Michael Porter's *The Competitive Advantage of Nations* probably marked the point at which it became obvious that there is no other way for a country to prosper than by considering itself as a competitor in a single marketplace.

## Marketing at the top

The elevation of ordinary commercial marketing disciplines to the dizzying heights of national strategy unavoidably creates certain tensions, chiefly between what branding experts believe their discipline can achieve, and what their clients in governments or city councils believe it is capable of achieving. This may have something to do with the quality of the people who customarily work in marketing, or it may not; it certainly has a lot to do with the poor "brand image" of marketing itself.

At the heart of the issue is the old question of whether marketing is merely about communications or something altogether more strategic. It does not help that so many politicians and statesmen, like most lay people, have little understanding of the proper meaning of "brand" and often believe that it is simply a matter of designing an expensive new logo for their country and a slogan to go underneath it. They barely distinguish between nation branding and tourism promotion.

Managing a national brand is both more complex and less glamorous than this. Most countries of any size or age already have a brand image, whether they like it or not. People have heard of them and believe certain things about them. In many cases, the country neither needs nor could sustain a new image, but it can benefit enormously by challenging people's prejudices and opening their minds to hearing something new and relevant about the place once in a while.

Many places suffer from an image which is out-of-date, unfair, unbalanced or cliché-ridden. This "starlight effect" occurs because the image of places which most people hold in their minds is often nothing more than the distant echo of associations created decades or centuries earlier. This makes the brand images of places incredibly hard to shift: some of them seem positively *rusted* into place. Of course, wars, catastrophes and World Cup wins can have a sudden and dramatic effect on the image of a place, but the more rapid the effect, the shorter-lived it often proves to be.

Naturally, there are widely different agendas to be found among the stakeholders of a national or regional brand. One common example of this is the disconnection between the tourism authority – which often likes to present the country as remote, unspoilt and sparsely populated by picturesque, warm-hearted rustics speaking vanishing dialects – and the inward investment board, which finds this kind of image most unhelpful when it is trying to persuade a Korean multinational to build its next semiconductor plant there.

So the kind of branding which nations undertake is much more likely to be brand management than rebranding. Brand management is quite a humble activity: the cautious husbandry of existing perceptions and the painstaking reconciliation of diverse elements into a harmonious yet distinctive whole. It is a process as unglamorous as it is unscandalous, and, not coincidentally, hardly the stuff to get journalists excited.

In many cases, place branding may be simply a matter of helping "consumers" to join up the dots between the things they already know and understand about a place, but whose relationship to each other has so far eluded them. The UK, for example, suffers from a widespread perception that it lives in the past, and yet surveys show that, once prompted, most people around the world are well aware of its modern fashion, design and youth cultures. A key component in "branding" the UK is therefore simply reminding people that Stratford-upon-Avon and Covent Garden are both to be found in the same country. Indeed, it was the recognition of this need to "join up" the traditional and the innovative in the UK's international image which gave rise to the public diplomacy programme which became popularly known (and derided) as "Cool Britannia".

There was little to fault in the strategic thinking behind this initiative; what went wrong was the way it was presented to the media and to the general public at home. In the UK, there is a widespread and perhaps idealistic or even naive feeling that public affairs and international relations are, or should be, purely about deeds and facts. Marketing, however, is seen by many as a dirty and unprincipled business, dealing with surface and illusion, vanity and deception: lies, in short. So the news that the Blair government was planning to *rebrand the whole country* naturally caused instant outrage, and the vital message was somehow never communicated that this was nothing more than telling the world some good, true things about the UK which they didn't already know.

In the end, of course, places are not soap-powder, and this is the central paradox of place branding: places are intensely complex and often contradictory, yet the essence of all effective branding is simplicity. To find a branding strategy which is believable, relevant to the "consumer", true to the reality and the aspirations of the place, yet capable of encompassing this variety without becoming a boring compromise or alienating the population, is a task far bigger and trickier than anything marketing service agencies have had to tackle before. Cultural relations can play a critical part here in helping to restore the richness and dignity to the place brand which the rigours of practical international marketing take out.[4]

### Is branding equal to the task?

It does seem an odd place for a humble commercial service like brand management to find itself: almost, in a sense, above national government. Yet there is a compelling case for the national branding strategy to direct, or at least embrace, the full gamut of political, economic, cultural and social development. After all, the argument for nation branding hinges on the acceptance that in a globalised world, all nations need to compete with each other for a share of the world's attention and wealth, and that development is as much a matter of positioning as anything else. So it makes perfect sense for governments to do everything possible to ensure consistency of behaviour in every area.

It also makes sense to say that anything which does not fall under the remit of brand is therefore a weak link in the strategic chain, and can undermine the efforts and investments made in other areas. There is, for example, simply no point in investing in a brand strategy which portrays the country as a peaceful and beautiful tourist destination and an exporter of ethically produced quality consumer goods if the government is busily oppressing minorities, polluting rivers or behaving belligerently towards its neighbours. This line of thought leads to the irresistible conclusion that place branding can actually encourage more moderate and benign foreign policy, because it concentrates the minds of political leaders so wonderfully on the real importance of their international reputation.

Furthermore, making ordinary citizens feel instrumental in shaping and realising the international aspirations of the country may help to create a stronger sense of national identity and promote social inclusion. The whole country can be united in an objective examination of its strengths and weaknesses through an open and public process of focus and improvement.

Everything hinges on the basic need for consistency of behaviour and the representations of that behaviour, and if there is no hope of achieving consistency, then there is no hope of building a brand. Just as the development of corporate and product branding has led to the conclusion that branding, if it is done properly, must affect every aspect of the corporation both inside and out, so the same conclusion applies to nation branding.

However, another paradox of place branding is that achieving this degree of consistency is likely to be a great deal easier under a contract of employment than under a social contract, especially a democratic one. In the commercial sector, it is openly acknowledged that a certain amount of heavy-handedness has often proved essential to achieve the kind of ruthless adherence to strategy which companies need to build their brands. There is, in fact, little that is democratic in the way that most companies are run, and powerful brands are often the result of a single-minded, even mildly deranged visionary, who tolerates no deviation from the company line. This is understandable, since so much of the success of any branding venture is attributable to the degree of consistency the company manages to achieve in its internal and external communications. It is also permissible to an extent, since, supposedly, the employees are there of their own free will and are being paid to perform in a way which the management decides is in the best interest of the company. It may not be nice, or ultimately very productive, but that is another matter.

Obviously, countries are different. The same approach by the leader of a country is called tyranny and is frowned upon in international circles, however good it may be for the national brand. Yet we know from experience that getting many independent people and organisations (all with very different interests, opinions and agendas) to speak with a single voice is a hard thing to achieve through consensus. But one thing is clear: unless a government can find a way of achieving in its committees the same single-minded sense of purpose and control that the crazy brand visionary achieves within a privately owned company, a national brand programme is guaranteed to fail.

## Hope for branding

When examining what is involved in branding places, it is easy to see why people without inside experience of first-class marketing can be sceptical about whether the discipline is really up to the task.

In reality, branding theory and practice have something of value to offer in virtually any area of endeavour. Few other disciplines so fully explain and allow for the management of human enterprise. Branding and marketing embrace scientific clarity of thought and rigorous observation of human psychology, culture and society with a deep sympathy for the mystery of creativity. They combine advanced knowledge management (as is found in the way the better brands are policed in all their complex variants) with sensitive intercultural management (as is found in the way the better brands are communicated worldwide). Branding is a clear set of universally applicable rules for building successful endeavours. It brings commerce and culture together as a potent force for creating prosperity. It can harness the power of language and images to bring about widespread social change. Good branding, uniquely, has the humanism and wisdom to know that there is a difference between what makes sense on paper and how people actually behave; it has the intelligence of academia combined with the worldliness of practice.

There are many people who feel far from comfortable at the thought of marketers mingling freely with politicians and helping them determine the fate of nations. It is possible to sympathise with this view, but the influence of the art and science of branding on governments, if responsibly and intelligently applied, can be enormously positive. If it is good branding, it will bring a much-needed dose of practical, rigorous, egalitarian, good-humoured, quick-witted humanism to an area where such qualities are all too often entirely absent.

Brand building is one of the great achievements of the western world, even if it has usually been used for somewhat trivial ends, merely increasing wealth where more wealth is least needed. Place branding is one of the ways in which the discipline can begin to realise its full potential, providing an opportunity for marketers to demonstrate that they have something to contribute above and beyond that tired old litany of "increasing shareholder value". Branding has a unique power to create a fairer distribution of the world's wealth by adding the miracle of intangible value to products, and the places that produce them, beyond the "first world". This process has just begun, judging by the success of Urvâshi noted earlier and the several hundred other nascent global brands created in developing and poor countries.

Place branding has big implications for the future role of brands and marketing in general, and is the industry's best and quite possibly last chance to create a lasting and significant future role for itself beyond its traditional boundaries of promoting products and services and helping rich companies get richer. During the last 100 years or so, much of the wealth of rich countries has been generated through marketing. These skills should now be transferred to poorer countries, and so help them graduate from being mere suppliers of low-margin unbranded commodities to brand owners and branded places in their own right.

Branding is part of the reason there is such a wide gap between the rich and poor places of the earth. It would be a fine thing if it could now turn some of its attention towards reversing that trend.

### The eight principles of place branding

*1 Purpose and potential*

Place branding creates value for a city, region or state in three main ways:

- aligning the messages which the place already sends out, in accordance with a powerful and distinctive strategic vision;
- unlocking the talent of the people who live there to reinforce and fulfil this vision;
- creating new, powerful and cost-effective ways to give the place a more effective and memorable voice and enhance its international reputation.

*2 Truth*

Places often suffer from an image which is out-of-date, unfair, unbalanced, or cliché-ridden. It is one of the tasks of place branding to ensure that the true, full, contemporary picture is communicated in a focused and effective way; never to compromise the truth or glamorise it irresponsibly.

*3 Aspirations and betterment*

The place brand needs to present a credible, compelling and sustainable vision for its future, firmly in the context of our shared future. This will support the overall aim of a real increase in the economic, political, cultural and social well-being of the people who live there, while contributing in a more than token way to the well-being of other people in other places.

*4 Inclusiveness and common good*

Place branding can and should be used for achieving societal, political and economic objectives. Inevitably, a workable strategy will favour certain groups or individuals over others, and this creates an inalienable responsibility to ensure that those less favoured are supported in other ways.

### 5 Creativity and innovation
Place branding should find, release and help direct the talents and skills of the population, and promote the creative use of these in order to achieve innovation in education, business, government, environment and the arts. Furthermore, only creativity of the highest order can "square the circle" of translating the complexity of a place into purposeful, distinctive and effective brand strategy (see Principle 6).

### 6 Complexity and simplicity
The reality of places is intricate and often contradictory, yet the essence of effective branding is simplicity and directness. It is one of the harder tasks of place branding to do justice to the richness and diversity of places and their peoples, yet to communicate this to the world in ways which are simple, truthful, motivating, appealing and memorable.

### 7 Connectivity
Place branding connects people and institutions at home and abroad. The clear and shared sense of purpose which good brand strategy engenders can help unite government, the private sector and non-governmental organisations; it stimulates involvement and participation among the population; externally, it helps build strong and positive links to other places and other people.

### 8 Things take time
Place branding is a long-term endeavour. It need not and should not cost more than any place can comfortably afford, but is neither a quick fix nor a short-term campaign. Devising an appropriate place brand strategy and implementing it thoroughly takes time and effort, wisdom and patience; if properly done, the long-term advantages, both tangible and intangible, will outweigh the costs by far.

Source: Placebrands Ltd, 2003

## References
1   Olins, W., "Branding the Nation – the historical context", *Journal of Brand Management*, Vol. 9, No. 4–5, April 2002.
2   See Ind, N., *Living the Brand*, Kogan Page, 2001.

3   Anholt, S., *Brand New Justice: The Upside of Global Branding*, Butterworth-Heinemann, Oxford, 2003.

4   Anholt, S., "Editor's Foreword", *Journal of Brand Management*, Vol. 9, No. 4–5, April 2002.

# 15 The future of brands

*Rita Clifton*

The future of brands is inextricably linked to the future of business. In fact, the future of brands is the future of business if it is to be about sustainable wealth creation. Further, because of the interaction of brands with society, and since so many socially influential brands are in the not-for-profit sector, the future of brands is also inextricably linked to the future of society.

This chapter examines some future trends and predictions, both in business and in broader society, and looks at how brands may affect and be affected by those changes. It also explores the categories and countries that seem likely to yield some of the world's greatest brands in the future, and makes observations on what brands of all kinds will need to do to be successful.

But first, it may be useful to recap on the main themes and arguments outlined in previous chapters:

- Branding has been in existence for hundreds of years and has developed into a modern concept that can be applied to anything from products and services to companies, not-for-profit concerns and even countries.
- Well-managed brands have extraordinary economic value and are the most effective and efficient creators of sustainable wealth. Understanding the value of a brand, and how to create more value, is essential management information.
- Brands can also have a critical social importance and benefit in both developed and developing countries. This applies as much to commercial brands as not-for-profit organisations.
- Most of the world's greatest brands today are American owned, largely because of America's "free" political, commercial and social systems. But the knowledge and practice of what creates great brands can be (and is now being) applied around the world.
- Every brand, if it is to be successful, needs a clear positioning, expressed through name, identity and all aspects of products, services and behaviour. For corporate effectiveness and

efficiency, the brand and its positioning should be used as a clear managing framework for portfolio management and business unit relationships.

◪ Increasingly, brands require a distinctive customer experience in the round. Indeed, increasingly a brand is that experience, not least through the behaviour of its people. The brand should be the central organising principle for everyone and then every thing.

◪ Every brand needs a strong creative idea to bring it to life through visual and verbal identity. This creative process needs not only innovation and imagination, but also the courage and conviction to carry it through.

◪ The strongest brand communications may work at the levels of information, fame creation and by creating (often unconscious) associations. Those elements which are harder to measure and justify are no less important; in fact, they are often the most important elements.

◪ Public relations for brands will succeed only if they are based on the brand promise and the internal reality of the company; people have become increasingly sceptical, and in a 24-hour news culture, organisations have nowhere to hide, either inside or outside.

◪ If a company is going to invest in a brand long term, it must give its "identifiable distinctive features" adequate legal protection; and it must enforce that protection vigorously, increasingly on a global basis.

◪ Leading global brands can, and should, help the wider public understand the benefits of globalisation and free trade. But they can do this only if they open up, behave well and collectively educate about their benefits. They must also ensure they continue to innovate.

◪ Brands need better and socially broader measures of success. Corporate social responsibility should be about genuinely solving problems, not just about brand reputation management.

◪ Asia shows every sign of becoming a global brand generator, not only in terms of cost advantage in manufactured product-brands, but also because of its heritage in areas such as personalised services and holistic health.

◪ In a "globalised" world, nations need to compete with each other for the world's attention and wealth. Active and conscious nation branding can help them do this, and at its best, it can be argued, it presents an opportunity to redistribute the world's wealth more fairly in the future.

If the last theme in particular makes anyone baulk, it is worth remembering the importance that China is attaching to growing its "branded commodities" as its way forward in the world and "so as to benefit the world's people"[1]. While many western nations are fashionably wringing their hands about the nature of capitalism, and about brands as their highest profile manifestation, developing nations are coming to see branded businesses, and indeed their own images, as their opportunity for development and more stable wealth and economic control. Whether it is ironic or not, western consumers' constant search for novelty and authenticity may also help ensure that the "newer" economies have an interested audience for their propositions.

But before reflecting on whether and how the main themes of this book may be carried forward in the future – and before speculating on the provenance of the world's most successful brands of the future – it is worth considering the broader future context.

## The future thing

The future certainly isn't what it used to be, but nevertheless a recent article by Martin Rees, the Astronomer Royal, made rather depressing reading.[2] The opening line was:

> I think that the odds are no better than 50-50 that our present civilisation on earth will survive to the end of the century.

He puts this down to the potential for "maverick" misuse of science and/or weapons of mass destruction. In the meantime, of course, there is always the possibility of super-volcanoes or asteroid hits.

At the other extreme, Watts Wacker, an American futurist, made it part of his working philosophy to encourage organisations to develop "500-year" plans. This was meant to be symbolic rather than literal, but does rather stretch the point.

Steering a slightly less radical course either way, it was interesting to consider a range of predictions for the year 2025, drawn from various think tanks and futurists.[3] These included market wars over ice on the moon; widespread "designer" babies; a truly pregnant man; a derelict Silicon Valley, overtaken by technologies such as quantum, optical and

DNA computers; and one which would bring Rees's doomsday scenario rather closer, widespread cyber-terrorism.

You only have to look at a random selection of sci-fi films and futurology books to understand the dangers of publishing-specific predictions. Even as recently as the mid-1990s, Nicholas Negroponte was reportedly predicting that by the year 2000, more people would be entertaining themselves on the internet than watching TV networks. We shall see whether Toshitada Doi, president of Sony's Digital Creatures Laboratory, is right in saying that robots will eclipse PCs in product growth worldwide within 30 years (or even within 10–15 years).[4] However, as Alvin Toffler says in his introduction to *Future Shock*, "The inability to speak with precision and certainty about the future ... is no excuse for silence."[5]

It is obviously important to try to understand general trends and possibilities in scientific, economic and social terms if we are to plan and adapt brand futures, whether for new or for existing brands. Even the strongest brands today can get stuck in a complacent time warp, overtaken by new and baggage-free competitors.

## Future brand issues

From past trends, the odds might seem in favour of the top brands today still being up there in 25 years' time. As the introduction to this book pointed out, over half of the 50 most valuable brands have been around for more than 50 years. However, it is difficult to see how past performance will give quite so much reassurance in the face of the extraordinary changes we are likely to see in world power and economics in the next ten years.

The most successful technology and telecommunications brands have already shown how quickly they can progress if they read and act on consumer and business trends in the right way (look at Microsoft, Nokia and Intel). Their challenge is to maintain their position and sustain their value. To do this, they will have to continue to innovate and, critically, to deepen and extend their brand relationships with customers well beyond the level of technological prowess; for long-term value, brands need emotional as well as technological appeal. Indeed, they will have to invest in their brand as their major sustainable competitive advantage.

It is not unreasonable, for instance, to imagine that a new killer application will emerge from somewhere like Bangalore in the near future. Nor is it unreasonable to suppose that the service and branding skills required to build that proposition into a sustainable brand will have developed to such a degree in India itself that global brand status is within reach. What is more, the "skill cost" difference between India and America or Europe, which has already seen global organisations such as Citibank and GE outsourcing their services to the subcontinent, means that price differentials will make their brands even more attractive. For comparison, look at the wages differential around the world: in 2003, the minimum wage per hour was $5.15 in the United States and £4.20 in the UK, equivalent wages in China 18 pence (29 cents) and in India 7 pence (11 cents).[6] As far as service expertise is concerned, a recent study by Deloitte Research concluded that in the next five years, 2m jobs in western financial institutions will be moved overseas, which means that around $356 billion worth of financial services activity will move away from first-world economies. Established brands will indeed have to continue to leverage their trust and heritage, even while the core of their own service offering is on a passage to India to cut costs and satisfy Wall Street and the City. To take up the opportunity properly, however, India will need to work on its nation brand in terms of reliability of infrastructure and the taint of corruption.

With 1.3 billion consumers, China is the world's biggest potential consumer market. It is currently difficult to attend a conference on world trade and financial issues without speakers speculating on the extraordinary impact China is having and will continue to have. A study by the Engineering Employers' Federation in the UK[7] suggested that one-third of manufacturing firms were considering shifting production to China. A vivid case study is Hornby, a venerable British company, manufacturer of classic toy train sets, owner of the Scalextric brand and recently brought back to fame by the Hogwarts Express featured in the Harry Potter films. In speaking about the advantages of moving production to China, the CEO says:

> The strain on the bottom line began to ease immediately. We were able to use the savings to increase the quality and details of the models so that sales began to pick up.

Essentially, the company retained just the designers and managers at its UK head office in Margate, reducing the head count from 550 to 130, even though some observers were sceptical of the long-term viability of separating innovation and production.

One other thing Hornby's CEO outlined was his view of the fate of the company had he not moved production: "Hornby would have closed, or been taken over by a Chinese company, if we hadn't moved." This was no idle boast in the light of the case of Haier. Almost 20 years ago the Qingdao Refrigerator Plant bought the production-line technology from Liberhaier, a German company, and used this as the basis for its brand name. As noted in the previous chapter, Haier is now the world's second biggest refrigerator brand. How much of this is to do with the 'borrowed' belief among some buyers that they are of German origin is debatable.

This kind of false provenance, whether real or assumed, is hardly a new idea. In the electronic goods category alone, it has been customary for UK electrical retailers to give their own-label products Japanese-sounding names, as this would give better quality associations than British-manufactured electrical goods. Think also of Haagen-Dazs, Estée Lauder, Hugo Boss and Sony as brands with a name at odds with the real country of origin and ownership. Clearly, although provenance, and authenticity in that provenance, is important in such categories as luxury and cars, so much depends on how the brands are built and managed. Many of the world's most valuable brands now transcend their country of origin. A Chinese company such as Legend computers will need all these world-class branding skills if its global ambitions are to be realised. As we have discussed before, its ambitions to become the world's biggest PC manufacturer within ten years will not necessarily make it the world's most valuable PC brand. However, there is a particularly strong Asian brand case study that may serve to inspire them for the future.

Samsung, from South Korea, is one of the most spectacular global brand success stories of recent years. From a brand value of just under $2.5bn in 1997, it grew to almost $11bn in 2003, and seems likely to continue its success. It is the reason for its success that is of interest here. In the mid-1990s, Samsung's managers realised that they would be on the commodity and low-price road to perdition if they did not develop their own brand. They saw a real opportunity in the digital platform, invested heavily in premium quality innovation and R&D and, most telling of all, invested in their own brand rather than be condemned to the uncertainty of OEM[8] status indefinitely. They built brand awareness around the world, and resolved to use their brand value (rather than just straight financials) as a key performance measure. As the company's president and CEO said at the time:

*Competing successfully in the 21st century will require more than just outstanding product and quality functions. Intangibles such as corporate and brand image will be crucial factors for achieving a competitive edge.*

This concern for other measures, and ways of measuring performance to ensure that everyone in a company continues to build brand value rather than trading on it, is perhaps something that more western companies, particularly publicly quoted companies, and the equity markets need to reflect on.

Brand America may appear to have taken a series of body blows in the early years of the 21st century. However, while it might be true to say that there are slightly fewer American-owned brands in the top 100 today compared with a few years ago, this is as much to do with market changes and self-inflicted corporate wounds as American heritage. More than 60% of the world's most valuable brands are still American owned. Despite opinion polls and anti-American demonstrations, consumers can be radical at the research questionnaire and reactionary at the checkout.

However, other countries are beginning to learn the global brand game, and companies such as Coca-Cola and Nike will need to keep on reflecting their sensitivity to local cultures and habits in their management and marketing approaches. It is interesting that, whereas for the past 50 years America itself has been a strong brand, standing for freedom and lifestyle aspiration, increasing familiarity and the spread of democracy have meant that these previously "magic" qualities have lost their cachet. American-owned brands will have to work that much harder on more imaginative positionings, operations and communications for their brands if they are to withstand the challenge from all comers.

An interesting battle of retail brands and operating philosophies is potentially emerging between the mighty Wal-Mart and Tesco, a UK-based retailer. In many ways, Wal-Mart is the archetypical American business success story. It has in Sam Walton a founder with a distinctive home-cooked philosophy, with a strong service and moral ethic, and a zealous evangelism for giving people American-style life opportunities. Wal-Mart's expansion internationally has been cautious so far, as has its behaviour around its purchase and management of the Asda brand in the UK. While the retail giant has made a simple philosophy of low prices and genuine customer service work well in the United States, and has made much of its respect for employees, there are perhaps lessons to be learned from the innovation, own-brand building and customer relationship management of the best UK grocery retailers. There are several margin-point differences between the average grocery retail businesses in the UK and those in America. While some of this difference is down to the dominant position of major retail chains in the UK, it is also because of their success in building their own brand values, and using their own-brand products and services to sustain their quality image, rather than just being price fighters against manufacturer brands. Tesco is now not only the UK's number one retailer and one of its most respected companies; it is also the world's largest online grocer, and its joint venture with iVillage.com has created the largest women's online destination in the world. Out of the ten countries in which it operates, Tesco is currently market leader in six. Its stated core purpose, to "create value for customers to earn their lifetime loyalty", has driven its ability to extend its brand well beyond grocery into banking, health care and mobile telephony. It is a brand that is trusted by people in whatever area it is operating.

This ability of a strong brand to transcend categories, and to be trusted by consumers in whichever category it chooses to involve itself, would seem to be an important property of the world's greatest brands in the future. In a hyper-competitive, over-communicated and complicated world, people will increasingly want and need to simplify their purchases and time management. What is more, in a blurring physical and virtual world, any brand will have the ability to be a powerful medium and a power retailer – if only in virtual space. Trusted brands provide ideal navigation for consumers across sectors, and as the strongest will be able to leap into categories without having a previous product or service track record, no brand will be sacred in its marketplace any more. Although it has its financial challenges, the Virgin brand is another good example of this "leaping" ability. It has a strong vision and values around being "people's champion", innovative and irreverent, and through popular support has managed to transcend markets from airlines to cosmetics, from financial services to mobile telephony, from soft to hard drinks and many more.

The issue of category-defying life brands is also relevant when looking at those new or growth categories that would seem most likely to produce strong brand growth in the future. These include:

- health and well-being, including more holistic and organic lifestyles;

- leisure, entertainment and "new adventure" experiences;
- physical and emotional security;
- services for a new generation of the "new old" (a critical trend in industrialised countries);
- lifelong education;
- information and lifestyle management (relevant to the prediction of Sony's "personal robots");
- biotechnology and genetics.

These areas could yield entirely new global brands in the future; it may well be that the most valuable brand in the next 25 years has not been invented yet. However, it is equally possible that an existing, trusted brand may extend or cross into these new areas. As part of this, the blurring of the online and offline worlds (a distinction that is already barely recognised by global teenagers) will mean that any brand can become powerful both as a medium and as a retailer, virtual or otherwise.

Current product-based brands will find it harder than service or retail brands to deepen and broaden their relationships with their audiences. This is not just because they are having to invest so much of their marketing support in retail distribution, rather than spending it on consumer communication. It is also because in their current form, they lack the ability to control the total customer experience, and so engage their audiences as fully as they would like. Chapter 6 of this book highlights the increasing importance of experience in building brands, and we should expect to see in the future many more "manu-retailers": product-based brand companies developing their own retail experiences and direct relationships with their consumers, both offline and online. Unilever's experiment with "myhome", a home cleaning and laundry service, was interesting in its extension of Persil and Cif as service brands. Although it did not progress beyond its test market, it nevertheless demonstrated the company's interest in developing core brands beyond the product form. To facilitate this process of concentration on resources, innovation and investment behind its most successful brands, Unilever has been culling its smaller and weaker brands in recent years, either selling them or dropping them. As other conglomerates have been doing the same, an interesting possibility is on the cards. Not only will we continue to see further brand consolidation and corporate "musical chairs", but some of the brands that are being sold off could end up in the newer economies, fired up by entrepreneurial spirit and a new angle for selling. Think of Haier many times over.

Other areas of brand activity that are likely to increase in the future are co-branding (for example, Sony Ericsson) and celebrity branding (as in current examples like David Beckham and Jennifer Lopez). The challenge for the former is to generate clarity about the joint brand proposition (never easy in partnership), and for the latter, to identify how to generate long-term sustainable value after the flush of celebrity fades.

It is also interesting as a trend that major corporations such as Mars and Estée Lauder have either launched or acquired brands which feel like explicit "social enterprises", and have allowed them to operate with no obvious brand connection with the corporate owner. Mars acquired Seeds of Change in 1997; it had been launched in 1989, with a stated purpose of preserving biodiversity and sustainable development. Estée Lauder later acquired Aveda, a brand connecting "beauty, environment and wellbeing". At a conference shortly afterwards, Leonard Lauder said that Estée Lauder itself was committed to phasing out synthetics entirely, following the lead of Aveda. Using new ventures of this kind as operating test-beds for new business principles indicates that major corporations recognise that business may have to be conceived and conducted in rather different ways in the future.

Another area to mention for brand growth is the NGO (non-governmental organisation) sector. When national governments, for whatever reasons, cannot or choose not to act, non-governmental and not-for-profit organisations can play the role of "guardian brands". A recent example is the role Oxfam has played in the developing-world coffee crisis, where coffee farmers in the poorest countries are facing falling prices and new levels of poverty. In a 2002 report, Oxfam demanded that the multinational companies involved in coffee purchasing and marketing demonstrate a "long-term commitment to ethical purchasing".[9] In the future, raising funds will be as much of a challenge for such organisations as it has always been. To avoid the danger of appearing compromised by expedient corporate partnerships, they should perhaps think more about "selling" or licensing their intellectual property about best practices in ethical processes and measurement.

### Further brand management considerations
In maximising and sustaining the value of brands in the future there needs to be more focus on:

- ◪ **Understanding the value and value drivers of a brand.** As can be seen from the Samsung case, a focus on brand value and measuring performance on the basis of the brand value added can build momentum and create sustainable growth. It is also crucial management information for mergers, acquisitions and divestments, which will continue in the future as markets shake out and consolidate. Few mergers currently deliver long-term shareholder value, largely because of overemphasis on financials and practical operations. Greater focus on brand value would help mergers succeed – as well as generating real organic growth.

■ **Clarity of brand positioning.** Clarity of vision, values and positioning overall are often given insufficient attention in practice. The majority of corporate and brand visions are interchangeable, bland and viewed with cynicism. In an over-communicated world, lack of clarity will substantially reduce effectiveness and efficiency; and complex brand and sub-brand structures without a real audience rationale will reduce this still further. Clarity of strategy is also one of the leading criteria by which companies are judged.

■ **Brands as total experiences, and as central organising principles, rather than just products and logos.** The success of experience-based brands at building deeper customer relationships at the expense of solely product-based brands argues strongly for every brand to think about its total "chain of experience" – from visual identity to advertising, product, packaging, PR, in-store environment – and increasingly round-the-clock presence and availability online. Technology will provide the opportunity to build an even greater sensory experience into brands through touch, smell and sound. Whatever emerges, distinctive value can and will need to be added at every stage of the experience, or at the very least, not lost.

■ **More compelling and more imaginative expressions of a brand's identity and brand communications.** Senior executives may not feel entirely comfortable in this area, but the ability to break through brand proliferation and communications clutter depends on imaginative and innovative creative expression. In the developed world, audiences are knowledgeable and savvy about marketing, and will increasingly "edit out" communications that they find boring or irritating. Imagination will need to be applied not just to the creative message, but also to the medium. Product placements in editorial and appropriate sponsorship of events, programmes and computer games will become more important. In particular, young people around the world have high expectations from brands, and are increasingly difficult to reach and satisfy.

◪ **The need for internal and external operations to be aligned – and transparent.** In an all-seeing digital world, and in a sharper business environment where employees at all levels can be ambassadors or saboteurs for the company's reputation, there really will be no hiding places any more. Organisations will have no choice but to be transparent in their dealings and fulfil their promises, or to have transparency forced on them. On a more positive note, numerous studies have confirmed that investment in a company's employees, and their good treatment, translates into significantly better customer satisfaction. Customer satisfaction and loyalty are, and will be, the drivers of long-term sustainable brand value.

◪ **Rigorous legal protection around the world.** It is estimated that 9% of world trade is counterfeited.[10] Although international law is increasingly being upheld, even in the previous counterfeiting capitals of the world, it is likely that while there are still brands to copy, there will be willing makers and buyers of copies. Brand owners must use the full weight of the law, quickly and publicly, to prevent value loss and degradation. Brand valuation, which can demonstrate how much economic loss might be attributed to passing off, is an effective way of supporting cases such as these.

◪ **Corporate social responsibility as a core corporate responsibility.** Corporate social responsibility (CSR) seems to be an overused buzz term in too many organisations today, and a whole new industry has grown up around it. Although good intentions may be there, all too often organisations look at CSR as an insurance policy, or a more sophisticated form of cause-related marketing, rather than as core to their operations. Many responsible companies produce elaborate CSR reports, including social and environmental performance. However, it is necessary to ask whether the basic principle of separate reports is the right one, or whether there should be a more integrated and central way of dealing with these issues in the future if we are going to have the kind of world we would all want. Or at least to mitigate the pessimistic scenarios of environmental destruction and terrorism breeding in areas of poverty and exclusion that we might all fear.

For those who would say "but what has this to do with business and brands", the fact that brands have the power to *change people's lives* and indeed shape the world we live in is not a fanciful notion, but a demonstrable fact. Brands have extraordinary economic power, often transcending national governments, and are able to connect with people's lives, behaviour and purchases across borders. If there are those who say that business's only concern should be to make a profit, then this would not only to be missing the point about CSR at its basic level – that CSR by definition demands more than the profit motive – but also missing out on opportunities for brand leadership in the future. From more than 3,000 studies of brands around the world, leadership is the characteristic most closely correlated with the strongest long-term value.

Any brand seeking to succeed and to be most valuable in the future will need to think and behave like a leader: at the basic levels of product and service distinction, and at the more emotional levels of creativity, values and core social contribution.

## The future of brand leadership

It is appropriate from time to time for governments, businesses and indeed any organisation to ask themselves what they are there for. Procter & Gamble recently restated its core purpose of improving the lives of its consumers; Samsung talks about creating superior products and services and "contributing to a better global society ... to the prosperity of people all over the world – a single human society"; and the UK government published its "quality of life" indicators in 1999 in answer to challenges on how to create a more sustainable society.

It is easy, but probably not helpful, to be cynical about these kinds of statements. Ironically, one of the brakes to progress on environmental and social issues for companies has been a fear that their actions will be interpreted cynically. Although the stick is an important incentive for companies not to misbehave, opinion-forming media might think sometimes about the carrot of encouragement for corporations trying to do the right thing and struggling to balance the interests of shareholders, consumers and the public at large.

This balancing act also leads on to discussions about how businesses (and indeed governments) are measured and rewarded, as well as how to truly measure the wealth and well-being of society in general. A recent study by the Future Foundation concluded that the increase in wealth and possessions in the UK was poorly correlated with happiness,[10] and the UK government's Sustainable Development Commission found the same in its study of prosperity.[11] While it is easy to sit in the wealthy west and philosophise about these things when people in developing countries are dying through lack of basic services, it does nevertheless raise questions about the goal of development. Will our prioritising of economic success in preference to any other be as appropriate in the future, in either developed or developing countries? There are several references to alternative, more broad-based measurement systems for business and society in this book. These would give a broader base to the priorities of CEOs and governments.

It would of course be better for organisations to take an active lead in setting standards in different markets. What can be termed a " leader brand" is not a brand leader in the old-fashioned sense, reflecting scale and muscle alone; rather it reflects a newer, restless and agenda-setting leadership across all areas of philosophy and operations, inside and out. Leader brands also need to take it upon themselves to explain the wider benefits of branding, and increasingly show sensitivity to local cultures, so that they continue to have licence to operate (and hopefully be welcomed) in even the most difficult parts of the world. As discussed throughout, brands can be uniting influences, and powerful social and economic developers. It is important for all brand owners and influencers to manage their brands well, and as a discernible force for good, and to ensure that they help people understand the benefits in a more informed way.

The balance of this book has been quite unashamedly "Pro Logo", but there is a conditional "Pro" here. Brands will continue to succeed if they deserve it, and, since the future of brands is the future of sustainable business and fundamental to developments in society, it is important to us all to see that they do.

## References

1 Chinese Vice Premier Wu Bangguo, reported in the *China People's Daily*.
2 "The end of the road?", *Sunday Times*, 20 April 2003.
3 "Chronicle of the future", *Sunday Times*.
4 "Sony re-dreams its future", *Fortune*, 10 November 2002.
5 Alvin Toffler, *Future Shock*, Bantam Books.
6 Quoted in "The great Indian takeaway", *Sunday Times*, 8 June 2003.

7   Ibid.
8   Original equipment manufacturer.
9   "Mugged: poverty in your coffee cup", Oxfam, 2002
10  "High anxiety screws up our hi-tech heaven", *Sunday Times*, 27 July 2003.
11  "Re-defining prosperity", Jonathon Porritt, Chair of Sustainable Development Commission, June 2003.

# Index

Numbers in *italics* indicate Tables; those in **bold** indicate Figures.